AROUND THE WORLD IN 30 YEARS

AROUND THE WORLD IN 30 YEARS

If I Can Do It, Anyone Can!

Harve E. Rawson, Ph.D.

Copyright © 2000 by Harve E. Rawson, Ph.D.

ISBN #:   Softcover   0-7388-5237-6

All rights reserved. No part of this book may be reproduced or transmitted in any form or by any means, electronic or mechanical, including photocopying, recording, or by any information storage and retrieval system, without permission in writing from the copyright owner.

This is a work of fiction. Names, characters, places and incidents either are the product of the author's imagination or are used fictitiously, and any resemblance to any actual persons, living or dead, events, or locales is entirely coincidental.

This book was printed in the United States of America.

To order additional copies of this book, contact:
Xlibris Corporation
1-888-7-XLIBRIS
www.Xlibris.com
Orders@Xlibris.com

CONTENTS

FOREWORD 11
ENGLAND 13
ISRAEL, SPAIN, AND MOROCCO 18
CZECHOSLOVAKIA AND THE U.S.S.R. 27
MOROCCO 39
"RED" CHINA 47
THE AMERICAN WEST & THE CARIBBEAN 66
PERU AND BOLIVIA 72
A FULBRIGHT SCHOLAR LIVING
    IN BAHRAIN: 82
INDIA 111
YEMEN 118
THAILAND 124
THE SOVIET UNION TWENTY
    YEARS LATER 129
GREECE, EGYPT, & JORDAN 137
DJIBOUTI 145
ZANZIBAR 148
MISSISSIPPI 152
COSTA RICA 159
AMTRAK IN THE U.S. 162
BRAZIL 165
GOREE ISLAND 169
MAURITANIA 173
PRINCE EDWARD ISLAND 177
ALASKA 180

CROSSING THE ATLANTIC IN THE
    LARGEST SHIP IN THE WORLD 183
ITALY 186
SPAIN AND PORTUGAL 190
AFRICA'S SLAVE COAST 194
NAMIBIA 204
SOUTH AFRICA 208
GREENLAND 211

APPENDIX 215
GOING WEST IN THE FIFTIES 217

FOREIGN LOCATIONS VISITED

1969: England, Scotland
1970: Israel, Spain, Morocco, occupied Jordan
1971: Greece, Israel, England
1973: Czechoslovakia, Soviet Union
1975: France, Switzerland, Italy, Liechtenstein, Germany, Luxembourg, Holland, Belgium
1977: Morocco
1978: Romania, The People's Republic of China [Invited Study Tour], Iran, Hong Kong, India, Pakistan, Greece, Switzerland (enroute)
1979: Canada (Eastern)
1980: Dominican Republic, Puerto Rico, Netherlands Antilles, Virgin Islands
1981: Peru, Bolivia
1981: Puerto Rico, Virgin Islands (US), Netherlands Antilles, Dominican Republic
1983: Alaska, Canada
1984: Canada (Cross Country)
1986: Martinique, Guadeloupe, Barbados, Netherlands Antilles, St. Kitts and Nevis, St. Lucia, Puerto Rico
1987: United Arab Emirates, Saudi Arabia, Qatar, Bahrain, France (Invited Study Tour)
1988: Bahrain (Fulbright Scholar for year), United Arab Emirates, Yemen, Oman, India, Thailand
1990: Czech Republic, Slovak Republic, Poland, Ukraine, Russia (Invited Study Tour)
1991: Turkey
1996: Mexico, Greece, Israel, Egypt (twice), Jordan, Djibouti, Kenya, Zanzibar (Tanzania), Mayotte, Comoros, Madagascar, Seychelles, England
1997: Mexico, Costa Rica, Panama, Jamaica, Brazil, Cape Verde, Senegal, Isle de Goree, Mauritania, Canary lands, Morocco, Gibralter, Portugal, Switzerland, Nova Scotia, New Brunswick, Prince Edward Island

1998: Spain, France, Monaco, Italy, Gibralter, Portugal, Azores
1999: Turkey, Tunisia, Morocco, Canary Islands, Senegal, Ivory Coast, Ghana, Togo, Benin, Walvisbaai S.A., Namibia, South Africa, Mexico, England, France, Belgium, The Netherlands, Germany, Denmark, Sweden, Norway, Scotland, Ireland (Eire), Wales
2001: Costa Rica, Nicaragua, Panama, Aruba, Bahamas, Virgin Islands, Sicily, Australia, Bali, Java, Malaysia, Singapore, Denmark, Norway, North Ireland, Scotland, Iceland, Greenland, Newfoundland (Canada)
2001: Italy, Sicily, Canada (Cross County), Mexico, Estonia, Russia, Finland, Sweden

FOREWORD

I first wrote about some of my travel experiences when I was a Fulbright Scholar on assignment to Bahrain, an island sultanate in the Persian Gulf. It seemed like a good idea in that I wanted to send back my impressions of living in this exotic and interesting country to my small hometown newspaper as well as my immediate family anyway, and this would be an economical way to kill several birds with one stone. So I wrote one article of my initial impressions of Bahrain as soon as I could buy a simple little Japanese typewriter/word processor I found in the Manama suq, and sent the article back to the U.S. I enjoyed writing the article and decided a month or so later there was more to say, and so I followed that up with a series of articles about various aspects of Bahraini life as my wife and I experienced the country. Our friends at home were quite enthusiastic about the newspaper accounts of life in the exotic country and urged us to continue.

While living in Bahrain, we took a "side trip" to the ancient country of Yemen—closed for decades to foreigners and only beginning to open up just a little at that time. In a strange set of circumstances, we were traveling there on visas issued in Kuwait with a venturesome British couple who also lived in Bahrain . The country was so different, it seemed a shame not to share this rare experience with the folks back home, so that led to another article. The same is true of another side trip from Bahrain—this time to India, where we were fortunate enough to book passage on the famed "Palace on Wheels" train tour. And still later, we traveled from Bahrain to see Thailand's palaces, canals, hill people, and drug trade at a time when very few people ever got to that part of the world. so another article was born.

When my wife, Joyce, and I got back to the United States from our nine-month stay in Bahrain, we were overwhelmed with locals telling us how much they enjoyed reading my accounts of life in the Arab sultanate and other countries we had visited. And they had really read them! They could recount many details of the articles and seemed genuine in their thanks for going to all the trouble to write them up. This "feedback" was so positive ("soul food for the ego" I called it), I decided to continue writing articles if I was fortunate enough to visit any more exotic and culturally-different nations of the world where most people wouldn't likely be able to visit.

Since that time, I have written many more articles on our travels, But I've limited them to describing only those places we've gone that are:

(1) really different from the usual tourist destinations and where I figured most people would never have the opportunity to visit; or

(2) something unusual or unique happened that warranted the telling of the tale. Most of the articles fit under category (1) above, but a few, in Canada, Alaska, or even one within the continental United States fall under category (2). Using this criteria, most of the many, many places I've visited around the world (112 countries to date) don't seem to warrant articles. Either a lot of people have visited the same spots and hence my travel is not unique; or I felt people just wouldn't share my interest and enthusiasm about that particular destination.

In this book, I'm sharing some of the "best" articles with you. I hope you enjoy them.

Harve E. Rawson

ENGLAND

THE FIRST VENTURE: A VISIT TO THE 'MOTHERLAND' or "HOW THE NAIVE VENTURE FORTH TO ENGLAND"

The first time we ever left the U.S. was to visit our "Motherland"—England—for our seventh wedding anniversary. My parents dutifully showed up to take care of our two sons, four and five at the time, so that we could take a two-week trip to visit one of my many cousins in England, see London for a few days, visit Oxford University and see some of the English countryside.

Knowing nothing about foreign travel at that time, we rather naively called the now defunct British Overseas Airway Corporation (BOAC) in New York and asked them if they had a two-week package trip. They eventually mailed us a "package" consisting of seven nights in a "guest house" in the Bayswater District of London with "full English Breakfast," hosted transfer from Heathrow Airport to the guesthouse with a guide, easily identified by "his yellow tie," a one-week motorcoach tour of Scotland with all meals included, and round trip airfare on the famed VC-10 BOAC aircraft from New York to London Heathrow. We signed on the dotted line and sent in our check for the first two weeks of June.

It's a wonder we ever went anywhere again. The famed VC-10 was broken by the time we got to New York and after waiting until 2 in the morning, BOAC finally fed us supper, and at 4 AM moved us to a run down hotel in the Queens. After two hours sleep, they got us up, fed us breakfast at the airport again, and after waiting seven more hours, we were finally on-board and winging across the Atlantic. By this time, all but about 20 passengers had wisely found passage elsewhere, so we practically had the plane to ourselves and the service was excellent since the crew, at least, was fresh and considered themselves lucky to have such a small load. At Heathrow, the "man in a yellow tie" never materialized despite our search of the entire airport, and somehow we found our way to the Bayswater area and our rundown "guest house," run by two Indians who spoke no English, a small room with a bed that resembled a hammock, and a bathroom for everyone fashioned out of a storeroom over the front stairwell which exposed its occupants to everyone passing by on the street since someone had decided it needed to be fully windowed with clear glass. Breakfast the next morning was two eggs swimming in lard, cold toast with marmalade made out of rotten oranges from Spain, acidic juice from green oranges imported from Israel, and "porridge" which had the consistency of concrete slurry and tasted exactly like that.

It was our introduction to English food and I attributed it to the Indians trying to cook English. But the pure English food was even worse and by the end of that trip, I was existing on Scottish shortbread in a "tin," Cadbury chocolate bars, and vitamin pills.

Nevertheless, London was the most fascinating city of the world. I couldn't help but agree with Samuel Boswell who allegedly stated: "He who is bored with London is bored with life." The museums, the hustle and bustle of the city, the palaces, the changing of the guards, London Tower, and all the other tourist sites were just as good as I wanted them to be.

The plays were cheap and good. I saw "Boys in the Band," a hit play about a group of homosexuals in New York buying a male prostitute as a birthday gift for one of their group as each character expounded on some Freudian reason as to why he was a neurotic homosexual. It seems silly now, but at the time it was a rather daring play and the admission in London then was a single pound (about $2.40 at the time). A very prim and proper English lady sat down next to me before the play started and said, "Oh, good, you're American. Isn't this play about John Philip Sousa, your own composer and bandleader?" I told her I didn't think so, but enjoyed her company until ten minutes after the play started when she just sort of disappeared.

My parents had always sung the praises of the delectable steak and kidney pie of their native land, and I bought one at a small restaurant in downtown London as my first British lunch. It, like the eggs before it, was oozing in lard and two bites were enough for a lifetime. Undaunted, I put the barely touched kidney pie to one side and ordered up fish and chips since in the U.S., I thought British style fish and chips were delicious. Apparently, "British style" was only known in the U.S., because those poor fish were swimming in lard and I found them totally inedible. That's when I discovered Cadbury chocolate bars as a good meal substitute.

We enjoyed visiting my cousin in Hereford, visiting Cathedral School where my grandfather and five generations before him had attended, and visiting the ancestral family home of my mother's side of the family, "Hereford Lodge," which was on the National Registry of Historic Homes. We even found my grandfather's initials carved into the brick by the front door since he'd been raised there along with all those generations before him. The large house and surrounding hops farm was a gift from George III to my great-great-great-great-great grandfather, who was wine steward to the King. Like all "gifts" of the monarch, the property was on perpetual loan to his family through the Church of England, a loan which expired as the Church of England began selling off its vast properties to keep going, starting at the end of World War II. So by the time we got there, the family no longer had "Hereford Lodge" as its own, but a lovely lady currently renting the place was gracious enough to show us through. She even served us "high tea" in the dark and rather gloomy old mansion.

The one-week motorcoach tour of Scotland was a hoot. My wife and I were one of three American couples crowded to the back of a jam-packed coach full of British on "holiday." All the way out of London, across the Lake District, and clear up to Hadrian's Wall, the Brits never said a word to the Americans, who were busy laughing and joking among themselves in the back of the bus while endlessly offering cookies, candies, and mints to the British who always politely but firmly refused to imbibe. But before another 24 hours was up, they begin to accept the culinary bribes and after a week it was hard to tell American from English as we commented on the Scots (the British had always been suspicious of them), the Vietnam War (most Brits were violently opposed to the "evil" war long before Americans came to the same conclusion), and crime in America ("I hear tell you can't even go up in a lift with impunity," one English nun proclaimed while others viewed our allowing citizens to carry guns as barbaric).

We got so far North there was only 5 hours of night up at Skye, saw definite movement in Loch Ness as "Nessie" did her stuff for the tourists, and my wife and I both commented on how, while most teenage girls are radiantly beautiful, the Scot girls certainly weren't. If anything, Scottish food was even worse than English food and we attributed their dour demeanor to their food, their gloomy weather, and the lack of human beauty in their immediate environment.

In a Scottish castle, I had the temerity to ask for ice in my water which produced one lonely ice cube. The tiny piece of ice instantly dissipated as I stared in dismay. But not without comment from a fellow Brit traveler sitting next to me.

"You know, chap, drinking all that cold is why all Americans have stomach trouble," he confided in me.

When I figured out he was referring to the long vanished speck of ice in my glass of water, I replied, "But Americans don't have stomach trouble—you're thinking of the French."

"No, all the French have liver trouble, but you Yanks all have stomach trouble," he said with finality.

"No we don't," I retorted. "I don't know of a single American who has stomach trouble," thinking that would forever stop such gross generalization among the uninformed.

"Yes, they do—and it's because of all that damn ice," as if my one little hint of frozen water, long gone, was somehow responsible for a national plague of some type on the other side of the Atlantic.

"Americans don't have stomach trouble," I responded with a clenched jaw. "None of them," I added for emphasis, even though I could think of a few always drinking milk for their ulcers.

But I had lost him—he was busily telling the person sitting on the other side of him that all Americans have stomach trouble because they want everything cold.

By the time we got home and found out my mother had forced my two sons to brush their teeth every night with hair cream because she couldn't see well enough to tell the difference between that and tooth paste, we were all enthused about taking another trip somewhere when we could afford it.

ISRAEL, SPAIN, AND MOROCCO

HOOSIERS VISIT THE HOLY LAND AND OTHER ALIEN PLACES

Right before I'd left for England, I was the first recipient of a teaching award set up by Hanover College, where I'd been "professing" since 1963. Somehow or another, I had been "elected" by alumni and current students to a $1000 prize which was to spent for "educational purposes." Upon my return, I discovered that a local minister was organizing a trip to the "Holy Land" which included a tour of modern Israel, Spain, and even a bit of Morocco. The price of the two-week venture, including airfare from Indianapolis and all meals, was under $1000, and it was taking place during the college holiday vacation so we could spend Christmas in Bethlehem.

I called my brother Paul, himself a professor at Northeast Louisiana State University, about him accompanying me. I knew he taught a course in geography of the Middle East, had long wanted to visit the Holyland as a fervent Presbyterian, and he would have the same time off for Christmas vacation I would. Unfortunately, he had even less money than I had, but the price was right and, with his wife's encouragement, we decided to go and room together since we both knew we'll never beat the price and it was economically impossible at the time to take our wives, let alone arrange for our children in such a venture.

All arrangements were made. I dutifully went to two "organizational meetings" with the local Methodist minister, about 20 aging widows who had never been out of Madison (Indiana) before, two really old married couples who could barely walk, and one rich matriach who was taking her son, his wife, and their six children, aged 16 on down, so they could see where Jesus was born. My brother Paul was to join the group in the New York airport before we started across the Atlantic, and we were to be seated together on our way to the Holy Land.

Two weeks before leaving, I came down with my seventh siege of pneumonia and X-rays confirmed the worst. Lungs full of water, no energy, barely breathing. I told the doctor I had paid my money and I was going even if I died. At least I would die in hallowed ground. Although he wanted to hospitalize me that very afternoon, I firmly told him that wasn't his decision: his job was to give me a sack of medications that would alleviate the symptoms until I died in the Holy Land. Having tried to argue with me before, Doc Harris promptly gave in and filled a huge plastic sack with samples of "goodies" courtesy of the pharmaceutical firms that plagued his office daily.

The day of departure arrived and I was worse than ever. In fact, my wife had to drive me to the Indianapolis airport with the two boys (now 5 and 6) in the back seat who first asked why I breathed so funny; then asked if I was dying; concluding with the question, "But why does he have to go to Israel to go to a hospital?" It was obvious they had concluded this was the last time they'd see me, especially since I was too weak to talk, but tried to hide this prescience knowledge out of respect for their mother. My wife helped me out of the car, to the terminal, and saw me shuffle slowly down the ramp to the waiting airplane to New York. I told her, "it's all right, Joyce. Paul will help me the minute we meet in New York, and he'll be my nurse until I get well."

Once I got to Kennedy Airport in New York, I hunted and hunted for my brother Paul. Just as I was beginning to panic, thinking he had missed his flight from Louisiana, I found Paul in the TWA men's room. He was on his hands and knees vomiting up all over himself and the floor and was pure white as he gasped, "Oh, Harve, I've never been so sick in my life. Thank God you're here to call the undertaker." I helped him up to the sink and got him rinsed off with cold water, got the vomit off his clothes, and was able to get two red pills down him out of my sack of samples—the little box I opened claimed it was for "severe digestive disorders. DANGER: Do not plan any activity upon medication." By putting most of his weight on one side, I was able to drag him out of the restroom and down the ramp to the TWA flight for Madrid where the rest of the Madison church group was told this was my long-lost brother. I'm sure all those Methodists thought he was a hopeless alcoholic who I'd cleaned up from his latest binge in the restroom. While most looked totally disgusted, a few were tolerant enough to look askance. Once we were seated on the plane, my brother announced he was dying and promptly went to sleep with his head slumped to one side.

Two meals and a movie later, he came out of his drugged coma ravenously hungry as the airplane was descending into Madrid. By the time the plane was refueled and on its way to Rome, he ate both his breakfast and mine as well, since breathing for me was now a sporadic affair at best. It was obvious he'd had a total recovery as he rambled on about Napoleon's exile at Elba, a well known palindrome phrase ("Able was I ere I saw Elba") as we flew over that island and, later, Corsica, Napoleon's native land. By the time we landed at Rome, his prescription for my total recovery was Italian espresso, the administration of which led to the discovery that Italian toilets are easier to vomit into because they are higher; that and the fact Italian men don't pay much attention to people gasping, retching and groaning in their toilets—some remnant of their Ancient Roman vomitarian heritage, no doubt.

By this time, I was so weak Paul had to sort of scoot and shove me onto the next airplane for Tel Aviv and within hours, I saw the plane landing. I looked out the window and saw the Parthenon! In Israel? The stewardess calmly announced we had a unscheduled landing in Athens and how lovely the Parthenon on the right side of the plane looked with its new lighting. And, by the way, we would be "discharging" a passenger here before taking off again for Tel Aviv. As the plane landed on the far reaches of the tarmac, the plane was surrounded with police cars with flashing red lights. The door was opened the minute the plane stopped on the runway, a person was ejected into the hands of the police, and, without further ado, the motors gunned up and we taxied around for a take-off. Once in the air again, the same cooing stewardness announced a person was on the plane who wanted to hijack the plane showing us the rifle the man apparently had hidden on him. Since terrorists were unknown at that time, everyone thought it rather demented, if not humorous, and the matter was dismissed with never a thought of imminent danger. If that same incident had happened ten or fifteen years later, we would have lost half our passengers to heart attacks if nothing else. As it was, everyone was delighted we had gotten to see the Parthenon with its new lights absolutely free, especially since "it wasn't even mentioned in the brochure" as the Rev. McKinney, the Methodist minister leading the group from Madison, pointed out to his appreciative flock.

Finally, we got to Tel Aviv at 1 A.M., then were shuttled to a bus for the drive to Haifa where our hotel was located and at 3:30 AM were told we would have a "wake up" call at 5:30 AM to begin our tour of Haifa and then off to Jerusalem for a full afternoon. At 5:30 AM, I felt I had died, but managed to stagger to a shower, fell down twice in the hot water spray, and then shuffled to the bus, thinking of death and the Holocaust.

Two days later, I wrote a postcard to Doc Harris at home: "Holy Land has cured me; threw bag of pharmaceuticals out of bus window today; relying on God's will in the Promised Land." It was a good trip. We retraced the ministry of Jesus, saw firsthand the rebuilding of a barren desert into the modern state of Israel, visited several kibbutzim, learned the Israeli's unique ways of farming and dairying, and picked up a lot of history about Tiberius Caesar, the Emperor Constantine, and his ex-prostitute wife, the Empress

Helena who'd made the first full-fledged pilgramage to the Holyland and identified and preserved many of the sites mentioned in the New Testament in the early 400's. We did spend Christmas eve on Shephard's Field in Bethlehem where the Star of Christmas shown brightly, and it was easy to feel just like the shepards must have felt almost two thousand years earlier. We saw the crucifixion site, the alleged birth site, the Wailing Wall of Solomon's Temple, the Sea of Galilee, the site of the Sermon on the Mount, the stations of the cross. It really did make the Bible come alive.

In Israel, one can easily get caught up in religion despite all the conflicting reports, competing sites, and juxtaposed theologies. There is a Catholic and a Protestant version of where the crucifixion occurred, with two opposing sites several miles from each other, and several of the "sites" of events are widely disputed by Biblical scholars. Nevertheless, most proposed sites of Biblical events I saw made a lot of sense from a geographical viewpoint, especially considering the transportation system present at that time.

But for some in our group with more rigid belief systems, the conflicts and controversies were just too much. One fervent Baptist in our group, a woman whose husband had refused to accompany her (I found out on the trip just why), limited her interest exclusively to Baptist missions staffed by "true Christians." Wherever we went, she demanded the bus stop at the two or three remote (and run down) Baptist missions she spotted. Finally, my brother, far less tolerant than I am, retaliated at her self-centered arrogance. In Tiberius, the ancient city built by the Emperor of the same name, he spotted a bombed out "Church of St. Andrews." He demanded the bus be stopped because "we will all want to visit the one true church left in this heathen land." As we trooped off the bus, to the consternation of our tour guide who simply had no idea of how to handle religious fanatics, and started picking our way through the rubble, my brother went on and on about the glories of Presbyterianism, Calvinism, predestinationalism, and the goodness of the Anabaptist movement which had, unfortunately, proven unsuccessful in replacing the Southern Baptist movement in the United States. The Baptist woman got the point as her eyes glistened with a most un-Christian hatred and I knew revenge toward my brother wouldn't be far off. That night, I heard her whispering conspiratorially to her lady friends about that horrible atheist and his fat brother in the group.

From Israel, we went to Spain, still under the tight Fascist regime of Franco. Our local guide was explaining how Catholicism was the state religion and so we should be most careful in any remarks we might make about Catholicism.

"For example," he extolled, "last year, an American group called the Southern Baptists sent illegal missionaries to Madrid to convert people away from the Holy Church. Unfortunately, they were all stoned to death which has led to some diplomatic tensions with the American Embassy."

"Could you repeat that," my brother yelled from the back of the bus. "I want to hear that again in that we've had that same problem in Louisiana and it sounds like such a good solution I want to make sure I remember it."

"You damn atheist," the Baptist woman turned toward my brother and screamed as her face turned beet red in rage until every vein in her face was outlined. "How dare you!" she gasped.

"You can see our problem," my brother again lectured the guide in the front of the bus. "It's all over the States, I'm afraid," he sighed.

The Baptist lady choked in rage and became speechless as her friends tried to console her. Three years later, I ran into her in our hometown. When she just glared at me, I countered with a friendly "Hello." Embarrassed, she stared coldly at me, but then said, "Maybe you're o.k., but that brother of yours will burn in the everlasting flames of Hell," she said with obvious delight at the prospect of his agonizing death.

Spain was charming at that time. Short, stocky, dark-skinned and obviously poor peasants were everywhere mixed with the light-skinned and arrogant landowners. Five percent of the population owned 95 percent of the land. As our grossly underpowered bus (taxes were based on horsepower) struggled over the mountains, we visited one beautiful, almost medieval city after another, complete with cobblestone streets, overhanging balconies, soaring cathedrals filled with relics, and never ending rain. Everywhere the "Guardia" (police) were present, always in pairs, with their unique three-cornered hats. Since each city's Guardia demanded and got our passports to hold in those days, foreign visitors always toed the line. How Spain has changed since the monarchy was restored.

From Spain, we crossed the Straits of Gibraltar on a smelly old ferry and landed in Tangier which, until just a few years before we got there, had been an "international free city." Let's just say, if something was for sale anywhere in the world, it was for sale in Tangier at that time. Piles of marijuana were on the street along with hashish. Every kind of opiate was offered, and as a result every American and European with a penchant for drugs lived in this city of abundant and cheap pharmacological escape. Whether prostitution had a connection with drugs or the fact Tangiers was also a big seaport, it was obvious it was a huge industry in that they were everywhere—female and male! A black American man in his early twenties approached me and offered himself for $10 U.S. dollars, and then, looking at my older brother, added "the two of you can have me for $15." My brother and I were both so speechless all we could get out was that we were married as if that made any difference to him one way or the other. "So what—don't you want to have some real fun?" To my brother and me, it would be an immoral, dangerous, disease-ridden, career-ruining, stupid, and unappealing thing to do even if we were interested. To him, it probably had no more meaning than picking your nose. Turned out he was from Alabama, moved to Morocco to get away from American prejudice since they certainly didn't care what a person's skin color was there, but apparently found selling his body was the only, or perhaps easiest, way to make a living. But he was one of thousands, male and female, we saw offering themselves during our brief stay in Tangiers where anything seemed possible.

Tangiers was, at that point in my life, more exotic than anything I had ever experienced before, and the experience left me with the desire to revisit this really different culture when I had more time. The Muslim religion, the ancient cities, the lack of racial prejudice, the Arabic language, their rigid marriage patterns—all piqued my curiosity.

When we left Tangiers, they opened our suitcases and dumped them right on the floor of the airport. The customs people then searched every piece of dirty underwear, every old pants pocket, every dirty shirt looking for drugs. I could see why. Since everything was totally open market there, a lot of people probably tried to smuggle drugs out to resell at huge profits just a few hours away in Spain, France, England, and the U.S. As a result, all the curious people in the Tangiers airport got a good look at what American men's underwear looked like.

Although I returned from the Holy Land cured of my pneumonia, the rest of the group wasn't so fortunate. Within one month of our return, one of the aged couples had expired while the other couple was still in the local hospital on the critical list. By the end of three months, three more of the group had died from various afflictions. Of those who lived, I don't think one of them ever left the county again.

I was so enthused about this trip, however, I talked my wife and mother into going two years later during the Christmas vacation while I stayed home and took care of the boys. "Ruth and Naomi returning to the Holy Land" was my label for this trip. Since both were good travelers and enjoyed each other's company, they had a great time even though the trip could have been marred by the fact a large number of their group were members of Aimee Simple McPherson's "Four-Square Gospel Movement," an evangelical remnant of the back-to-religion movement of 1930's Los Angeles. But that didn't seem to bother them. My wife met a famous Hollywood movie producer in a night club outside Jeruselum and my mother bought the biggest Alexandrite I've ever seen (which she willed to my wife upon her death) and both returned as healthy as horses.

CZECHOSLOVAKIA AND THE U.S.S.R.

THE SOVIET BLOC IN BREZHNEV'S DAYS

In 1973, I ran across an announcement of a professor organizing a trip for professors and physicians to visit the Soviet Union. The Soviet Union at that time was certainly at least the second world power, covered one-sixth of the world's surface, was imperial in its expansionism, maintained the world's largest army by a huge margin, and was as rigid as its ruler, Premier Brezhnev. The trip was scheduled for the Christmas vacation most professors would have, and would feature visits to schools, universities, colleges, hospitals, and clinics to accommodate the professional interests of both physicians and those in higher education. The all-inclusive trip was subsidized by some Soviet-American exchange agency, so the price was low enough to allow college professors to go. Determined I was going, I needed a roommate and my brother Paul, now teaching a course in "Geography of the Soviet Union" at Northeast Louisiana State University" was the logical choice.

When I called Paul, he was as eager as I to go, and we quickly made all the arrangements to pair up in New York to start on this new venture. The trip was routed to London and then to Moscow, then flying to Leningrad, Kiev in the Ukraine, and finally another flight out of the U.S.S.R. to Prague, Czechoslovakia. From Prague, we would take a flight back to London and then home.

This time, both my brother and I were well. It was a good thing since visiting Russia in the dead of winter is a challenge few travelers are willing to take. For us, it was about the only time we could go where we wouldn't be teaching and we thought it would be interesting to visit the "real Russia"—the land of snow and ice that had stopped not only Napoleon's but Hitler's Armies dead in their tracks. It wasn't just a rationalization. I've visited Russia at other times since this trip, and Winter is the best time to go—it's when you get a real feel for the country and its people and winter weather is far more typical of Russia and the Ukraine than the two months of decent weather in the summer when almost all tourists visit.

There was only one American plane a week between London and Moscow in those days of the Cold War and when it landed in a snow storm, the Boeing 707 was surrounded with an entire squad of Soviet troops armed to the teeth. When the door opened, the cold rushing into the plane was unbelievable. As we were marched under bayonet across the tarmac, in what seemed like a blizzard in the total darkness of 4 PM, I knew we were in the home of Fyodor Dostoevski's "Crime and Punishment" and the mother lode of all Communism—the Soviet Union. The scene exactly fit my expectations.

After all sorts of tiresome paperwork, we were finally delivered to our hotel in Moscow, the Hotel Ukraine, built in the Stalinist era with massive reception rooms, huge wide halls, 20 foot ceilings, three-foot-thick walls, double windows, and electronic bugs everywhere. It was where all foreigners were housed so they could keep an eye on us. Each floor had its own receptionist/ concierge / spy—an ugly old woman who searched your luggage when you were out on field trips, listened in on your phone calls, arranged laundry service as well as issued fresh towels and soap, and could be bribed with old American bras (bras had been completely forgotten in the last two "five-year plans" and consequently were impossible for Soviet women to buy), Kennedy half-dollars (even then worth more than any amount of Soviet rubles), and chocolate bars (unobtainable in the Soviet at that time) we'd been told to bring for just that purpose—always wrapped in white tissue paper as the local custom prescribed.

The trip was extremely well planned: we visited hospitals, clinics, schools covering all ages, children's "Pioneer Palaces", universities, and colleges extensively. In between we visited housing projects, theaters, ballets, folklore and popular shows, power plants, factories, the Kremlin, Lenin's tomb, the famous GUM department store, and even a few local restaurants outside our hotel. Intourist, the state operated tourist agency, kept close track of our whereabouts at all times, but in return delivered a tight, pleasant, and well-scheduled display of what they wanted to show us about the Soviet Union. Everywhere, Intourist sponsorship of our tour gave us top priority: we were taken to the front of the line at Lenin's Tomb so we didn't have to wait like the thousands of Soviet citizens in a line that stretched clear across Red Square, the Kremlin tour was private so that we would get to see, as special guests of the government, more of the treasures than most mere tourists, and our visits to universities, colleges, and schools were always hosted by the President or Director of that particular school with every professor, teacher, and even students at our disposal during the visit. The same was true of our hospital visits: physicians in our group conversed with their Soviet counterparts relatively unchaperoned as we did with our Soviet professorial colleagues. It was during a conversation with a psychology professor at a college for teachers I found out special education was taught under the "Department of Defectology" and that all statistics were ordinal, rather than interval, in that the "classless" society didn't allow researchers to make assumptions that one person could possess a given quantity of a trait (such as intelligence or blood pressure or number of blood cells) compared to someone else. All the researchers were allowed to assume was to say one person had more of the trait or less of the trait in a rank-order style, but never a precise measure. The resultant statistical methodology was so weak it was hard to see how they proved anything compared to Western science. It was a political system that forced the concept of all people being equal to an extreme—especially in a country where party officials lived high off the hog relative to everyone else. But I must admit I liked the idea of college professors being granted the best housing, chauffeured limousines, and salaries six times higher than the average Soviet worker. What a sharp contrast with the U.S., where two faculty members I knew at Hanover College were eligible for food stamps. And the fact that physicians, most of whom were women, were paid much less than professors was somehow delicious to me, especially when I thought how in the U.S. they earned three to four times as much as any professor despite the same level of training.

The elementary and secondary school systems offered some really great ideas I thought we could profit from. It was obvious the Soviets were pumping a lot more of the public budget into education than we were if the equipment, number of teachers, class size, and conditions of the buildings were any indicator. One concept that intrigued me was the idea that schooling was really in two parts: the academic part in one building with well trained no-nonsense teachers being asked to teach only what they knew within a specialized discipline (mathematicians taught math; writers taught writing; historians taught history, etc.) while all the rest of what we call school was shunted off to the Pioneer Palaces located adjacent to the academic school. In the Palaces, children were taught ballet, physical education, given their meals, taught simple household economics, sewing, small motor repair, household repair, campcraft skills, sex education, political ideology, art, radio and TV, and music. Again, all training was done by teachers who had actually reached a high skill level in their own lives: former ballet artists taught ballet; retired engineers taught radio and TV; retired performing artists and musicians taught art; retired political administrators taught communism; semi-retired professional athletes taught physical education; and retired social workers taught sex education and basic household economics. Children were taught by people who knew what they were talking about and demanded respect for their topic of expertise; the teachers felt purposeful and socially needed in the beginning stages of a multi-stage retirement, starting at 50. I thought of my wife, an elementary school teacher in America, charged with teaching all subjects (including subjects she really knew little about), and then being responsible for music, art, playground supervision, and even collecting the lunch money for each student. She was asked to be a nurse, a mother, a Renaissance scholar, a babysitter, a coach, an artisan, and a social worker—all with her required teaching certification based on having taken a few "methods" courses in college with such gripping titles as "Audio-Visual Presentations" (how to run a slide projector); "Media Display" (bulletin board management); and "Children's Literature" ('kiddie lit' as everyone called it to be polite, grateful for the usual guaranteed "A" if they just came to class). And sports were completely separated from the academic school. No athletic competitions in the school; but all you wanted in the Pioneer Palaces. One didn't contaminate the other. Yes, I thought we could gainfully borrow some ideas from our Soviet neighbors when it came to education.

When we visited a nursery school, I saw one of the most effective, but frightening, examples of childhood training I've ever witnessed. It was explained to us the same lesson was being taught to three years old throughout the Soviet Union that very day out of the state-prescribed curriculum. A large boulder, patently manmade apparently just for this lesson, was in the middle of the playground right in the way of everything.

"This rock is ruining our play. We'll have to move it," the teacher exclaimed, obviously from a memorized script. "How can we move it?" she asked the children.

When one said to shove it out of the way, she asked him to try it.

"I can't," he reported after pushing a short while. "It's too heavy."

"What can we do?" the teacher asked the group.

"Maybe two of us could push it," another student suggested.

"Try it," the teacher hopefully responded.

The two pushed and shoved and nothing happened.

"What should we do?" the teacher prompted.

The group of three-year-olds talked among themselves and then one said, "Maybe if we all push together, we can move the rock."

"Try it," the teacher responded.

Obviously the concrete "rock" was designed to be heavy enough to not be moved by less than 15 to 20 three-year-olds, but when a larger group, such as enrollment at the state-run nursery school allowed, the rock was easily moved and the children were excited and enthused by their success.

"Congratulations," the teacher said proudly. "What did you learn by this?"

Eventually, one kid said something like, "If we all work together, we can do things we can't do as an individual," in the words of a three-year-old.

"That's exactly right, Ivan," the teacher said as if he had discovered the meaning of life. "That's what we call communism and that's the way our government works. Communists working together in a socialist country can move all obstacles toward a better life."

I could almost hear the theatrical music swelling as she reached the last line of her script, but it was a lesson in political dogma I'm sure those children never forgot—especially taught at the tender age of three. When communism collapsed 20 years later, I could see why that generation of children were so bewildered.

When we visited the space program museum, my brother noticed the simplicity of the cosmonauts' outfits as they were sent into space: ordinary shoes, ordinary pants and shirts, ordinary cans of regular food, etc. "Why do we have to spend $10 million dollars on a contract with Goodyear to develop some special shoes? If they were so necessary, why don't the Soviet cosmonauts have shoes at least similar to the $10 million specials?" After studying that exhibit, one did have the distinct impression there was perhaps a lot of feather bedding in our space program to the great benefit of some of our giant business corporations.

While wages were extremely low, so was housing and food

costs, and most public transportation was either free or a very small token charge. No one seemed to be starving, there were no slums quite as bad as one sees in New York City, there were no areas quite like the burned out Bronx, and education was totally free—no book rental fees, no candy sales to support the band, no college tuitions, etc.

On the other hand, housing, though dirt cheap, wasn't worth much more than that. We were fortunate enough to have a person in our group who had a brother living in Moscow and several of us were invited by the Muscovite to visit his apartment. We walked up to the sixth floor (the elevator was broken) of the huge housing complex and crowded into the small two-room apartment he shared with his wife, mother, and two children. A shared kitchen served four apartments while each two apartments shared a bath consisting of a sink, commode, and shower. It was crowded but comfortably furnished, warm despite the subzero weather, and noisy since the walls were paper thin. They said their biggest problem was plumbing and roaches.

Moscow's subway system was a marvel of engineering and provided swift, pleasant travel throughout the city. But private cars were practically unheard of then and I couldn't imagine a car lasting very long on Russia's horrible roads anyway. Electricity was practically free, as was natural gas, to the country's citizens but, even then, choking clouds of pollution were omnipresent.

My brother and I were so sure we were being bugged in our hotel room, we only conversed with all the water turned on full blast in the bathroom and even then whispered. When I asked to call a former student now working in the U.S. Embassy, I was glared at as if I were a known C.I.A. spy, elaborately shown to a special red phone in a private room on the first floor of the hotel, and two Russians stood by me as I placed the call. Thank God the former student happened to be on vacation at Yalta or God knows what would have happened if I had actually talked to an employee of the Embassy. Our fears of being harrassed were reinforced when two physicians, bored with the tour of Moscow State University, wandered away from the group, and upon their return to the hotel outside the watchful eye of Intourist, found all their cameras, film, and personal items mysteriously gone from their luggage. When they reported the "hotel theft" to the Intourist guide, she airily replied they must have lost it and walked away. One day, they refused to take any American money or travelor's checks without any explanation whatsoever so for a day we were penniless. It turned out later that Nixon had devalued the American dollar that day and the Soviets, not being involved with the World Banking system, decided to freeze American assets without even telling anyone why. They changed their minds the next day, but it certainly made you feel helpless in a hostile land.

The people's gloomy demeanor couldn't all be attributed to the weather. There was little incentive to do a better job, since promotions were more political than skill based; career choices were determined by the state, based on national manpower needs, so free choice was eliminated at the very beginning of a work career; consumer goods were shoddy, if available at all; and service was invariably surly and disinterested at best.

A week later, we arrived in Leningrad (now St. Petersburg) in another snowstorm and the military plane transporting us actually skidded on the runway landing. The plane was obviously designed for paratroopers in that the seating consisted of long metal benches against each side, no windows, and a red hot charcoal stove in the center of the aisle the only heat source. I never knew you could have an open flame in an airplane; I never knew of a plane without seatbelts; and I'd never ridden in a plane without windows. There was no restroom and no beverage service, let alone food, mainly because the plane had no service personnel—just a couple of unfriendly pilots and us. We discovered on that flight that one of our group, a nun/professor from Puerto Rico, had a bad case of claustrophobia. When the doors shut on the windowless plane and we sat in total darkness until the engines were started, the nun went into a hysteric panic and we smelled her loss of control all the way to Leningrad as she shrieked in terror.

The Winter Palace, the Hermitage, St. Michael's Cathedral, the Fortress of Peter and Paul, the Pavlov Institute, the universities lining the frozen river, and the Europa Hotel across from the cathedral were all high points of this fabulous port city built by Peter the Great. The 400-day siege of the city by the Nazis in World War II was still fresh in the citizen's memories, and we were shown the sawdust and bonemeal "cakes," no bigger than a bar of soap, that was the total food supply for each citizen per day. The populace ate rats until they were all gone, and then watched each other die of malnutrition until nearly half the population was gone. Nary a family escaped loosing someone.

One incident I will never forget. An American physician in our group had stopped over in Denmark on his way to Moscow for our trip. Denmark, at that time, was the only place in the world where you could legally purchase pornography and the physician had bought up a lot of it and was carrying some of it with him. In the lobby of the Europa hotel, I saw him sidle up to our Intourist guide when she was alone, a beautiful young woman of about 25 to 30. He reached in his coat pocket and brought out a small stack of his treasured pornographic photographs he'll already shared with anyone who would even glance at them in our group . He obviously expected the Soviet girl, brought up in one of the most puritanical societies in the world, to gasp with shock or even revulsion. Instead, much to his consternation, she took the whole pack and carefully, slowly, and methodically looked at each photograph with little apparent emotion. When she had looked at each one studiously, she handled them back to him with the comment, "Conditions must be very bad in your country for people to have to do that for a living." She obviously thought the people in the pictures were American, but it was the first (and only) time I've ever heard people react to pornography with some concern over the actors involved, rather than the acts being performed. It was a different way of perceiving the world than one got in the West and puritanism had little to do with it. At any rate, it certainly defeated the physician who folded his wares and sneaked off to his room.

We didn't get to leave Leningrad as scheduled. A storm hit the city and even the Soviet pilots couldn't get the aircraft engines going in the minus 30 temperatures. So we were stuck in the Leningrad airport, locked in a unheated reception room for foreigners for the next 18 hours with one restroom, no blankets, no food, and questionable water. But we slept in our coats (the women with fur coats shared them with the rest of us), people shared the food they had in their luggage and coat pockets, and we worked out arrangements for men and women to time-share the bath, while others organized bridge, gin rummy, and even solitaire tournaments with the decks of cards the bridge addicts always carried with them. It was American organization and good will at its best and we actually had quite a good time, despite the crappy treatment by our host country.

Regardless of the weather, we finally got into a turboprop plane that took us to Kiev, the capitol of the Ukraine (now a separate country). This plane was billed by Aeroflot as a "luxury flight" and was to feature windows, unholstered seats facing forward, a stewardess, and a meal. The first two features were as advertised. The stewardess was an old crone with hairy legs and sagging breasts who offered us a wormy apple from the Georgia's out of a rusty bucket for our meal. To eat the apple, she passed around one paring knife as rusty as the bucket and a small 6x6x6 triangle of wax paper to eat it on. The procedure, when the knife was passed on to you, was to cut the worms out of the apple, slice the small remaining part onto the tiny wax paper triangle and enjoy.

Fortunately, Kiev had delicious food so we made up from the "starvation flight," as my brother had labeled it. "Chicken Kiev" in Kiev is nothing like the dish in this country and is, in my opinion, far superior. In Kiev, it always came in an earthen pot straight from the oven with a thick "lid" of yummy crust covering a savory blend of chicken, broth, vegetables of all types, and a dash of cheese melted in.

We got to see the remains of St. Nicholas, preserved in tons of salt in an ancient monastery catacomb deep beneath the earth, the largest apartment building in the world housing a cool 500,000 people with buses and trolleys running through the second floor of the buildings so no one had to go out in the bitter winter to wait on public transportation; the River Dnieper; many strange "department stores" crowded with shoppers for "New Year's Day" complete with gift giving to all members of one's family, gaily decorated New Year's Trees which looked identical to our Christmas trees, and Father Frost who delivered the New Year presents to all the children in the middle of the night. All the stores were decorated with toy reindeer, brightly colored tinsel decorations, and even painted pine cones. For an atheist country, the people seemed to have created a Christmas season whether the government approved or not. I strongly suspect behind locked doors, dolls of the baby Jesus and nativity scenes were secretly admired and a few old Russian Orthodox Christmas tunes couldn't have been completely forgotten, even 56 years after the Revolution. I could envision Grandma Borinsky leading the family in a few forbidden hymns down in the basement just for the spite of it since the Holiday season called for a little singing.

We saw a Communist style wedding in a marriage parlor and later, by sheer good luck, my brother and I got invited to a wedding reception in a hotel after sending the wedding party a bottle of champagne. Although not a soul spoke English other than "hello" and "American", we had a great time toasting the newly weds, kissing the bride, and hugging the proud parents.

Our hotel in Kiev was interesting. The lobby was filled with mattresses lined up vertically. They had been shipped there by mistake three years ago but since the hotel already had new mattresses at that time, they were still there sitting in the lobby. And the checkout counter computed your bill on an abacus used at the time of Ivan the Terrible while an electronic digital clock blinked at us from that same counter.

Our final stop, Prague, in what was then the united country of Czechoslovakia, was oppressively occupied by 20,000 Soviet troops at the time we were there. The Czechs let us know the best they could how much they resented the Soviet presence all around them. When our Czech government guide asked if anyone had been to their country before, my brother perked up and said he had been to Pilsen with the U.S. Army in World War II. We both heard the guide say under her breath, "Pity you didn't get 100 more kilometers down the road" with a knowing look. And when my brother and I took our usual mandatory streetcar ride to the end of the line and back to see where the people actually live, we observed even more resentment. At the end of the line, the car was placed on a turntable and swept out. Then Soviet troops entered the cars and busily pasted the government propaganda slogans above each inside window. I thought they were new, but I soon learned otherwise. As the trolley began stopping on its way back to downtown, each person that got on always managed to get their fingernail on one of the slogans and stripped a small piece off which they balled in their fist. By the time we got downtown, all slogans were completely gone and we saw another contingent of soldiers enter the streetcar with paste buckets and new slogans and replace the ones they obviously expected to be stripped within the past 30 minutes. It was Soviet planning at its best.

Prague, with its medieval castles, the beautiful river flowing under the artful stone bridges, and its magnificent downtown was a real treat despite the Soviet Army ever-present. It reminded me of a Sigmund Romburg operetta like "The Student Prince." I was able to buy some beautiful native garnets for my wife—an opportunity denied the citizens of the country which produced the garnets to start with.

I loved Prague and wanted to stay but it was time to get back to the U.S. and my work. At the time, few people were able to go to the Soviet Union or Czechoslovakia and here I was one of the lucky ones. It was a great adventure. Years later, I returned to the Soviet Union just as it was breaking up into all the countries now dotting the map. It wasn't the same country at all. I visited Brezhnev's Communist state at the height of the Soviet Empire and a country with more control over its citizens than any nation on earth outside of Mao's China. To a psychologist, it was fascinating.

MOROCCO

TRAVELING THROUGH
THE SAHARA WITH NO LUGGAGE

One bright Fall evening, I realized my two sons were referencing all events as to how it would be evaluated by their peers at the local junior high school they attended. What they wore, how they talked, what activities they choose, even whom they befriended—all was relative to that damn junior high crowd.

How provincial they were becoming! I decided it was time to open their eyes beyond the scope of their Midwestern junior high school. While we were at it, we would visit a place about as difference as could be imagined that very Christmas—Morocco.

The National Educational Association at that time arranged all-inclusive tours designed just for teachers on Christmas vacation and Joyce, as an elementary school teacher, was eligible. They offered a brand new one to Morocco that Christmas and the price was right—low enough to allow all four of us to go on our first trip outside the U.S. as a family. Joyce was apprehensive about being a woman in a Muslim country, and the two boys couldn't understand going to a country their friends had never heard of—let alone a country where the people were so ignorant they didn't even speak English. But they were used to going on a trip at Christmas since it was the only time all of us had off. And they knew Morocco was in the northwest corner of Africa, had a lot of desert, was Arabic, didn't celebrate Christmas, and that I had been there a few years before and had returned intact. As the trip drew nearer, our enthusiasm drowned out any last-minute qualms.

Royal Air Maroc had one Boeing 747 that winged back and forth from New York to Casablanca three times a week and we, along with 420 others, crowded on as soon as the four of us were out of school. Little did we know our luggage would never leave the New York airport even though we'd checked it through to Tangier from Cincinnati. When we arrived in Casablanca, we were hustled to another small jet which was taking us to Tangier for the beginning of our tour.

It was there we discovered our "luggage hasn't yet arrived," "it will come in, no doubt, on the next flight out of the New York" (3 days later), and that Morocco had no phone books, no phone information service, and that we would have to call the airport every day to check on our luggage arrival if we could ever get a phone line free. Fortunately, we each had a flight bag filled with our toilet kits, one change of clean underwear and socks, the camera, passports, credit cards, and money. So we didn't panic—we thought we could wait out the next airplane and the arrival of our luggage.

Joyce and our son Reed went for a walk on the beautiful beach of Tangier while Paul and I went to the airport to fill out the paperwork for the missing luggage. When we got back, Joyce and Reed arrived back at the hotel ashen with a police escort. The walk had started innocently enough, but within a half-block they noticed men following them; within a full block, the crowd of men had increased to at least one-hundred. Frightened, they headed back to the hotel. The crowd got ever larger and the police had joined them.

The local populace, unused to tourists (at that time), was totally unaccustomed to a woman and child being in public alone, let alone with uncovered lower legs and arms. Their way of objecting was to follow them with the correct assumption that such an action would scare the woman and make her go back where she came from without the necessity of direct confrontation and stoning her as they would have done a hundred years before. It was a bad start for Joyce and to this day, she's hesitant about being alone in Morocco.

That evening, while waiting for dinner, two Moroccan men got in a heated discussion in the hotel reception room, and, in true Moroccan style, their voices got louder and louder in harsh-sounding Arabic as their hands waved all over in dramatic gestures. To an outsider, it seemed like they were going to immediately kill each other, especially since both were wearing the traditional dagger and both displayed large interesting four and five inch scars on their faces which could easily be souvenirs of previous discussions. Several people in our group turned their heads and made every attempt to pretend they weren't there; others fled the room, giving up any prospect of supper in the process; while the Rawson's glared at them, fascinated at their lack of emotional restraint. My sons had never seen anything like it, and when the two men made a final lunge toward each other in a volley of Arabic curses, then paused and walked out together as if they were long-lost buddies, they begin to understand what I was talking about when I mentioned "cultural differences." The look of wonderment on their faces is something I will never forget and I made me glad we chose Morocco for our first foreign venture.

I had warned the two boys earlier that Moroccans were very free with their hands in touching your body as part of their way of communicating, that Moroccans did not share our sense of "personal space," and that Moroccans didn't share our aversion to homosexual liaisons prior to their eventual marriage in their late twenties or early thirties. As such, they should not be shocked when other men touched them, but they should pull away and not allow fondling. All this could be avoided if they stayed very close to me throughout the trip as no boys, Moroccan or foreign, got touched when they were with their father.

Even by the first night in Morocco, it was becoming obvious that our "delayed" luggage might never catch up with us since we would be in a different city every night from then on. I suggested we just buy some clothes for the boys at the local "suq" (marketplace) where we had spotted some German clothes for sale. The sizes were all different than ours, the prices were outrageously high, and before buying a shirt for Reed, I insisted he try it on. There were no dressing rooms and people just tried clothing on in the dimly lit store front on the street. Meanwhile, forgetting my own advice to the boys, I had wandered off to look at the offerings of an adjacent shop. Reed was a very well built boy for his age (13) and as he took off his old shirt and his athletic upper torso was displayed before he could get the new shirt on, he was instantly surrounded with a number of men feeling his chest, his shoulders, and even pinching his nipples. He let out a small yelp but was so startled he was actually speechless in a state of paralysis before I could rescue him. We bought the shirt just to get out of there, but I never had trouble with the boys sticking with me from then on. They were like dogs trained to "heel." And they both kept their bodies covered like monks from then on.

After those initial adjustments to the culture and discovering that Morocco had delicious bread and butter, at least, along with Coca-Cola, we relaxed a little and began to enjoy the country. The tour was on an old Volvo bus, complete with a native driver dressed in a shabby robe, well-worn scandals, and a smile that revealed he'd lost at least three-fifths of his teeth already; a baggage "boy" (at least 35 years old) dressed in rags who dutifully gathered up all our baggage and put it on the roof racks each morning, took it off each night and lugged it to the rooms (at least for those who had luggage), and who kept the bus clean inside and out despite swarms of dust everywhere; and our tour director, a young college-educated Moroccan who spoke Arabic, English, French, and German. Only the tour director slept in the hotels with the rest of us; the driver and baggage "boy" literally lived on that old bus with their portable stove for cooking, dirty old blankets for sleeping, prayer rugs, and a bucket for taking their baths.

The bus tour took us to the five "Imperial" cities of Morocco: Meknes, Fez, Marrakech, Rabat, and Casablanca along with Tangier. En route, we crossed the Atlas Mountains on a one-lane highway covered with powdery white snow, saw the amazingly preserved Roman ruins at Volupolis, the thousands of orange groves just at picking time, the Sahara sweeping right up next to the camel markets of Marrakech, and the semi-arid desert that makes up the largest part of rural Morocco.

Meknes was where the current royal family got its start hundreds of years ago. The palace there had been built by tens of thousands of Christian slaves brought from Spain and the Mediterranean who, when collapsing from overwork, endless beatings, and exhaustion, simply became part of the walls themselves. The ruler was fond of horses, apparently, in that his stone stable, attached to the palace, held 10,000. And he had all who opposed him woven alive into raffia bridges leading in and out of his palaces so that he could watch them suffer as the horse hoofs trampled them to death. Not far from this city was the ancient Roman city of Volupolis, amazingly intact in the Atlas Mountains despite all the earthquakes in that area. Our son Paul suddenly realized the cover of his Latin Book at home featured the very scene he was looking at. What he didn't know until he was there himself, however, was that the scene was primarily of a luxurious brothel, ever-present in Roman cities of that time. In fact, our local guide was so explicit on the goings-on of the Romans in their resort cities our children thought life back in Madison, Indiana, was pretty tame indeed by comparison.

Fez featured the largest suq I've ever seen: a tangle of shops all shaded by a huge roof of grape vines and which guaranteed I would get lost. At one point, I leaned back to avoid being overrun by a heavily laden donkey and suddenly found myself flat on my back in someone's living quarters. They screamed; I gawked and gasped for air; and they pushed me back out the inward facing door into the narrow little alley from whence I'd come with a rain of Arabic curses. Finally, a small lad of about 10 took me by the hand and announced: "You American—you lost—me get you to bus." I didn't argue, and that little tike led me like a small child through one alleyway after another after another. until I was convinced either he too was lost, or he was literally leading me to a quick robbery and early death. Then, suddenly, we emerged right into the bus parking lot outside the suq. "See, bus," he stated with pride and sure enough, out of all the buses on this lot, it was the very one I had come in. He smiled in pride as I showered him with sincere gratitude in the form of several U.S. dollar bills. I figured he did this for a living—watching foreigners emerge from a given bus, following them until they got in trouble or hopelessly lost, and then leading them back to their buses knowing they'd get well paid for their efforts. Smart kid. My wife and boys managed not to get lost, but they didn't have the excitement of seeing someone's living quarters up close and personal either.

Marrakesh was the most exotic city I'd ever been in. It was just like visiting a scene out of "Arabian Nights." The great square there had every known drug for sale, snake charmers, dancing boys, story tellers, colorfully costumed men selling you drinks of water out of goat's bladders, knife and rifle sellers, belly dancers, spices of every taste and color, little boys trained to pick pockets, huge crowds of natives in from the adjacent Sahara desert, the baying camel market, and a couple of merchants with straying hands looking my two boys over with avarice in their eyes. Since my wife had witnessed a Muslim women having stones thrown at her the night before in that she had dared to go out without the presence of a man, she remained uneasy in this medieval setting. Reed, who said little under most circumstances, did state emphatically that we were a long way from Indiana.

On the long bus ride to Casablanca, a group of French Canadians joined the NEA tour (they had missed their plane and came in three days late). They were mad at being late and took it out on the guide. Claiming they were assigned the worst rooms in the Marrakesh hotel (their rooms were the same as ours—marginal), they refused to go to bed and finally had to be put up in a different hotel before they would settle down. The next morning, the guide explained everything in English and then French. They then demanded he explain in French first, which he did, but that didn't satisfy them in that they said it wasted their time to have to wait while he spoke to us in English. It would have to be French only, they claimed. They refused to rotate seats, claiming they were entitled to the best seats permanently because they didn't want to rotate. Refusing to eat anything Moroccan, they demanded that familiar French foods be specially prepared for them. If you've ever heard of "The Ugly American," a book depicting Americans as the most insensitive, demanding tourists in the world, I could suggest a different nationality for the title. One could only pity the poor guide who looked like he was convinced Allah had cursed him with something called French. When he started getting a strange rash all over him as they continued their endless whining and complaining, he finally, out of his own pocket, rented a separate van to carry them on the remainder of their trip: from one French restaurant to another and from one French-run hotel to another. Good riddance, I thought, but the guide told us this would be his last venture as a tour guide. His uncle owned a tannery somewhere and even the horrible smells of camel urine they used as tanning agents would be better than this.

The guide and I searched the back rooms of the Casablanca airport, a relic left over from World War II, for our missing luggage but to no avail. But Casablanca was fascinating. A huge city with a literal polyglot of nationalities and races living there, it somehow mixed medieval Arabic customs with a thriving modern metropolis. The Atlantic was a beautiful blue there with sandy beaches in front of sun-drenched white adobe houses. Modern businesses in air conditioned buildings stood next to ancient suqs and casbahs, and the people were colored from snow white to ebony. The post office was a good example: a beautiful marble floored lobby with modern fans and crisply uniformed postal clerks. But, turning to the right, there was a little man dressed in rags handling parcel post on a loading dock. He was armed with a paste pot, old boxes he'd collected from around town, and a walnut drawered cabinet to keep all the stamps in next to an ancient scale with a set of weights that looked like something Benjamin Franklin would have used in setting up the first American Post Office.

Early in the trip, I'd spotted a small box of TIDE on the back of a donkey and, with a wild set of gestures, bought the detergent with a wad of Moroccan money. My wife discovered bidets made great wash basins when fortified with TIDE, and with both boys now gone native with robes generously loaned by our guide, who was no bigger than they were, we managed fine with no luggage. When we got back to New York and were marching through the U.S. Customs with no bags, the man looked suspicious until my wife imperiously informed him we always travel in just the clothes we wear because it's so much simpler. He waved us right through rather than argue that one.

From then on, my boys never thought the world orbited around the goings on of the Madison schools and took a somewhat more global view of events. They became more interested in affairs of the world, confided to their non-traveling friends there was a world beyond Indiana, and, horror of horrors (in Indiana at least), that not everyone in the world thought a basketball game determined destiny. The trip had been a big success.

We even got our wardrobe back. Four suitcases arrived at our house 63 days and 42 phone calls later—it had never gotten any further than New York.

"RED" CHINA

A MONTH IN MAOIST CHINA
UNDER A ROMANIAN VISA

Shortly after Richard Nixon and Henry Kissinger visited Chairman Mao's "Red China," a country closed to all foreigners for 30 years, I saw a strange little notice buried in the back pages of the *Louisville Courier-Journal*. It stated that anyone wanting to visit China someday should write the "People's Republic of China—United States of America Friendship Association" at a certain post office box in a small town in Florida. I didn't know if it was a front of the C.I.A., a ruse of J. Edgar Hoover's F.B.I. to flush out communist sympathizers or what, but couldn't resist writing. Months later, a 13-page questionnaire arrived with instructions to fill it out completely. It asked all sorts of things I thought were illegal to ask such as "Who did you vote for in the last election?;" "What church do you go to and how often do you go?;" "Do you believe everything your church tells you to believe? If not, what don't you believe?;" "Do you agree with the way the United States treats its criminals?;" and so on. After looking the questions over, I was convinced it had been written by Sen. McCarthy before he died of alcoholism or, more likely, the very much alive J. Edgar Hoover, the ancient Director of the F.B.I., so he could send me to prison as an "Un-American" which he seemed to label anyone who disagreed with him on any matter. Still, I wanted to someday go to China, so I gritted my teeth, answered the questions honestly, and sent it back to the strange post office box number in Florida.

I wasn't arrested so I forgot about it until a year or so later when a letter arrived in late June:

> "Dear Dr. Rawson:
> You are selected as one of 100 Americans to visit the People's Republic of China in July and August. In this tour, you will be a guest of the Ministry of Culture of the People's Republic of China who will make all arrangements for your 25 day stay. You will visit Peking (Beijing now), Canton (Guangzhou now) and other places to be announced upon your arrival. It is anticipated you will be allowed to visit schools, factories, universities, sites of political importance, and important historical sites. All transportation from Atlanta, Georgia, U.S.A., will be arranged by the Friendship Committee of the People's Republic of China—United States of America Friendship Committee. A charge of $2950 U.S. dollars will cover all global transportation from Atlanta, Georgia, all meals, all transportation costs within the People's Republic of China, and all meals within the People's Republic of China. Please forward your check made out to the "The People's Republic of China—United States of America Friendship Committee" to PRCUSA, P.O. Box 123456, Los Angeles, California."

It was 1978. No one but the President, the Secretary of State, Shirley McLaine and a few movie producers had ever visited behind the "Bamboo Curtain" as it was called then. I couldn't believe the letter and just sat there in shock. Finally, I let the others in my family read it, who were equally stunned. But everyone said to go. When I pointed out the money would mean sacrifices from all family members—no fancy athletic shoes, no vacations for them—no new 10-speed bikes—I remember my son Reed looking me straight in the eye saying, "No one gets to go to Red China—it's worth it to have a father who gets to go."

The next day, I tried to get information to yield a phone number so I could talk to someone in Los Angeles to see if the place was real before I sent my money. They couldn't give me any listing, but they did get a hold of someone in Florida listed under "People's Republic of China—United States of America Friendship Association" who seemed incredulous that I would be checking up on them before sending in a check to a post office box in Los Angeles. I had just a couple of weeks to prepare: Wade Clapp and Joyce were willing to take over Englishton Park, the Children's Program for behaviorally-disoriented children I was running, I could raise the money by dipping into savings, and God would have to take care of the rest of it.

The next morning, the *Madison Courier* had bold headlines: DR. RAWSON TO VISIT RED CHINA followed the next day by the *Louisville Courier-Journal*'s announcement: HEAD OF INDIANA CHILDREN'S PROGRAM ENROUTE TO RED CHINA—PROFESSOR GUEST OF GOVERNMENT. With all the publicity, I couldn't back out now.

About a week before departure, a letter arrived explaining only a few more details. All air travel would be by SwissAir since Switzerland was a neutral country that recognized the People's Republic. Since SwissAir didn't have flights across the Pacific, we would fly from Atlanta to New York on a domestic carrier, then SwissAir to Zurich on a U.S. passport; then a Romanian airline to Bucharest, where we would stay a minimum of 24 hours to be issued "temporary Romanian citizenship" and then travel on Romanian visas to visit the People's Republic of China. Since there were currently no flights to the People's Republic from Romania, the Chinese government would send a plane to Bucharest for the 100 of us at the appointed time and that military aircraft would transport us to Peking. We would depart China at Canton with train passage to Hong Kong, where we would be flown back to the United States by SwissAir through Bombay (India), Karachi (Pakistan), Athens (Greece), Zurich (Switzerland), New York City, and then Atlanta, Georgia through a domestic carrier. Transportation to and from Atlanta, Georgia, was to be arranged by each individual of the tour group. Upon arrival in Atlanta, we were to gather at a Ramada Hotel near the airport for three days at which time we would be given further details of our itinerary, plane tickets, instructions in the Chinese language, and an introduction to the current political culture of the People's Republic of China.

That's all they said, other than warning us that some areas would be hot, hotels in China were "not Western in accommodation", and we could not bring Poloroid cameras, traveler's checks other than Cook's (England) or Bank of America (California) would not be honored, nor would any credit cards. American money or the two types of traveler's checks could be exchanged only at specified times and places, and no pictures could be taken at airports or from airplanes, train depots, ports, military bases, or power plant installations.

I left for Atlanta on my birthday and found there 100 people gathered for the "orientation." It was kind of silly as I look back on it. The People's Republic of China, in this grand experiment of dealing with Westerners, had selected four of each of twenty five categories of U.S. citizens. There were four physicians, four judges, four professors (of which I was one), four American Indians, four American Blacks, four "union members," four "entrepreneurs" (defined as those who didn't work and lived off of unearned income), four capitalist businessmen, four museum curators, four millionaires, etc.—all drawn from the pool of thousands who had applied to go at some point or another. What Chinese political scientist or sociologist had come up with this scheme I'll never know, but to be selected to go just because you happened to be black or happened to be a millionaire or happened to be in a union or happened to be a Native American seemed strange. But there we were.

The next thing was to teach us Mandarin Chinese in three days. By the second day, they had come to the conclusion this was hopeless. So they worked us around the clock simply learning to say "hello" and "thank you" and expounding on the differences between the People's Republic and the United States. [The overwhelming "differences" in those days included practically every topic currently taught in higher education. It was like comparing America to a country from outer space at that time]. Taking in our obvious excitement at the adventure, the Chinese looked more and more worried. Most questions such as: "Could we send mail back to the U.S?" "What if someone got sick?" "What would we be fed?" "Where would we stay at night?" even, "What cities are we going to visit in China?" were all met with an impatient stare and a curt "It will all be taken care of." In other words, they didn't have a clue. Their job was to get us there.

The plane took off with the 100 of us and at New York, we were put onto SwissAir and eventually we were in Zurich, being hustled onto an old Russian airplane that was part of the Romanian Airlines headed for Bucharest. The seats in the plane were about three inches narrower than our seats and I found myself jammed between a huge Soviet businessman and an equally huge Romanian woman with a lot of hair on her legs and arms, neither of whom had ever heard of deodorants, but compensated with a bottle of perfume dumped on each of them. The seats were upholstered in what I swear were cotton Indian blankets like you used to buy at a dime store like Kresge's or Woolworth's, and instead of carpet, it had linoleum floors colored bright yellow. The seat belts were far too narrow to go around any of the three of us in my row (which was sort of embarrassing) and when the steward noticed this, he just ignored it since the belts fit less than half of the people in the plane. The interior temperature got so hot, even the bottle of perfume failed on each of my partners long before the flight reached Bucharest, which negated eating, but a meal was never offered anyway.

When the plane landed, we were lined up to go through the Army's immigration control and then whisked into little curtained stalls one at time for the most thorough, intimate, and prolonged frisking I'd ever experienced. [In hindsight, if you weren't so intimidated and shocked at the time, you would have screamed, hit the person fondling you, or balked and walked out of the booth.] The middle-aged pervert, with an automatic rifle strapped across his back, stunk on top of everything else, and when he finally slapped you on the rump to indicate he was through with you, gave you a farewell smirk daring you to complain about his gross indecencies with your body. With that over, we were marched through a long double line of armed men, taken to a bus with bars on the windows, and driven to our downtown Bucharest hotel.

The hotel, the tallest and finest in Bucharest, had been patched together after a serious earthquake two years earlier but huge cracks, broken windows, and falling plaster still predominated the decor. Even more intriguing were all the rubber tires stacked to the ceiling on each room's outside patio. The elevator was broken but fortunately I was only on the ninth floor so after a hour or so I managed to get all my luggage up to the room and could explore my little patio all my myself. The tires were new but had been on the patio for ages going by all the plaster dust coating them. In fact, I suspected they had been there before the earthquake. By supper that night, I found out the manager of the state-owned hotel was a brother of the Transportation Minister and, for a steep price, you could buy a tire from him if you were lucky enough to own a car. Judging from the thousands of aged tires on those balconies, I concluded that few people owned cars, the price wasn't right, or people were unwilling to risk illegally trading in such a visible black market, brother of the minister or not. I found out later all three conclusions were correct.

The furnished dinner in the hotel was inedible with the exception of the bread and salad, but breakfast the next morning was "on us." I choose coffee, orange juice, and a Danish. When I got the bill for $45 U.S. (they wouldn't accept their own money), I offered them a U.S. $5 bill which was accepted as full payment without question. Even though I felt taken at $5, some of my fellow travelers actually paid the outrageous amounts billed.

The rest of Bucharest was similar. There was really nothing of any value for sale in the stores other than a few second-hand goods left over from a happier time, the people look gray and glum, and the tourist attractions were totally phoney. Our group was shuttled to a "typical Romanian village" a few miles north of the city. When the buses arrived, peasants in native costumes were gayly singing folk songs as they swept the streets with huge handmade brooms. Children in bright colors sang as they walked to a large cathedral, presumably to pray, while old people sat in rocking chairs on the streets chatting to each other in a highly animated fashion. It was like a scene from the German operetta "The Student Prince." We weren't allowed off the bus, but I happened to be in the last bus and, as it turned the corner, I saw the actors abruptly stop singing, the old people and children headed for a truck to take them to the next assembly or back to their farms, and everyone was stripping out of the peasant clothing to reveal the ordinary clothing they wore under their "costumes." Our government guide was busy explaining how this was how life was in a typical Romanian village and how freedom of religion, speech, political expression, and individual lifestyle were all enhanced by the glories of their socialist government. Never mind the Party Chairman had held a firm grip on the country since the end of World War II—he was a kind and benevolent father who put his people's welfare before all. Next, we visited a construction project which would house over 15,000 people when completed. Each family assigned would have about 700 square feet to live in with a shared bath and kitchen. It was the only "new" housing available and I suppose was appealing compared to the antiquated and overcrowded pre-World War II housing available throughout the rest of the city. But newness has its price: window openings were trapezoidal guaranteeing the windows didn't fit, plaster was already peeling, and plumbing, made out of a cheap plastic, was exposed to the elements. After that, we visited another carefully choreographed event, this time a "spontaneous celebration of Romanian culture," before visiting the Chinese embassy in Bucharest where we were issued People's Republic of China visas as temporary citizens of Romania and told we would be leaving for China in the morning. As we returned to our rooms, I witnessed people not in costume selling pint-sized glass jars of gasoline they had thoughtfully siphoned out of government trucks that day.

After waiting about six hours at the airport the next morning, a lonely Boeing 707 appeared with Chinese military markings. There was no one on it—it had been sent all the way from China just to pick us up. Being a old military aircraft had its disadvantages. In this narrow-bodied plane, they had somehow put four seats on one side of the aisle and three on the other. I was wedged into a narrow seat next to the window and knew I'd just have to hold it until we landed for fuel somewhere. There were no overhead luggage racks, no galley, no stewardess or stewards, no snack tables. But strangely, there were six wide and luxurious first class seats up front in this military airplane from a classless society. I found out those were for Chinese military officers or party big wigs when the Communist party used the plane. I thought only capitalist societies provided different accommodations for different statuses, like AirForce One or General MacArthur's plane. I knew a 707 couldn't make it all the way from Bucharest to Peking without refueling, so I silently speculated on where we'd gas up. The straightest route is over the southern portions of the Soviet Union, but since China was into serious quarreling with the Soviets at that time (several armed border skirmishes had recently occurred), I knew the Chinese wouldn't risk flying over the Soviet Union, let alone land there. So I figured we would refuel in Afghanistan or Pakistan or, more spectacularly, refuel in midair. I never dreamed we would refuel where we did.

After all feeling had left me from the chest down and all thoughts were narrowed down to controlling my bladder, I felt the plane began to descend in the dark night. We landed on the outskirts of some airport but never taxied in. Soon the door opened and we were told to walk across all the runways to a distant building where there would be restaurant and bathroom facilities. We didn't mind the walk with our paralyzed legs, but holding it in any longer was out of the question. The women took one side of the plane, the men the other and bodily needs were met in the dark of night before any walks anywhere commenced. As we neared the terminal, we found ourselves staring at a huge portrait, at least two stories tall, of the Shah. It was my first visit to Iran.

It was two in the morning and the airport was practically deserted. Using a real restroom was exciting and finding a functional water cooler was even better. I joined the long line to buy a Coca-Cola to fortify me for the rest of the trip when I heard shouting and screaming in Farsi coming out of a small shop. Suddenly, all shops closed by pulling the iron grates over the openings to the lobby of the airport accompanied by dark looks, a lot of cursing and handshaking, and a few scuffles breaking out as the Persian merchants began pushing and shoving members of our American group. But one word was understood by all: "Jew." It turned out one of the categories of four was Jews (along with blacks, lawyers, etc.), so four Jews were apparently in our group. The merchants had "spotted" those looking like Jews, asked them if they were Jews, and when they replied yes, the demonstrations broke out against these Jews while the Iranian police stood idly by watching. Even though all our group had in common was that we were adventurous Americans, I'm proud to say our group sized up the situation instantly, surrounded the besieged "Jews," and the whole group marched back en mass all the way to the airplane parked at the end of the tarmac. Since we couldn't get back on the plane until they were through refueling, we stood as a group around the Jews, now crying in their fright, that dark night. The angry Iranian merchants shouted and screamed at us while the Shah's police held their distance and passively watched the scene. It was Americanism at its best in my opinion. That constituted my first and only visit to Iran.

Wedged back in my window seat, we were crossing the Himalayas just as the sun was coming up and I'll never forget the beauty of the sun's rays first striking the rugged snow-covered peaks of the highest mountains in the world. I thought it was a sight I'd never see again and I made sure I'd always remember it. By afternoon, we descended into a huge brown dust cloud which obscured any particulars and I correctly guessed we were landing in Peking. By this time, all of us looked bedraggled and weary: deodorants had failed; the men badly needed shaves, clothes were permanently and forever wrinkled, and, by the look on strained faces, everyone needed a restroom.

When the door opened and we staggered out, I looked up and saw a huge poster of Chairman Mao hanging from the roof of the airport along with a block-long banner welcoming the 100 Americans written in both English and Chinese. Then I saw what looked at first like thousands and thousands of black and white dots on window ledges, balconies, and porches. As I got closer, I realized those dots were Chinese, all dressed in Mao's prescribed dark trousers and white shirts gazing silently at these aliens from another world. Apparently, half the town had turned out to see us, and had probably waited for hours since our plane had left Bucharest long after schedule. It was my introduction to Mao's China and prescient of things to come.

Within a hour, we were divided into four groups of 25 (The "Greens," "Reds," "Blues," and "Yellows") and herded into small buses holding exactly 27 people: 25 Americans, one Chinese "guide and translator" and a driver. Twenty minutes after that I was standing in Tienemen Square facing the entrance to the Forbidden City, unbelievable to an American who for thirty years hadn't even seen pictures of the famous square until Nixon's visit. A shiver went down my back as I thrilled that a person who never dreamed they could—let alone would—ever visit this mysterious and forbidden country was now actually standing in its most famous spot. I was really here! The overwhelming and very personal sense of conquest, of supreme satisfaction, of satiated curiosity, I'll never forget.

The Forbidden City was in the process of being restored in 1978 and still showed signs of Japanese occupation during World War II when they had used it as a horse barn for their calvary. The parts that had been restored were fresh and magnificent. The Temple of Heaven, the Empress' Park, the Great Wall, and most other attractions now familiar to foreign tourists were all uncrowded, freshly restored, and mainly filled with the Chinese people themselves, all dressed in loose fitting dark colored trousers, plastic sandals, and white shirts regardless of gender. Some still faithfully carried their copy of Mao's famous "Red Book" with them at all times, and most parents proudly took their allowable "only child" with them everywhere. The government's policy of "one child, one family" to control overpopulation was already well in place. In those days, we weren't allowed into the Great People's Hall on Tienemen Square where Nixon had been entertained, but we were right there the first day Mao's mausoleum opened right next door to the People's Hall. Our group of Americans was ushered to the front of the line so we ended up being the very first people to see the magnificent building containing Mao's corpse.

The numerous public parks were "sponsored" by school children. This meant a given school class was responsible for keeping the park in great shape and they got the credit for it. In one park, I saw a class of eight-year-old's eagerly picking up the litter and washing the sidewalks. The next time I was about to throw a gum wrapper down, I thought of those kids' efforts and put the wrapper in my pocket instead. The Chinese must have felt the same way: I never saw much litter anywhere despite the hoards of people. What an effective program: the children had a sense of purpose, responsibility and possession; the adults learned to monitor their own behavior for the public good. How different from our system where we just discard our waste without a thought and then expect low-level paid workers to resentfully pick up the leavings of others, consequently taking little pride in their status or their work.

A visit to several schools was also instructive. At the first one, the entry way was lined with uniformed five-year-old's waving little American flags shouting "Welcome, American aunts and uncles" in English they didn't understand. When I asked the director (principal) why they were doing this when only a year before they had been practicing bayoneting American mannequins, he quickly smiled and said, "Because it is to our advantage to do so now" with nary a sign of moral ambivalence in his expression. I soon learned that Chinese, if nothing else, are very flexible and can apparently with no visible qualms change values as the wind changes direction.

In China, what went on in a school in a given grade was the same throughout China whether it was some remote village in Manchuria or in the urban sprawl of Shanghai due to strong central control by the government. That day, the children in the second grade were presenting a musical for the other students (and all children's parents that night) which didn't need much translation. People in a village were starving, sick and desperate as a result of a cruel and greedy capitalist landlord prior to the Revolution. Enter the People's Liberation Army of Chairman Mao. The evil landlords were promptly executed and the people were provided land of their own, medical care, freedom from hunger, and even schooling. The saga ended with a rousing hymn of thanksgiving for the Revolution. Although the scenario seemed trite to us, the point is that historically the musical was more accurate than not and there were plenty of older Chinese around that would testify as to its basic truths. The source of musical accompaniment was an old Estey organ made in the U.S. My childhood church was always raising money for an Estey organ (which was portable and cheap) for the Chinese missions at that time. As I looked at that old battered Estey wheezing away to the modern Communist paeans, I was just sure that was the very organ my church had paid for out of the proceeds of many covered dish dinners back in the Ozark Mountains.

Even more jolting was a lesson for six-year-old's I witnessed in another school. At that time, toys weren't available in China and could only be found in school settings (which made school even more appealing to children). Along the wall on the shelves of this classroom were some really nice toys, one of which was a beautiful metal scale model of a Rolls-Royce. The teacher picked the valued toy up and passed it around the room so each child had a chance to play with it a bit and study its fine details. Then the lesson began: "What is it?" A car. "Where is it made?" No one knew. This quickly produced a world map and the tiny island of Great Britain was located and compared to the vastness of China. "How much does the car cost?" Again no one knew. The teacher pointed out the car costs more than both their parents would earn working hard over their entire lifetime. Unbelieving gasps could be heard around the classroom. Eventually, one child asked "But who could afford the car?" Great Britain wasn't a socialist country it was pointed out—it operated under an old system called capitalism which used to be practiced in China before the Revolution. In that system, some people "have enough money to buy such a car and drive right by others who are so desperately poor they are sick and starving." The gasps of disbelief turned to a few utterances of outrage. "Would you like to live in a capitalist country like Great Britain?" the teacher coaxed. Hearing the thunderous and unanimous "no," she then summarized "Aren't you glad you live in the People's Republic of China?" A look of good fortune settled over the class and the Rolls-Royce was put back on the shelf to remind all of the horrible excesses of an unfettered economic system. [Actually, the teacher *understated* the case. At that time, the Chinese worker was averaging $25 a month or both parents $50 a month for a total of $600 a year. Assuming they were able to work 40 years each, their total earnings would be $24,000—far, far less than the $180,000 cost of the car at that time. She should have said "Seven and a half sets of parents would have to work a lifetime to pay for the car."]

In yet another class, we saw toy building blocks being distributed to a group of eight-year-old's along with the "blueprints" of a bridge. The task was to build the bridge using the building blocks. Most of the children quickly put the bridge together following the blueprint diagrams. But one child put the bridge together a different way than the blueprint demonstrated. The teacher quickly spotted the deviancy, sternly told the boy to stand up, face his colleagues and apologize for selfishly building the bridge to meet his needs, not those of the collective group. Whereas we would likely praise that child for their originality, their creativity, their inventiveness, in that classroom such behavior was characterized as selfish, immature, self-centered, and irresponsible to the overall needs of the society. As I heard the boy's voice quiver in his public shame, I knew from then on he'd carefully monitor any individuality that might wander to the surface in the future. The end result would be a society of obedient and highly conforming citizens regardless of what the presented "social needs" were. And a society where inventiveness, creativity, and discovery were strangely absence. [Twenty years later, that's exactly what you do observe in many, many cases. They are expert at copying the best efforts of others, are masters of working together, and are easy to control for a population exceeding one billion, but inventive, creative— hardly!]

Our group traveled over 3000 miles by train throughout China. Enroute, I got to know the assigned guide for our group of 25. He had recently graduated from a university majoring in English and hoped to be assigned to handle tourists (as he was doing with us) if the state decided to allow that in the future. He was good looking, pleasant, and articulate, so he'd make a good tourist guide in any country. But he was a recent university graduate and I was curious as to what he knew. Not much in my opinion. He'd never heard of Plato, the Pharaohs of Ancient Egypt, Alexander the Great, Julius Caesar, Jesus of Nazareth, Mohammed, Shakespeare, or even Hitler. He had heard of Karl Marx (but didn't know of his main work, the *Manifesto*), and certainly the Chinese dynasties of the past. I asked him why I knew of the long histories and contributions of the various Chinese dynasties, the major religious thought of historical China including extensive knowledge of Confucius and Taoism, and even the suffering of China prior to the Revolution, and yet he had never heard of any of the major influences on Western Culture. Was he really educated or just trained to think one way? He blanched at such heresy and said his education avoided "confusing and erroneous thoughts." I assured him I was smart enough to handle the confusions and who was to say what was erroneous? Was his education really honest? He said he liked me but we couldn't talk this way anymore. He was right of course, but

I knew I'd made my point and he'd wonder forever after about what he had missed out on. No wonder fifteen years later it was the students who were demonstrating against the government.

Each sleeper car on the train also carried an old Chinese woman who prepared hot water for the tea morning, noon, and night in a big aluminum kettle over an open flame toward the back of the car. She also fixed the meals when due, made up the beds, swept the floor, and cleaned out the primitive toilet facilities occasionally. Even at night she didn't rest: she monitored all sleeping arrangements by stationing herself holding a club in the middle of the car. Men at one end of the car, women at the other and nary the two shall cross regardless of whether they were married, 70 years old, or crippled. There would be no sex on her ship regardless. In that sense, she was reflective of the Puritanism so rampant in Mao's China. When I asked the good-looking unmarried guide about sex, he turned bright red and looked like he was going to die so I changed the topic before he suffered a heart attack. Yes, these are the same people that will kill to obtain ground-up rhinoceros horn for its alleged aphrodisiac effects and avidly buy up all the ginseng root they can find, because they believe eating the penis-shaped root leads to a bigger penis. It reminded me of the Victorians who fainted at the mention of sex, but supported more prostitutes than any other Western society at the time.

In Dalian, near the Soviet border, we visited the largest bomb shelter in the world. They had schools, hospitals, vast mess halls, and endless dorms carved out of a nearby mountain which would protect all two million citizens when the Soviets attacked them. They sported a system of public announcement unparalleled anywhere else. Loudspeakers were placed every few hundred feet throughout the city to instruct the people in case of attack, but it also served as a "voice newspaper." We heard the word "American" over and over as our visit to the city was announced to the populace. As a result, everywhere the four little buses went, we were surrounded by thousands and thousands of curious bystanders who hadn't seen a Westerner in over 30 years, so well over half the population had never seen a foreigner at all. When I stepped off the bus, I became an anatomical sensation: they'd never seen anyone as fat as I was; they'd never seen anyone with red hair; they'd never seen anyone with blue eyes; they'd never seen anyone with lots of hair on their arms and chest; in fact, they'd never seen anyone with white skin. When they ascertained I wasn't dangerous, the more aggressive began to feel my red hair, gently poke at my blue eyes, and feel the hair on my arms as they excitingly reported their findings to others. When I decided to see what was in a nearby neighborhood store, they followed me in until the store was jammed as I purchased a metal rice bowl for two cents which led to a flurry of Chinese jabber presumably about why I would want such a common bowl. When I picked up a small child and hugged him, the crowd clapped its appreciation. I felt like Marco Polo! It was on this segment of the trip I discovered Mao had set the price of a pack of cigarettes artificially low (one-fifth of one cent) so the people would have at least one evil available to them since liquor was taxed out of reach, opiate usage led to immediate execution, and prostitution led to a life sentencing. But each cigarette package was used to teach reading, geography, or mathematics since Mao's China was still struggling with its inherited educational problem of illiteracy among adults at that time.

In Manchuria the rice was seasoned well and peppered with tiny bits of chopped meat I later found out was dog. [Somehow I was sure my own dog at home innately knew of my indiscretion and was deeply ashamed for me.] There, we visited a regional technology university which specialized in research on water usage. All the students at least read English well and I was astonished to discover all our scientific journals on physics, computers, chemistry, and even psychology were on the shelves there and were widely read (going from their well-curled and smudged pages), even though we had no diplomatic relations with China at that time and our government had been openly hostile toward China since Mao's takeover in 1949. Professors were held in high regard and were relatively well paid, but all had to pass tests of "political correctness," got their appointments through the Communist Party, and even they had to participate, along with their students, in the hard manual labor of harvest one month a year to remind them of their proletarian origins.

In Canton, we visited a number of homes with their caged chickens inside, their charcoal cookers, and their heated beds. Mao had outlawed humans being used as draft animals to transport other humans, so the rickshaws were now used to transport goods rather than wealthy individuals. The streets were so crowded they had turned into pedestrian thoroughfares which precluded motorized traffic and it was interesting to study how people could live so close together and maintain any privacy. From my lodgings, I could look down on the crowded neighborhood surrounding the hotel. I found people taking baths naked with their bucket of water in totally public places since there was no room to be private, but no one really looked at them and everyone kept their eyes diverted. The same was true of disciplining errant children, times of personal intimacy, and normal family interactions. Humans make social privacy when it can't be arranged physically.

Like most places in urban China at that time, water was only available one hour a day, dependent on which district you lived in. During that allotted hour, everyone did the washing, bathing, and cleaning which required flowing water. After their hour was up, the water was diverted to the next sector of the city.

In Canton, I learned how you maintain close discipline in classrooms holding 50 or so children two to a desk and one teacher in a very crowded room. If a child causes a problem in the class, his entire family (parents, grandparents, brothers and sisters) are all called to a neighborhood council held that night and are required to tell their neighbors and friends why that child will not disturb the classroom again, how he or she will learn better, and how she or he will become a better citizen. This involves some brow-beating also on how they can be better parents, how the family can direct the child better, and so on. Others in the council are encouraged to offer suggestions to effect change in the child. All the while, the child being discussed is not only present, but required to stand facing the whole neighborhood as well as his entire family and all the school personnel. There just weren't many continuing behavioral problems with this system but if they did continue, the child was expelled for life from further schooling. "Schooling is a privilege; not a right" was the curt answer to my inquiries.

I also discovered that quickness of judicial decision was more valued than safeguards of innocence. The Chinese seemed to find torturous and inhuman our system of lengthy trials and endless appeals before final decisions are made. "How can you stand the indecision?" was the common observation on our judicial system. When you answered "To always make sure the person accused actually is guilty" seemed inadequate to them, who pointed out the people appealing usually were guilty anyway and, for those who weren't, it still ruined their lives with long periods of imprisonment awaiting trials. In China of that time, every criminal defended himself (Mao had banned lawyers as "agents of social decay"), trials were held the same day as the person was accused, and the sentence was carried out "before the sun set." It was efficient. In the old China, the judicial system had become paralyzed with one lawyer for each ten people, delays running into years, and where only the wealthy could hire lawyers. The reaction to this corruption was their system in the late seventies which stressed equality of defense, efficiency, and timeliness. Safeguards to protect the innocent took a back seat.

When I left China weeks later, the train tracks abruptly ended at the Hong Kong border. We got off the train under guard, walked across a small bridge separating the People's Republic from Hong Kong, and got on another train owned by the British to whisk us to the capitalist Mecca of Hong Kong. I can't describe the contrast—in societies, in economies, in culture—jolting you within 15 minutes from each other. In Hong Kong, I saw a gold-plated Rolls-Royce within blocks of the most miserable slums in the world. I saw some of the world's most luxurious hotels next to squalid disease-infested dumps where thousands of people lived. I thought of the little toy Rolls-Royce way back in that little Chinese classroom and the lesson that went with it.

When I checked in with SwissAir for the flight home the wrong way around the world, I was politely told it would be over 32,000 miles non-stop and I couldn't physically endure such a marathon. I told the agent I had to because my classes began three days later. He shared a few really good tips on how to survive long flights, wished me luck and I was on my way home. I went to India, Pakistan, Greece, Switzerland, New York, Atlanta, and finally home where my wife was faithfully waiting with a wheelchair in that she was convinced I wouldn't be able to walk by that time. But I could and within a day was back in my classroom doing what I always did, but I knew I'd never be the same after this great adventure of going to Mao's China.

THE AMERICAN WEST & THE CARIBBEAN

HOW TO TRAVEL WITH

TEENAGERS AND SURVIVE

At some point or another, most middle-class American parents seem to think they are obligated to show their children the marvels of the American West. We were not immune to these parental urges and so, when our two boys were 14 and 15, we decided the time had come if I could find a competent person to run the summer children's program I was forever involved in, while we would be gone.

The replacement problem was easily solved. Mike Rees, an extremely competent person who had worked in the children's program for two summers before, decided he wanted to apply for the Director's job the very summer we hoped to take off a short while. He was the kind of person who had great common sense, a genuine love of the program, and in whom I had complete trust. It seemed our time to travel to the West had come.

A close psychologist friend of mine in another town who had three teenage boys of his own had attempted a "family trip" the previous summer to the Canadian provinces of Ontario and Quebec. Before they were 80 miles down the road the bickering and fighting between the boys had reached a crescendo, he admitted he'd "lost it" as a psychologist, and had even stooped to the old parental trick of pulling the car over to the side of the road, expelling the oldest from the car, and threatening to drive away without him. After 200 miles, his wife was in chronic tears, his blood pressure was reaching heart-attack level, and most in the car weren't speaking to each other. By the time they reached Niagara Falls, my friend admitted going over in a barrel sounded "refreshing," especially if he didn't have to continue on the "vacation." In Montreal, the boys found themselves suddenly enrolled in a very expensive residential ice hockey school for a week so he and his wife could rest up for the dreaded trip home together in the car. When I told him we were thinking of driving to California, he firmly told me it would be an emotional disaster of epic proportions, dysfunctional for even the best of family structures, economically catastrophic in view of teenage demands and eating habits, and the anti-depressants required for months afterwards for both my wife and I would be expensive. It wasn't a happy tale and we took his warning seriously.

We planned to take six weeks off for the trip. We would cover the Midwest and Southwest going out to Las Vegas and San Diego, then up the California coast to San Francisco, then head East through Yosemite, Sacramento, the Sierra Nevadas, Reno, then the Rockies, Denver, Kansas City, St. Louis, Hannibal, Milwaukee, and any other places along the line that warranted a visit. It was the standard "loop" trip to California from the Midwest. We had saved $5000 for all expenses of the trip and had a new car ready and waiting. But, according to my psychologist friend, all this meant was we would be paying out five grand for "six weeks in Hell." My wife and I hesitated, but plunged ahead anyway since she had never seen the West herself and thought we might be able to circumvent some of the problems due to the nature of our boys (although the psychologist friend's children seemed very nice on the surface), clever preplanning, and trying out some ideas we'd been harboring for some time.

First off, we switched the tables on our boys. Instead of us planning and being responsible for the trip and then being blamed for its shortcomings, we made them responsible for all planning, including all money expenditures. Second, we gave them the hard-earned $5000 and told them this was all we had—it was their job to make sure we had enough to eat and buy the gas to get home and if they ran out, we'll all be stranded somewhere. If we returned with money left over, it was theirs to split between the two of them. Third, both my wife and I gave them a list of things we wanted to see ourselves whether they did or not—adult things, like Hoover Dam, the John Paul Getty Art Museum, Gunnison's Canyon, Harrad's Auto Collection in Reno, a meal at the Coronado Hotel in San Diego, the San Francisco Opera, the Mark Hopkins Hotel. Although my wife's and my lengthy lists didn't match, it didn't matter—these were musts. The rest of it was up to them and, if they would go to all our events, we would go to theirs. Fourth, they were to make all decisions as to where to stay, what and where to eat, and to pay for all car expenses, allowing enough to pay for an emergency such as a new tire, a broken water pump, etc.

The boys bought this concept 100 percent and a flurry of activity followed in the privacy of their rooms. A book "Free Tours of Industrial and Manufacturing Sites" arrived in the mail; the Mobil "Motor Guide of the West" also arrived whereupon it was explained "so we'd know what was expensive;" calculators hummed as gasoline costs were compared to estimated mileages; and each day new "guidelines" from the two of them were issued.

It was announced that Holiday Inns, long the mainstay of overnight lodging for us up to that point was "a ripoff" as was any other motel that was located on major highways, had a national reservation system, and featured swimming pools. Motels "just as nice" but far cheaper could be found on minor highways or at least a few blocks off a major highway; non-chain motels "weren't wasting a lot of money advertising nationally;" the costs of national reservation systems was "passed on to the consumer and who needed reservations anyway if you stopped early before supper;" we would "only use a swimming pool every two or three days to save money so why pay for it if you didn't need it."

Restaurants costs were too high for long travel they announced.

To save money, we would buy a portable icebox and stock it with milk and fruit which, with dry cereal and some sugar we'd also buy at a local grocery, would do fine for breakfast. Lunch could be prepared out of the icebox also what with the purchase of bread, cheese, salad dressing, lettuce, and luncheon meats for a variety of sandwiches along with potato, ham, and chicken salad we'll also get at a supermarket along the way and keep in our icebox. Pop, which they claimed had a 500% markup in restaurants "for what you get after you take the ice away" would be bought by the case and we'd cool it ourselves in the icebox filled each morning out of the motel ice machine.

Plant tours were free and would be interesting. Besides, they usually gave you a free sample when you finished the tour. We would be taking plant tours of everything from Ocean Spray cranberry juice to Hershey's Chocolate to Jockey underwear to the San Francisco *Daily Examiner* newspaper. And when they found out what the fabled "Disney Land" actually cost for even a one day visit, Walt Disney was labeled as one who was "a creative, but totally greedy capitalist exploiting little children." We would be visiting the Universal Studios tour in Los Angeles instead—"a much better buy and far more interesting." A few compliments were passed our way in that museums seem to have relatively low admission charges for what you get to see; that a few restaurants on my list were expensive but probably worth it compared to the "slop you get at most highway places" and "it'd be neat to have eaten there just once at least." Even the all-day $80 fee for the four of us to see the largest auto collection in the world (since broken up and sold off) seemed "reasonable" since it would take a full day to get our money's worth and we'd carry our lunch with us to save an hour and the costs of the restaurant inside the grounds so we could see more and spend less at the same time.

The Oldsmobile 98 would get better mileage if we kept the speed down to 55 or 60 and we should only use the air conditioner when it got over 80 outside. If I went my usual speeds, the gasoline consumption would be higher than they wanted to pay for. What a switch from the usual: "Are we in a funeral procession?" "Why is everyone passing us?" etc.

As they worked away in their planning, it became obvious to them they needed to divide up the work. Consequently, they decided early between them that one would be in charge of routing, car expenses, and lodging. The other was in charge of food expenses, entrance fees, and scheduled activities although major disagreements could be negotiated not only when it was planned, but later if the reality didn't match the planning.

The time finally arrived and the boys carefully loaded the car with the purchased icebox, the initial groceries, all the luggage necessary for six weeks of continual travel, and their maps, guide books, and all their carefully made plans laid out in the back seat. This was clearly "their trip" and they were assuming responsibility from the beginning.

We visited all the places of the West most people visit and then some and we saw more sights and took in more events than I thought possible within our time frame. We never had a quarrel, never experienced whining or nagging, never heard any complaints, and never heard any regrets about things they felt we couldn't afford. We did have a wonderful trip that drew us together in our shared experiences, we learned to appreciate each other's values and peculiarities along the way, and, best of all, loved each other's sense of humor and adventuresomeness. We did twice as much as we thought we would, had done it all in four instead of six weeks, and returned home with over 40 percent of our money intact.

"It's your money," I told the boys when they tried to give it back to me. "You delivered everything you promised; your mother and I got to see everything we had on our lists, and a lot more we really enjoyed. You saved it through your good planning. You can do with it what you want—I'm good for my word."

About that time, the boy's favorite TV show was "The Love Boat" about life on a cruise ship. "Let's all go on a cruise at Christmas," they suggested. "We'll pay for it as long as you get the best buy possible."

"Sounds good to your mother and me," I countered, "as long as you'll pay."

"I hear Carnival Lines only charges full fare for one party, two-thirds fare for the second party, and kids under 16 can go free if the adults book a room holding four," they started in and that very Christmas all four of us were on a fabulous seven-day special Christmas cruise of the Dominican Republic, the Virgin Islands, San Martin, Puerto Rico, and a number of other interesting stops. All four of us were in one room, but we had only paid 1-2/3 adult fare for the four of us including all the airfare to and from home. It was such a great buy, they still had enough of the California money left over to pay for another Christmas cruise the following year on the same boat.

Again, it was "their cruise". The boys had chosen the boat, the destinations, and the activities and we all loved both of the Christmas adventures. We saw children with beri-beri and rickets amidst the horrible poverty in the Dominican Republic where both my children realized a two cent vitamin pill a day would have prevented such tragedy; we saw adults driven to begging in their hunger alongside people living in great wealth who seemed totally uncaring of the human need often all around them; we saw women driven to desperate prostitution; we even saw people so poor they had no clothes. All this contrasted mightily with the luxury of an American cruise ship. They weren't oblivious to these contrasts and wondered aloud about the injustice of such inequities. They were learning lessons no regular school could teach them.

PERU AND BOLIVIA

CROSSING THE ANDES MOUNTAINS

I was most pleased when my oldest son wanted a foreign trip for his high school graduation present instead of the more traditional gifts such as fancy clothing, a gold class ring, a watch, or even a car. All those things would wear out or get lost—the value of travel, like all education, would go on forever.

When Paul said he wanted to cross the Andes Mountains, I knew he was my son! He wanted to see the homelands of the Incas, the "hidden city" of Machu Picchu, cross the second highest chain of mountains in the world, and sail across Lake Titicaca, the highest lake in the world, to Bolivia, the land of political revolutions, cocaine, and blue potatoes. And he wanted me to accompany him on the trip. Perfect, I thought, in that I couldn't think of anyplace I'd rather go! We set about planning the trip immediately.

In those days, not too many people were interested in such a trip, and it took a long time and a lot of hunting to find a tour that would take us where we wanted to go. Finally, we spotted a tour led by an anthropologist at U.C.L.A. and sponsored by American Express. This tour was primarily focused on the "non-Spanish" areas of South American Indians and led by the anthropologist who spoke fluently all five of the non-written Indian languages prevalent in the areas we would be visiting. Twice the trip was canceled for lack of interested participants, but the third date selected attracted the necessary minimum of 15 or so. We were scheduled to leave the last week of August which interfered with the beginning of Paul's senior year of high school, but that would be mainly review anyway so we decided to go ahead rather than risk yet another cancellation.

We flew to Lima to meet our group and found the city paralyzed by a "general strike" against the current government. Welcome to the realities of South America. Nevertheless, we were able to see the government palaces, the cathedrals, the museums, the opulent homes owned by some of the world's richest landholders side-by-side to the continent's worst slums inhabited by some of the world's most desperate peoples. The social contrasts were jolting. The museums reflected these contrasts. The Gold Museum dazzled the eyes with tons of the stuff, while outside the gates scabby diseased children were dying of malnutrition. The nuns running the Archeological Museum wouldn't allow my 17-year-old son inside, because they displayed the erotic and explicit clay statuettes Incas used to teach sexuality to their children. So he was forced to wait outside in the streets where children, much younger than him, were openly selling their bodies to any and everyone for a dollar bill, a bar of soap, or even a scrap of food. The paradoxes of South America were all around us.

We first headed south to the Plains of Nasca where the unexplained sand writings of some ancient people are still there in the desert. About the only way to view them is from an airplane, so we climbed into the first one available: an ancient Piper Cub that seated four. My son and an adventurous cello player from the St. Louis Symphony climbed into the narrow back seat, leaving the front seat for my girth. As I gripped the passenger grab-rail to pull myself in, the whole dash moved out a few inches—an ominous beginning. When the pilot tied the passenger door shut with some baling wire, I knew we were in trouble. Then I noticed that on the pilot's side, the door had just fallen off long ago. When I stated I'd changed my mind about the ride, the pilot laughed and said "You Americano", starting the sputtering engine before I realized he understood not one word of English. As the plane taxied forward, I thought I better fasten my seat belt before discovering it had long ago been replaced with a simple rope which you just tied around your belly.

Amazingly, the plane got off the sand airstrip without too much trouble and soon we were winging across the famed desert plains. As the first drawing came into view, the pilot motioned over the roar of the engine to look down and then abruptly tilted the plane 90 degrees, presumably to offer us the best view. The small rope strained against my belly and I felt Paul's hands grip the back of my seat for all he was worth. We saw the drawing of the "Eagle" splendidly, but not before Paul shouted out he was getting sick and the cellist was frozen in a catatonic reaction to extreme fear. Her eyes didn't even blink. I motioned for the pilot to land as best he could, but he interpreted this as enthusiasm for his piloting and proceeded to flip the plane 180 degrees to its other side. Thirty minutes later, we had seen all of the famed sand drawings from every possible angle and the pilot celebrated by withdrawing a small flask from his jacket and helped himself to a big swallow before preparing to land. I was so scared my hands trembled as I tried to unknot the rope around my middle; Paul was white from airsickness and threw up the minute he lunged out of the backseat, while the cellist remained frozen in position and had to be bodily lifted out of the plane. Amazingly, within five minutes recovery time, the three of us all agreed the plane trip was wonderful and well worth any "inconveniences."

On the Pacific coastline next to the Chilean border, we were shown the spot where the penguins of Antarctica migrate at a certain time. In an amazing feat of timing that would be the dream of any travel agent, just as this was announced we spotted some tiny dots in the distance which turned out to be the first of a huge wave of migrating penguins. I always wondered if the guide had someone letting them out of a cage just around the next bend of bluffs, but decided later this couldn't be in that there were just too many of them. At any rate, we were impressed with the tour's timing and paid rapt attention to anything the guide said after that remarkable demonstration.

In a small coastal town nearby, the roasted chicken served that night had orange-colored meat but tasted fine. Our guide explained the chickens were feed marigold flowers which were grown commercially just for this purpose. The flowers allegedly made a healthy diet for chickens without any supplements necessary, but the flower's orange permeated all aspects of the chicken. Our guide further explained we were lucky. In the winter, the chickens were fed anchovies instead of marigolds. The meat then was the normal ivory color, but the meat had a distinct fishy flavor—"take your choice," he said with a laugh.

In Cuzco, the ancient capitol of the Incas, the rarified air took its toll. Despite drinking copiously the coca-leaf tea prescribed for "altitude sickness," Paul passed out in the bus while I lectured him about how teenager's just don't hold up to serious travel, a lecture I regretted later as my health very slowly but steadily deteriorated in the oxygen-poor environment.

We marveled at the ancient temples constructed of huge boulders placed together so tightly and without any mortar whatsoever. They were still in perfect place hundreds of years and scores of heavy earthquakes later—so tight we couldn't stick a piece of paper between the foundation stones. Everywhere, we heard the Incas singing their plaintive songs accompanied by lute and harp, just as they had for hundreds of years. And the regal looking llamas were everywhere—the source of the bright wool clothing all the Indians seemed to prefer. As we got further and further into the Andes, we heard less and less Spanish, until by 15,000 feet we heard nary a word, and our interpreter became vital. In the small remote Andean villages rarely visited in these high altitudes, we went to Mass at the only church—nominally Catholic but you wondered. We witnessed the all-Indian population simultaneously worshiping Jesus, the Mother Mary, the Sun, the Moon Goddess, and the last Emperor of all the Incas. And we became aware of an infant death rate of 50 percent before the age of two, mainly due to starvation. It seemed everyone packed their cheeks with coca leaves on one side, white lime on the other to break the coca leaves down into cocaine. Mothers carefully packed the cheeks of their infants; adults packed the cheeks of the few aged people around. It wasn't just an antidote for altitude sickness; far more important, the cocaine dulled the hunger pangs. So a baby starving to death never cried out in his misery and a starving mother with dried up breasts could face the fact she was dying along with the child in her arms. When the Inca Empire was flourishing, birth control was taught from the cradle on, and the population was carefully tailored to the available food. In the modern era, birth control was condemned by both church and government while antibiotics had extended the life-span. Unfortunately, the food supply was no greater than it had ever been so pandemic starvation was the result. Infants, being the most fragile, were the first to go, and we saw it everywhere.

Machu Picchu is as close to heaven as man is likely to get in this world. Once you see it, it's obvious why the Incas built a great city at this spot. Forgotten by time and distance, the entire place was unknown to the modern world until an American discovered it toward the beginning of the twentieth century. Now you reach it by rail only. In 1981, few world travelers made the trip and you had the distinct feeling you were experiencing something totally unique and special in that so few ever made it there. From the train depot at the bottom of the canyon, you make your way up on ancient school buses via a zig-zag road to the city itself high in the clouds and you got the feeling the old buses would never make it, but they did. Coming down, an Inca boy bet me one dollar he could beat the bus to the depot at the bottom. Looking at the buses, I doubted if they had any brake linings left and thought surely I would win. But when we rolled up at the train station with the brakes stinking with black smoke, the boy was standing there smiling with his palm thrust out for the dollar. Since he wasn't even panting in altitudes that had me gasping at rest, I told him I would give him free room and board in Madison, Indiana, if he would join the local high school cross-country and track team. Why university coaches don't recruit down there I'll never know.

Back in Cuzco, we boarded the once-a-week narrow-gauge train that actually crossed the Andes. But not without incident. At that time at least, the train was routinely four times oversold by corrupt government officials. Our tour company, knowing this, had hired a mean-looking man with a machine gun to "save" a passenger car for us. After we boarded under cover of his gun, he calmly locked the car doors from the inside, and are seats were "saved." As the train took on speed, he started pushing away the many people clinging to the bars covering the windows with the barrel of his gun—unless they had placed a silver or gold coin between their teeth. In that case, our gunman let them hang onto the window bars after taking the bribe coin from between their teeth; the others he threatened to shoot if they didn't let go. If this didn't work, he jammed his right foot against their chests and sent them reeling backwards from the moving train.

The group of seated Americans, stunned by such actions, were shocked into inaction. Should they stop the man hired by their own tour company and lose their place on the train? Or should they "close their eyes" to the sordid scene on the grounds this procedure had obviously gone on for generations? They turned to the train conductor for guidance. He was taking half of the coins from our gunman and helped him push a particularly strong and obstinate peasant from clenching onto the bars of the last window. The whole world seemed corrupt and none in our group intervened beyond noting the moral injustices of a society where "might makes right." Our moral chagrin seemed strangely divergent to the physical sights all around us: truly the most breathtaking scenery in the world as the train chugged up to 17,000+ feet among the snow-capped mountaintops.

Since no food or water was available on the train, you had to purchase these from vendors at everyone of the 14 stops along the way. Most of the Indians on board had no money for this luxury and watched you eat each bite with hunger written on their faces. It wasn't long until you couldn't stand to eat in front of them and you either stopped eating yourself or you hid the food until you got back into the locked passenger car and then ate it with guilt so strong you could barely digest it. Between stops we saw Indians living so remotely it was obvious the government had changed many times over and they probably knew nothing about it.

Thirteen hours later, we were in Pisco, close to the shores of Lake Titicaca. It was two in the morning but the train station there was teaming with people awaiting the weekly train. One Indian woman in her late fifties departed the train and looked frantically for the son who promised to meet her. It was obvious she'd had nothing to eat or drink the entire trip and the look on her face went quickly from anticipatory to desperate to despair. After inquiring of everyone if they'd seen her son, she piteously clutched at the few who would listen, and finally, when it was obvious he wasn't there, she threw herself on the tracks in heart-broken sobs of total despair. I always wondered if there was any resolution to this mother's plight and feel guilty about it to this day.

Our tour director shocked us back into reality by telling us thievery was rampant in this station and ordering us into a tightly formed human triangle with our luggage carried on the inside of the triangle, we shoved our way through the crowds of grasping hands. Despite everything, a small bag was grabbed and, when I realized it was mine, I gave chase. Within one block I collapsed in the 14,000 foot altitude and realized, laying on the ground, that the travel bag contained my credit cards, $300 of U.S. cash, my camera and film, my medicines, and all my toiletries. What a fool I'd been to let the bag out of my grasp somehow. At least my passport was safely in the secret zipped pocket of my coat. But luck was with me. The tour guide had also given chase, but to the nearest policeman, and the police caught the thief almost instantly in an outdoor all-night movie theater another block away. I saw with tremendous relief the policeman return with my bag. I checked the bag quickly and saw all was intact—the thief hadn't had time to do anything with the contents and I looked to the tour guide for direction. He said quietly to get out some $10 bills and put them in my pocket and when he nodded to give them one at a time to the policeman or I would be detained to fill out endless papers and reports, possibly for days and days. After at least 10 minutes of uninterrupted discourse between the guide and the policeman in rapid Spanish, I saw the first nod. I delivered the first $10 bill to the outstretched palm of the policeman. After another five minutes of rapid dialogue, another nod came and I produced the second $10 bill into the ever-present palm. More talk followed, reaching new crescendos, but no nods came and finally I saw the guide shake the hand of the policeman. The guide practically thrust me on the bus and ordered the driver to get out of town as fast as he could. As the bus careened into the dark of night, I wondered what happened to the thief. Assuming he stole because he was desperate, I was sure he never saw one cent of the $20 bribe. Knowing you have to pay for your food in most South American prisons, I wondered if he ever survived his imprisonment through one hustle or another, if he was able to bribe his way out of a sentencing somehow, or if he was now working for the policeman in some sort of indentured arrangement common to that area.

At Lake Titicaca, we crossed in the iron ferry brought piece by piece up into the mountains and then bolted together to serve as the main transportation for the next 40 years. All around us were the famous woven reed boats that lasted a few months, then rotted and sunk to the bottom as the Indians simply wove a new one.

Once we crossed the deep blue waters of the lake into Bolivia, we were taken by train to La Paz, one of the highest cities in the world located in the crater of an ancient volcano. Once there, we marveled at the 100 different types of potatoes for sale (including potatoes preserved through "freeze-drying" by laying out in the fields where the temperature in this highlands on the equator ranged from 100 degrees in late afternoon to below zero each night), the women all wearing felt hats which denoted their family clan, and the "magic market" where supplies for placing and lifting curses and charms (such as llama fetuses for blessing a new home) did a brisk business. While we stayed in a luxurious Sheraton hotel, many in the suburbs were lugging water in plastic jugs from the one spigot available every two blocks.

Common to both the American travelers and the natives of La Paz was the revolution that took place the first night we were there. When I heard gun shots in the streets below and saw army trucks go roaring by with screaming soldiers in the back of them, I asked the clerk at the hotel desk what to do. He yawned and said, "Nothing. The General has left for Switzerland with all our money. His cousin, another General, is taking over. It will be O.K. by morning. Go back to sleep."

The hotel clerk was right. Nothing did happen—to us or to anyone else. I read in the morning papers the good General was now in Switzerland $40 million happier; his cousin was in place for another siphoning of available funds.

From La Paz, we headed for the interior of Bolivia where the original Asian immigrants to South America had allegedly first settled thousands of years before—the Aymara (Americus). En route we traveled for hundreds of miles on the bleakest, most barren dirt roads I'd ever seen. At one small town, we stopped to take in an Indian market where colorful dyes and cloth, along with llamas, were being sold. Everything was going fine until someone said the word "Americano" and suddenly the place was alive with threats, shouting, shuffles, and hostilities everywhere. We ran for the bus which had barred windows, so common in South America, and quickly locked the bus door from the inside. The Indians proceeded to smash every window in that bus but the windshield (which was laminated and too strong for their clubs) and the only thing that saved us were the bars on the windows and the sturdy door locks. The driver had run for cover with the rest of us and was finally able to start the engine and gun us out of the place before they rolled the bus over or, worst yet, set fire to it. To this day, not one of us has the slightest idea of what sparked the riot, why they were angry at "Americanos" (since none of us had been anything but courteous and polite that day), or why their feelings ran so strong. I suspect it was because American government agents, under orders from President Nixon's "War on Drugs," were burning their coca fields without reimbursement in a desperate, but futile attempt to stop the infiltration of cocaine into the U.S. I'd be mad too if some foreign government agents were burning my cash crop and not paying me for it—especially a crop my people had grown for hundreds and hundreds of years. After that, we didn't stop to mingle with the friendly natives anymore.

Back in La Paz, which means "Place of Peace," we were taken to the airport for our flight home under the tutelage of hundreds and hundreds of soldiers, all heavily armed with submachineguns and all noticeably unfriendly. It was with relief when our plane finally took off on the longest runways in the world—they have to be twice as long because the air there is so rarified the jets can't develop enough thrust to get them off quickly. For the past several days I had been feeling poorly. The bad water had finally caught up with me when I refused to drink any more warm beer, and the diarrhea, lack of water, lack of air, and exposure to 100 degree temperature swings a day had taken their toll. My son Paul was more of less nursing me home at this point and I barely remember the plane transfers at Lima and Miami before we got home.

After a week of rest, I failed to get any better and checked in with the doctor. At first, it was lamentably diagnosed as "fungus of the lungs" which is incurable, but later the diagnosis was changed to my eighth case of pneumonia—fortunately the bacterial kind that antibiotics (at that time) could tackle. My son Paul and I had experienced the adventure of a lifetime. I knew he'd never be the same again, after witnessing such scope of human suffering parallel with some of God's most awesome beauty. We ofttimes must live with such incongruities, and he had learned first hand what some of them were. We had shared this together as father and son. He had chosen the best graduation gift possible.

A FULBRIGHT SCHOLAR LIVING IN BAHRAIN:

"INITIAL IMPRESSIONS"

[Written in late August, 1988]

Although my wife and I had read everything we could get our hands on about Bahrain before leaving the United States, the written word alone could not prepare us for the actual physical experience of Bahrain in late August when we arrived. When we stepped out of the airport about 8:00 P.M., we were encompassed by a mass of hot, humid air which was like opening the door of a sauna. My wife and I looked at each other in disbelief and could only speculate what the next morning would bring. As I looked at her, I knew what she was thinking—had we made one of the biggest mistakes of our life?

I had stayed overnight in Bahrain a year and a half before as part of a study tour for a few selected American professors sponsored by the National Council for U.S.-Arab Relations. In that tour, we had visited the United Arab Emirates rather extensively, took in ARAMCO (Arabian-American Oil Company) headquarters and a university in Saudi Arabia, and stayed overnight in Bahrain. So I had an intriguing glimpse of the Arabian Gulf. But that was in the relative cool of March—a "cool" that was like early summer back home in Indiana. I was stimulated and challenged by this study tour—so much so that I decided I would celebrate my 25 years of teaching American Midwesterners by teaching entirely different students from an entirely different culture in an entirely different setting. The challenge excited me and one way to do this was through the Distinguished Lecturer Program of Fulbright Scholars where, in essence, our government sends American academics to foreign "host" universities where they serve as visiting lecturers, researchers, and academic consultants. In essence, Fulbright Scholars are a "gift" from the U. S. government to cooperating countries and their universities abroad. Fulbrighters are awarded a grant (roughly equal to about an assistant professors' salary in the United States) plus a modest travel, dependency, and "settling in" allowance which varies with each country. Although you have enough to live on comfortably, a Fulbright grant does not really allow you to "make a profit" nor should it be viewed that way. Your job is to represent America abroad and contribute American "know-how" as appropriate to the host country.

Bahrain is a small set of islands (about 214 sq. mi.) located in the Persian (Arabian) Gulf about 23 miles off the shore of Saudi Arabia. It is a separate Islamic country which has been governed by the Al-Khalifa family for almost 200 years. Bahrain is noted for its rich cultural and trade history. Amazingly, archeologists have uncovered advanced civilizations on Bahrain over 5000 years old, including Western civilizations such as the Greeks and Romans, as well as the legendary empire of Dilmun. The British established a naval base in Bahrain at the height of the British Empire and served as advisors to the Al-Khalifa family for about 100 years until 1971, when Bahrain became an independent state. For thousands of years, Bahrain was noted for three things: a flourishing center of trade, its natural pearl industry, and its dates (possible due to a supply of natural spring water). But Bahrain was the first Gulf country to develop an oil industry and set up the first refinery, export facility, etc., in the 1930's. Unfortunately, it will also be the first Gulf country to run out of oil, expected within 15 to 20 years. Currently, Bahrain is wisely in the forefront of exploring non-oil income sources, e.g., it has built an aluminum smelting plant, it has a huge ship repair yard, and it has developed an "off shore" banking industry attracting over 100 international banks.

Bahrain is best noted, however, for its people. Long noted for their tolerance of foreigners, Bahrainis are also noted for their politeness, their friendliness, their trust, and their remarkable ability to accept the best of Western technology and information while retaining the best aspects of Bahraini culture. Bahrainis are not a people who are overwhelmed by the West nor are they "stick-in-the-mud" traditionalists. They accept the West, but are not in any way suffering from an "identity crisis" as a result of that acceptance. The end result is a very high literacy rate (73 percent), a relatively advanced modern educational system, and a deep seated sense of social and cultural values. Hence, the American "Dairy Queen" store looks like a slice of America until you realize hamburgers are appropriately called beefburgers, there is no pork in the hot dogs, and an attachment to the toilet allows compliance with Muslim sanitary prescriptions. Here you see both Arabic and Western dress and hear both Arabic and English (but also many other languages). A Filipino serves you, an Indian clears the tables, a Sri Lankan is the main cook, a Bahraini family is in one booth, a British family in the next, a group of Saudi men are in the next booth, a Pakistani family is across from them, and so on. The newly-arrived American tends to become overwhelmed with the cosmopolitan aspects of this multi-cultural country.

Since I'm a psychologist, my appointment was at the College of Health Sciences which is run by the Ministry of Health. As such, my housing was provided by the Ministry. After spending the first five days at the Bahrain Hilton (yes, the same Hilton as in the U. S., but considerably more expensive and luxurious), the U. S. Embassy Information Services Officer took my wife and I to our new home within easy walking distance of the college. Again, we were overwhelmed. We had expected a small one-bedroom apartment since there was just the two of us. Instead, we were in a huge "villa"—huge, at least, by American standards. Within the walled compound, we found ourselves lost within about a 7000 square foot four-bedroom house complete with twelve tons of air-conditioning, thick concrete walls, Bahraini sugar cane growing by our entry walkway, tile floors, and individual rooms so large we felt lost within each one. We even had a flat roof where in the winter we could play tennis if we wanted on one wing and have a badminton court on the roof of another wing. In the back of the walled compound was a long deserted servant's "house" which was tiny, but still air-conditioned. The villa was wildly overgrown with all sorts of vines and weeds, so obviously it hadn't been occupied in some time. My wife couldn't imagine how all of this could grow with no water and such heat. A friendly neighbor arranged a gardener for us who amazingly had the "garden" conquered within a week. But getting the electricity, water, and phone connected wasn't easy and getting this done was one of the major milestones of our settling in: endless lines, forms to fill out, language difficulties, and a lot of frustration—all done in the "cool" of one six-hour morning where the heat hovered around 100 degrees and the humidity ranged from 80-90 percent (that's before you get into serious afternoon heat!). After this episode, my wife and I felt strangely proud. We had accomplished what seemed impossible and if we could get this done, we could do anything! Buying a much needed vacuum sweeper, the TV, a videocassette player, word processor, washing machine, installing an aerial and rotor, buying dishes, pots and pans, groceries, and all else were trivial by comparison.

Most things on Bahrain are imported, of course, and are expensive by American standards. We found you can get almost anything here you can buy in the U. S. (and then some!) but you may have to pay dearly for it. We found Kroger's canned soup, all types of ice cream, popcorn from Indiana, and even Kellogg's Corn Flakes. But all cost much more than in the U. S. Fresh vegetables are reasonable, a huge variety of fish is both cheap and plentiful, and the recently introduced Coca-Cola (bottled in Oman) strangely costs little more than in the U. S.

I wish that my Buick setting in the garage at home could be flown here on a magic carpet—I could sell it for a small fortune. My rental Avis car (a small Japanese car which was very well used) cost me $254 for a week. And my long-term leased car cost me

$360 per month for a two-year-old Toyota Cressida. What amazes the car enthusiast is the sheer variety of makes and models of cars. Apparently, every car in the world is here, but in very small numbers, so parts must be a chronic headache. I notice almost every car has the same muffler hooked up underneath, so that tells you something of the problem. And the intense heat is murder on the interiors: the plastic dashboards and steering wheels simply melt sometimes and few dashboards are not covered with felt or other substitute materials after a few years of this punishment. Hub caps rust, air filters get clogged with dust, and shops abound devoted to fixing the all critical car air-conditioners which run under maximum capacity most of the time. When planning this venture, we thought a car would be unnecessary in that a small island would most likely have an advanced mass transit system and cheap taxis. How wrong we were! A car seems to be a necessity to get places when you want to get there. Taxis are relatively expensive, and buses are infrequent and not air-conditioned. Nor is it very easy to walk places due to the custom of walling in most compounds—too often you have to walk clear around them rather than through them.

By far the most favorite saying in Bahrain is "No problem." It's the answer to most inquiries and often, but certainly not always, it is true—what seems like a problem to the newcomer really isn't, if you're dealing with forthright, honest people and that's usually the case. As a psychologist, I was amused at how untrusting we Americans have often become—I'm afraid we appear cynical and suspicious to a gentler people. On the other hand, things do often move noticeably slower, sometimes bureaucracy takes its toll, and occasionally events which really are a problem and could be effectively managed are simply prematurely dismissed as "no problem!"

Family life seems to be a major focus in Bahraini society and family privacy and activities are obviously given top priority. Americans tend to be open, including their families, and to Americans I'm sure Bahraini family life seems closed and guarded. Initially, I got the distinct impression one's family was most private and even "off limits" to a degree. When inquiring about children, parents are polite in answering your inquiries, but I get the impression I'm pushing the limits of courtesy if my inquiry goes much beyond the surface.

Every European or American I've met who has lived here a while is almost evangelical about living in Bahrain. I don't know whether they're simply self-validating their career choices (and thereby lowering their anxiety) or whether it's totally sincere. One American serviceman told me, "If it weren't for this God-awful summer weather, it'd be perfect." Another U. S. Embassy worker told me "Other than the heat, it's perfect. The Bahrainis are the best people I've ever met and I've lived all over the world!" A few grumble of course. The summer heat is terrible, there are language problems at times, it's hard to get things done with high efficiency, and things are expensive in U. S. dollars.

At the university, I've found my Bahraini colleagues to be very friendly, hard working, and cooperative. We work six days a week with Friday off. Students attend classes five days a week—Saturday through Wednesday. Thursday is for administration of exams, department and faculty meetings, meetings with deans and other administrators, and simply catching up with office work. So it's a rather long week compared to the American system. Telephones, typewriters, and paper are noticeably scarce as compared to American universities. And textbooks seem to be a chronic problem: they are expensive, hard to come by at any price in many cases, and often relatively dated. Library resources are also extremely limited by American standards. But the college is just opening a very well equipped computer center and offering appropriate training in their use to all students. Although the courses are primarily conducted in English here, almost all communication outside the classroom is in Arabic. Classes at my college are small by American university standards: I have one class of nine in research methodology; another class of 11 in psychology; and my largest class (Social and Behavioral Aspects of Medicine) has only about

20. In addition, I'll be running workshops for the faculty here on how to do research; for the psychiatry faculty and other medical staff on therapeutically working with children; as well as running a number of workshops for Bahraini teachers on therapeutic intervention techniques with children. In addition, I'm to consult with the faculty here on setting up and reorganizing courses within the behavioral sciences.

My wife has accepted an appointment in the English department of the same college I'm located, so we will be able to go to and from work together. Unlike me, she's an actual employee of the university and was hired like a native Bahraini would be. Her classes will be primarily at the first level (freshmen) and consequently her classes are larger (25 to 28) but still small by American standards. Many freshmen students here have considerable trouble with English, despite the fact they've all had it repeatedly in secondary school—hence most English classes here are what we'd call remedial English.

The whole style of life is wisely dictated to a large degree by the weather. People get up every early—it's full daylight with a bright sun by 5:30-6:00 A.M. Many Bahrainis start work at 7:00 A.M. and work straight through until 12:30-1:00 P.M., then take about three hours off and work again from 4:00-7:00 P.M.—a lot like Spain. But almost everyone here goes to bed very early—10:00 P.M. at the latest (the *late* movie starts around 8:30 P.M.). Friday is the Holy Day, but many shops are open in the afternoon and evening. To an American, the days initially seem very long, probably because you get up so early. My wife and I have still not adjusted to this so we always work through the afternoon—the result is we're tired by evening. Bahrainis wisely rest in the afternoon and are much more lively in the evening. We get television from Qatar, Kuwait, Saudi Arabia, the United Arab Emirates and Iran as well as Bahrain's two channels. About half the channels are in English and show primarily British and American shows (I saw *Golden Girls* the other night!). But so far we have found the Arabic channels more interesting to us, simply because they're so different. We were really thrilled to be taken by television right into the Grand Mosque at Mecca for evening prayers! These same channels show a lot of different Arabic dances and music, which we find most intriguing at this point. The news is really different: first you have a man newscaster who reads a statement. This is followed by a lengthy scene of what he talked about without sound. This is then followed by a woman newscaster reading the next item of news followed by a lengthy scene of what she has just read, again without sound. No cutesy jokes, no "selling" of TV personalities, no advertisements cutting in, and heavy emphasis is placed, of course, on Arabic countries. There is surprisingly little news about America although Bush and Dukakis are mentioned about every third day or so (I was struck by the thought that we Americans think we're so important that of course everyone is interested in everything we do!). On the other hand, the coverage of the Bangladesh flood was excellent—probably much better than American viewers ever saw. But my wife and I still wonder if those men and women newscasters are in different rooms!

Driving *is* different, at least initially. Many Bahrainis learned to drive later in life—they didn't necessarily grow up with it. They tend to drive fast by our standards, especially for in-town driving. Traffic is often heavy in Manama (they too have rush hours) and the "turnabouts" (in lieu of intersections) and "giveaways" are straight from England. But Bahrainis are very polite drivers (they often let you merge into a line of traffic by patiently waiting) and there seems to be surprisingly few accidents. I have a theory they drive so fast subconsciously because it's cooler—the air-conditioner compressor goes faster and puts out a lot more cool air.

Fulbright Scholars can get a lot of help from the United States Information Service (U.S.I.S.) of the U.S. Embassy, who actually sponsor the Fulbright programs. We received all sorts of settling in help along with social support. Getting us through customs, having us for dinner, helping us buy the initial household items, taking us grocery shopping, introducing us to other Americans, even helping us get the TV antenna installed and leasing a car gave us that invaluable support we needed to get settled and comfortable. Our greatest asset came from the fact that the U.S.I.S.'s administrative assistant turned out to be a close neighbor. This remarkable lady seemed to be able to get anything done, and done fast and done right. What a stroke of good luck for us! With her help, we felt settled within a few days after leaving the hotel.

All in all, we look forward to a most interesting academic year. What a great way to celebrate my 25 years of teaching college. And the educational challenge is intriguing. The Arabian Gulf is a most inviting place for the American educator who wants to experience some enriching experiences along with considerable personal growth.

"TEACHING IN BAHRAIN"

"Teacher Teacher!" "Teacher Teacher!" It seemed like everyone was talking at once! Chairs were being scraped across the floor as the girls moved their seats separate from the boys. Although "Teacher-Teacher" was in sing-song English, all else was a babble of Arabic. No one was in their seat and chaos seemed to prevail. Thus began my teaching career at the College of Health Sciences: I was meeting my first class!

Although I can now look back with humor at those experiences four months ago, I will never forget the absolute panic I experienced at the time. I had expected a challenge, but not one of classroom management! I'm sure everyone has had a few episodes where they sincerely wished they were somewhere else—at least for the moment!

To make my life as a Fulbright Scholar interesting and educational, I had worked out a scheme with the University where I would teach at three different levels: (1) the lowest level of beginning student; (2) the highest level of graduate student; and (3) college faculty and physicians in both research methodology and child psychology.

What I didn't know at that time was that there is a huge difference in classes dependent on the level of the student. The second-year college students I was meeting at the time are as different from the bachelor degree students as night is from day. And the faculty (that I teach more than any other group) are yet another story.

My lower-level (associate degree) class of 17 nursing trainees range in age from 19 to 35. All were recruited by the Ministry of Health to be nurses. All had graduated from government (rather than private) schools and most of them were from small village backgrounds. None have every been off this small island. Their government "job" is to go to college. They are paid the same as if they worked at a regular job (about $600 a month) plus all transportation to and from their homes every day. Uniforms and books are supplied free. There is no tuition. Once they finish their 2-1/2 to 3-year program, they are placed directly into nursing positions at the Health Center—usually replacing a hired foreign nurse who is then sent home. My job was to teach them a little social science, but at this lower level what is taught, when and how they are taught, when they are examined, what is on the examination, what constitutes passing or failing, and all other major academic decisions are pre-determined by departmental chairmen who report directly to the Dean of the College. This degree of "course control" would be unheard of in the United States where generally these decisions are left up to the professional competence of the instructor. Textbooks are rarely utilized. Instead, "modules" of specially prepared materials presumably better adapted to Bahraini culture, Islamic values, and where English is a second language serve as instructional material. Of course, these locally prepared materials sometimes miss the mark: in my social science class, the modules mainly discuss a little cultural anthropology in other Islamic countries, a smattering of sociology of the Arab family (complete with multiple wives), and a little social psychology—mainly on how to change attitudes. There are no copyright laws here so a great deal of material is lifted directly or indirectly from other published materials. The course attempts to cover four or five entire disciplines in 54 class hours, and fails miserably: far more learning would take place if you covered a lot less but had at least some depth. Memorization of definitions and terminology are heavily emphasized. Examinations contain practically no items measuring application of the material learned, analytic skills, or synthesis. Students tend to memorize definitions, take the exam, and promptly forget the whole ordeal! This level of student is almost chronically late to all classes, often pays little attention in class, and most shocking to a Hanover College professor, tends to cheat on examinations if given the slightest opportunity.

The students selected to pursue a regular four-year college degree are an entirely different breed. Here classes are kept very small—mine has only nine. Students are mature, well-motivated, and able. They are highly selected and they know it. They are destined to become the future leaders of their country and they shoulder the responsibilities seriously. By contrast with my associate degree class, they are generally married with children, have had at least five to eight years of work experience, are extremely well-traveled (seven out of nine have been to the U.S. and everyone has been to Europe at least twice!) and most speak three or four languages fluently. They too have been recruited by the government, but in this case for future leadership. Nominated by their employers, "sponsored" by various government agencies, it is proving to be a most exciting class. Since I teach this group how to do research, I always have the feeling that what I'm teaching will someday be put to use. The research proposals this group submits are exciting, well thought out, and have definite practical applications. Bahrain has done so little research almost anything is new, needed, and appreciated. It's an ideal climate for a stimulating learning experience.

The bulk of my time is spent teaching the faculty of the college, however (this includes a lot of physicians). This generally takes the form of voluntary seminars or workshops on selected topics within my area of professional competence. Faculty seem very eager to register for these "classes" which are scheduled "off-hours." So eager, in fact, I've had to repeat several of them because more people sign up than the room holds. Faculty, like the students they teach, are often late, are sort of noisy in class, but they do pay better attention. Asking questions is viewed as being a "show-off" so few are ever asked. And almost everyone expects a diploma-like fancy certificate attesting to the fact they completed the workshop along with a mini-graduation ceremony. Physician's "buzzers" are always going off in class, but nobody every seems to leave so I assume they're just status symbols. Examples utilized in class must be from their culture, so my "old standards" from American colleges had to be shelved and new ones substituted. And humor is not a common classroom commodity. How I long for a really good American belly laugh! But considering where I'm from and considering how little I really know, the faculty is very accepting, gracious, forgiving, and hospitable. I've even been elected by the faculty to their "Faculty Senate," a dubious honor according to some of my Hanover College colleagues, I'm sure.

The greatest problem I've had is my "accent"—anything other than pure British English is viewed as a strange accent and I have to remember to use British terminology and pronunciation in my lectures and to speak as slowly as possible so my students can follow me.

The greatest thrill is when a student or faculty member comes into your office and thanks you for giving them a new thought or a new idea. It doesn't happen every day but it happens often enough to make you feel worthwhile and effective. What better reward could a professor have?

"CHRISTMAS IN MANAMA"

My wife and I entered the empty restaurant at noon (everyone else in Bahrain eats lunch at 2-3 p.m. and supper around 9-10 p.m. so we often eat in empty restaurants!). Since we were known to the staff as American, we soon heard a scratchy old record of Gene Autry singing "Jingle Bells" coming over the sound system. Shortly thereafter, a decorated Christmas tree suddenly appeared from some back room and soon the chef had conjured up a meal of turkey, dressing, and even a hot cranberry sauce. What a treat!

The fact that Christmas can be "produced" on short order here is no mystery when one realizes it is "Festive Season:" a term that covers National Day (the 17th of December) like our 4th of July, New Year's Day (which is a national holiday), the summit meeting of the Gulf Cooperation Council (G.C.C.), and Christmas for at least 500 Christian foreigners in a total population of 400,000. People give gifts, cards are exchanged with "Season's Greetings" on them, and restaurants and hotels offer "Festive Dinners." We've received a number of Islamic cards wishing us a good "Festival." But December 25th *is* a working day. My wife and I both teach classes until 4:00 p.m., then a quick Christmas dinner with a British friend, and off to the only English-speaking church at 6:15 p.m. for the Christmas service.

Despite the fact that this is an Islamic country, Christmas appears regardless. My faculty colleagues who are in the same building are quietly having a special "pitch-in" dinner at 10:00 a.m. Christmas day in one of the empty classrooms even though most of them are Muslim. And several of them have suggested I cancel class because it's Christmas for me.

We were able to buy a frozen turkey through the American Embassy along with cornbread stuffing mix, cranberry sauce, and pumpkin pie mix. All the other "fixins" are available in local stores. And the Manama Singers, a British choir I joined, gave a rousing public concert of traditional Christmas music to an audience of 1100. Some American friends invited us to a great Christmas dinner in the background of 90 degree heat in a land where it has never snowed. Somehow, it's just not the same without a cool snap in the air.

But just when we were feeling a little sorry for ourselves—after all, our children aren't here at Christmas, Christians form just a small minority, and we are a long way from home—a package arrived from Madison, Indiana. Jack and Betty Rivers, neighbors of ours at home, played Santa Claus and sent us a small Christmas tree with a string of lights, some Christmas napkins and paper plates, some Christmas "scents," and some Christmas M&M's. What fun we had decorating the tiny little tree and what a pleasure to have some uniquely American aspects of Christmas celebrations. As my wife said amid her tears of joy: "It's like a portable Christmas just for us!" I don't think she every got such joy from any Christmas gift before.

After that, everything was uphill. Gifts are exchanged, people are in a holiday mood for whatever reason, and the weather dipped down to 86 degrees for the occasion. In Bahrain, the "cold spell" as it was known, produced coats, mittens, and even earmuffs! I suppose everything is relative!

"PUBLIC SCHOOL IN BAHRAIN"

After meeting our students at the college, my wife and I became very curious about their education before college. What *had* they been taught? And how? The answer lay in the government public schools as this is where 80 percent of Bahrainis go to school.

We quickly found out that all government schools are segregated by sex, grade levels, and neighborhoods. Hence, there are separate schools for primary levels (grades 1-6) for girls and for boys, separate schools for intermediate levels (grades 7-9) for both boys and girls, and each school handles between 200-500 children and are arranged by neighborhood, so all schools are "walk-in's." Only the private schools (handling about 20 percent of the children) utilize busing, as they have to collect children from all over the island for one building. There are then secondary schools, again segregated by sex (grades 10-12) but also segregated by curriculum (technical, pre-college, or general studies).

Bahrain spends about 25 percent of its total budget each year on the education of its children. If the U.S. spent that same percentage, every educator's dream could be fulfilled. Considering this country was largely illiterate just 35 years ago, how much progress can be expected? We knew, of course, that Bahrain, of *all* the Arab Gulf countries, was the first to set up public education and was the first to offer education to women. But had these pioneering efforts paid off?

We also quickly found out that few Westerners are ever allowed into these government schools, where access and security are tight. Most of my colleagues at the University said I would never be allowed to visit, and no one knew of anyone who had ever seen them. Using my credentials as a Fulbright Scholar, I appealed directly to the Minister of Education in a 10-page letter explaining exactly what I wanted to see and why. Furthermore, I wanted my wife to accompany me, since she had taught in public schools for 27 years and would know exactly what questions to ask of school staff. [My colleagues had also told me that never would a woman be allowed in the upper-level male-only schools.] Within 48 hours, the Minister called to inform me the visits had been arranged to four different types of schools (2 male, 2 female) exactly as I had requested, that my wife was welcome to accompany me, and that I would be visiting some of the best "model" schools and some of the schools with the greatest number of problems. The visits would take four full days. Everyone at the University was astonished and I was primed with questions to ask, things to look for, etc. Before I knew it—48 more hours to be exact—we were off on our first visit in a chauffeured college van since we had no idea of where the schools were even located.

I asked my wife to comment on these schools since she would have a professional perspective. Her comments follow.

"The first school we visited was in Isa Town—about seven miles from our home. It was a fairly new school (about five years old) for primary age boys. The schools do not contain kindergartens or pre-schools as this is left to private concerns. The primary schools are first through sixth years. As we were expected, the head mistress and her assistant were waiting for us.

"The first surprise was the headmistress' office: sofas and overstuffed chairs lined two walls, lovely rose carpet with a pink and white Persian carpet on top, glass coffee table, her desk at one end and lovely woodgrain files and credenza at the other end. We were ushered in and coffee and tea offered. As we sat and talked, the tea was served by a female "laborer." A laborer, it seems, is hired by the Government just to help out around the school—run errands, serve, keep the administrative area neat and pleasant. They are not the custodians.

"The headmistress was not totally fluent in English but the assistant was, so we had no difficulty communicating. The school had approximately 500 boys and 20 teachers. There were six Egyptian teachers and the rest were all Bahraini. All teachers had at least a four-year college degree. They were all female. All classes are limited to 30—only in rare emergency conditions will they allow 31. They have art, music, and sports (physical education) teachers. The rest of the classes are self-contained just like in many schools in the U.S. The building itself is what I call "motel style." It has outside halls with individual rooms opening off them. The rooms are large, terrazzo-floored, and have big windows. They have individual air conditioners and ceiling fans. Each room has its own small library and a beautiful Persian carpet for the children to sit or lay on as they read. There are large bulletin boards and whiteboards that you use felt markers on instead of chalk.

"As we toured the building from room to room, we were greeted in each room by the children rising and saying "Salaam alay-e-kum" meaning "Peace be upon you." Believe it or not, I was able to respond "Wa alay-e-kum salaam" which means "and upon you peace." The children and teachers seemed pleased to have visitors and were proud of what they were doing. As we left the rooms "Shukran" was called to each other: "Thank you."

"The schools' academic areas cover: Arabic-Islam-History as one subject; English language starting in the fourth year; mathematics; science; geography; art; music; and sports. The last three classes are out of their regular classroom just as it is in the U.S.

They have a large well equipped gym with no difference in equipment or program between the boys' and the girls' schools as we saw later. I was truly impressed with the music class, not because I am a music teacher, but perhaps because I am not. The children copy the music from the board into their own notebooks on blank staff pages. Then they play or sing from their own book. Again, no copyrights respected! The instruments also seem to me to be uniquely suited to Arabic music. They have electric keyboards, drums, tambourines, accordions, violins, mandolins, flutephones, guitars, zithers and marimbas. Needless to say, the children were delighted to play for us and we were a most appreciative audience.

"Midway through our tour, we returned to the headmistress' office where we were again served Arabic tea or American coffee and a large array of Arabic sweets including a kiwi-fruit cheesecake (I must add—if one loses weight here, they're sick!).

"We saw many dedicated and innovative teachers. The media specialist/librarian helps children and teachers alike with computer work, projects, reports, puppet shows, bulletin board displays and visual aids. Any teacher willingly helps and contributes ideas and materials to another. The headmistress looks over the children's work and can talk to them individually about what they are doing. The children are a joy to watch explaining what they are doing or what they just did. My favorite remembrance was in asking a teacher what she did with children who misbehaved and she truly could not comprehend what misbehaved meant.

"We also visited the Al Adawly Primary Girls School in Manama, Un Salama Girls Intermediate School in Al Hura, and the Hamad Town Intermediate Boys School located in Hamad Town. Each school was similar in building design, curriculum, and goals as are all the government schools. The only difference was in the closing gestures of again offering coffee or tea and presentations of gifts from the children and staff.

"I would like to add that the Un Salama Girls School's practical arts class was really something to behold. When we walked into these two classrooms the girls were knitting both by hand

and by machine, crocheting, making dried flower arrangements and pictures, and making their own perfume and fragranced soap. Samples of each were presented to us. The beautiful sweaters, doilies, afghans, baby sets and stoles all go home with the girls. Perfume and fragranced soaps are very expensive here but are not difficult or expensive to make, so when these go home they are really appreciated. Now THAT'S PRACTICAL ART!"

"BAHRAINI SOCIAL LIFE"

By now, I've visited over 50 countries throughout the world. But being a tourist and actually living in a country are two different worlds. As a psychologist, my greatest treat in living in Bahrain has been the opportunity to share and observe the personal, everyday routines of social life among average Bahrainis.

Actually this opportunity does not come easily to an American in a culture as different as Bahrain's. Most foreigners live with like kind in compounds and rarely mix with the local population. Americans and British are notorious for this and, indeed, many Americans choose to live in segregated compounds allowing little real social integration with Bahraini locals. It minimizes the adjustments necessary, avoids cultural conflicts, and eliminates the language problems. It's the easiest thing to do.

Both my wife and I have the tremendous advantage of working side-by-side with Bahrainis. Most of our fellow faculty are Bahrainis, our housing is with the local Bahrainis (we're the only Americans in our "compound"), and most Bahrainis, being the best educated of any Gulf Arabs, speak at least some English. Thus a lot of our social life is with Bahrainis rather than other foreigners.

Most social life among Bahrainis revolves around the family. By family, I mean extended family—real extended by American standards. Remember this is a very small island (less than 300 square miles). Families can't move away from each other. So close and very frequent contact between brothers, sisters, mothers, fathers, cousins, aunts and uncles is kept throughout a lifetime. It's like a city the size of Louisville, Kentucky, was a unique country totally separated and isolated from the rest of the U.S. for thousands of years. Almost everyone is related somehow or another, and marriages are seldom outside the local islanders.

And even immediate families are very large by American standards—it's not unusual to have 8 to 10 children in a Bahraini family. Population growth staggers the imagination. It's doubling every 30 years at the current rate! At least Bahrain, unlike India, the Philippines, and many South American countries can afford to support that increase although environmental pollution, land usage, traffic, and scarcity of the precious water is bound to be drastically effected.

Thursday nights and all day Friday (the "weekend") is usually reserved for family activities. Family obligations tend to run through the sons, although daughters stay close to their family also. Hence married sons, their wives, and their children visit his parent's home. But there are many variations: we were with a family last week where a daughter and her husband hosted all her sisters and brothers as well as her parents. And on another occasion, we were at a home where a son and his wife hosted his wife's brothers and their wives, and all the children involved—over 30 children in this case!

These occasions require large houses and Bahrainis generally build large homes. The usual newer house has a very large entry hall that also serves as an informal "family room," a very large formal dining room, a "ladies room" where women often go to visit, a formal reception room, i.e., a "parlor," a huge kitchen (often two rooms) with eat-in room for at least 10 to 12 people, and usually a study and laundry room and/or pantry. Upstairs they usually have 5 or 6 bedrooms (much larger than in our homes) along with an upstairs family room with TV and hi-fi. Outside are garages, servant's quarters, and often a "summer kitchen" to keep cooking odors out of the house. So there's plenty of room to entertain, and entertain they do!

Let me describe last Thursday night as an example. We arrived about 8:00 p.m. in that no one here dreams of eating much before 9-10 p.m. After being greeted by the hosts (a family of six), we were introduced to her parents, her sister and brother-in-law and their four children to date, her brother and his wife and three children to date, his brother and sister-in-law and their four children to date, and two more brothers and sisters and their families.

The women were dressed in typical Bahraini attire: beautiful full-length, brightly colored, highly embroidered gowns decorated with many beads and baubles. The men were dressed less formally in the traditional "thobe"—a full-length white, blue, or tan robe with the usual head covering that flows down their back—and sandals, although two of the men were attired in "western" dress, i.e., shirts, trousers, no headdress, and regular oxford-type shoes although all Bahrainis always leave all shoes and sandals outside the front door.

Three of the five women under 40 were pregnant. There were 16 children under 16 years old.

After introducing us to all—the introduction of their children (of whom they are terribly proud) takes even longer than introduction of adults—we were served five different types of "starters" (appetizers). What they call "starters" constitutes a meal for a snack-ridden American! Shortly thereafter, the men disappeared and started barbecuing mutton, chicken and fish on large outside charcoal grills.

While the meal was being prepared, both the mother and father made sure we met every child, told us the special "talents" or abilities of each child (often having the child give us a short demonstration of this talent), and, especially impressive to a psychologist, explained in great length why they were proud of this child and the special unique ways this child brought happiness and joy to their family. It was great to see the children beam as their parents bragged about them! No one could say that a child felt unappreciated, ignored, or depreciated. Bahrainis openly state that their children are their finest accomplishment. And, despite what I had previously thought, daughters seemed to be just as appreciated as the sons—at least here in the more progressive Bahrain. No wonder family ties are so strong here!

After several hours of visiting, meeting everyone, and touring the house, the food was ready. A huge plastic tablecloth was spread over the reception room's carpeted floor and more food than you can imagine was spread out picnic-style. The typical American saying is: "You could feed an Army with that much food," but lavish amounts of many different kinds of food seems to be Bahraini's version of Arab hospitality. There were huge platters of chicken, mutton, Gulf fish, rice, Arab bread, and condiments. Everyone sits down on the floor around the cloth and "digs in" without ceremony. Arabs love to eat and the food was truly delicious, and by this time it was 10 to 11 p.m. so I take it everyone was as famished as I was. For whatever reason, huge amounts of food were consumed. Originally, it was hard for me to get used to eating on the floor (my wife claims her bones just don't bend that way), but after a while it seems natural and relaxed. Bahrainis don't rush their meals—they talk and joke throughout their meal—and most meals take at least 1-1/2 to 2 hours before one literally gets back on their feet.

After that, a large brass charcoal incense burner was passed around with some Bahraini "scents" and everyone fanned some of the smoke into their clothes and hair. That was followed by passing aromatics around with which to anoint oneself—one bottle of heavy oil of frankincense for men; another of rose water for women. After this ritual (the room smelled like a perfume factory by this time), the men went to one side of the room and started vigorously playing a card game named "Hands" similar in many respects to our poker. The women cleared the food away and then visited among themselves while the children played upstairs. As the children got tired (by this time is was almost midnight) a few simply went to bed while others fell asleep on the floor. Others, having long naps in the afternoon, were just getting their "second wind."

"Sweets" were then served. An array of choices were put before us on a tray. It was like a "dessert cart" at a fancy restaurant. I counted at least six choices and every encouragement is made to try "all of them." Most were not as sweet as our desserts but equally delicious. Our fondness for chocolate does not seem to be shared by Bahrainis, so almost all had some form of nuts, dates, honey, or coconut in them. Their version of ice cream is so good here—the best I've every had—I usually forget other desserts are available.

After sweets, our "second wind" had clearly died out, and we were graciously excused to go home. But their visiting and card games continued. It's my understanding that these family visits often extend to 3:00 a.m. or so with a late sleep the next morning.

Fridays (the one "no work" day here) are often a repeat of Thursday nights, but this time revolving around lunch (2-4 p.m.) rather than supper. In between these feasts, individual families visit the very popular amusement parks, go shopping together in the ancient "suq" or at the modern shopping malls (called shopping centers here), drive out on the new 24 mile long causeway connecting the island of Bahrain to Saudi Arabia, or visit friends outside their family. It's not common for families to split up during this time to pursue individual interests as in America. Generally families do an activity together—at least on the weekends. This is an expected social conformity.

The weekday nights are much more varied. Since the working day in many jobs is 8-1 and 4-7, evening free time starts late as does dinner.

There's really not too much time in the evening, but certainly television ranks as the number one family entertainment as it does in the U.S. Bahrain has its own good Arabic channel, an English-speaking channel that's really not very good, and good reception of many Arabic, but also some English-speaking channels, from Saudi Arabia, the United Arab Emirates, Qatar, Iran, and Kuwait so there's a huge choice available. "Football" (soccer to us) games are extremely popular as are Arab soap operas, camel races from the U.A.E., Koranic teachings from Saudi Arabia, and, of all things,

"Dallas" and "Falconcrest" from the U.S. Also, old wrestling (WWF) shows from the U.S. seem to be on every night (but are banned on Saudi Arabia TV). Our version of football and any form of basketball or baseball seem to have little appeal or popularity here, but because of the British influence over the past 100 years, rugby and cricket do have a limited following.

Hoosiers would be interested that after basketball was introduced here with great fanfare by Americans, most Bahrainis were so bored they couldn't possibly understand why anyone would do that instead of playing "football" (soccer). As a result, basketball and baseball is never shown on TV. So, if you're from Indiana or Kentucky, you better bring basketball videotapes with you when you come!

But "football" is taken most seriously and men (not women) frequent the games on weekday nights in huge stadiums built just for this sport. Many, many Bahraini men belong to "sports clubs" which sponsor the games and players and arrange all the events. Colleges, universities, and professional organizations do not sponsor competitive sports—all sports are performed at the private club level. I wanted to attend a "football" game at the National Stadium—a huge coliseum-like structure rivaling the Rose Bowl. Two Bahraini clubs were playing each other—the usual arrangement. I had to have a Bahraini friend, who was a member of one of the clubs playing, invite me to the game as his guest—it's the only way a ticket was available. Since the games are sponsored, the fans wear the team's colors and cheer their team on in very organized, ritualistic ways. These "sports clubs" also sponsor many family events, however, such as picnics, holiday celebrations and banquets, children's folk dances, and other cultural events. So by no means is all social life organized solely around the home.

Bahrain does not honor any copyright laws. As a result, pirated videotapes from all over the world are readily available for as little as two dollars a week. Almost everyone has a VCR machine and people typically rent tapes by the bagful so a lot of people are watching an awful lot of movies somewhere or other. Almost all

American and British TV miniseries are available on tape along with all Olympic events, all the German and Italian movies, and, of course, thousands and thousands of Egyptian movies in Arabic. Movies that have just been released in the U.S. are available here on videotape within days—long before they are released on videotape in the U.S. Of course, they have been pirated illegally by some rascals in the U.S.

But books are hard to come by—paper is expensive, most books are printed in English, and few people here read English that well, or prefer Arabic writings. Hence there is little market and relatively few books are imported.

Almost 40 percent of the population here is comprised of foreign workers. Of these, Americans are probably one of the smallest but most affluent groups. For the foreign worker, social life takes on a different cast. Most non-Bahrainis here are separated from their families, which are left in their native land. Since most of these workers send as much of their wages home as they possibly can to support their families, there is precious little money left over for a social life. Nevertheless, many foreigners belong to clubs centered around nationality which celebrates and cherishes their own customs, national holidays, and even food preferences. Americans cluster together to celebrate Thanksgiving; Indians celebrate Mahatma Gandhi's birthday; and Filipinos celebrate their Independence Day. Indians, by far the largest group of foreigners here, have their own churches, social help agencies, and recreational events as well as many social clubs.

Overall, our social life has been extremely active—too active for a prolonged period—but very enjoyable for the short time we will be here.

"FAREWELL TO BAHRAIN"

Twenty-one hours after we started our trip home, the plane finally landed at the Cincinnati Airport where our two sons were waiting for us. As we headed toward our home in Madison, we were overwhelmed by all the green (everything in Bahrain is usually some shade of brown), all the rain (we experienced far more rain on our short trip from the airport home than we had altogether in the previous nine months), the "sexy" tight clothing Americans tend to prefer (Bahrainis wear very loose flowing clothes and tend to always keep "covered up"), the sensible driving (by no stretch of the imagination could driving in Bahrain ever be labeled "sensible" or even "sane" in most cases), and the cool weather (it was 108 F. when we left Bahrain).

On the flight home, I thought about our last church service in Bahrain. The Emir himself had donated the land on which the church was built and had personally dedicated the building—a gesture modeling tolerance and openness for his Islamic people.

The building was used every night for a different congregation based on the language: Arabic on Monday, Urdu on Tuesday, Hindu on Wednesday, etc. The English-language service was on Sunday night since Sunday is a working day in Bahrain (Friday is the Holy Day in Islamic countries).

The church was located right next to a beautiful mosque (there were over 300 mosques in Manama alone) and sometimes our hymn singing had to compete with the evening call to prayer next door. The church was always jammed beyond capacity so my wife and I always went early for two reasons: first, to get a seat; and secondly, we got to sing hymns of our choice before the service.

The congregation looked like the United Nations. Only seven of us were Americans. All the rest (out of about 350) were Indians, Sri Lankans, Filipinos, and various Africans along with a few British, New Zealanders and Australians. The minister was a rotund jolly Canadian who obviously loved his congregation and what he was doing. Since everyone in the congregation was as grateful as we were that such a church even existed in an Islamic country, there was always a joyful evangelical enthusiasm that one literally felt.

And such singing! Everyone sang at the top of their voice

whether they could sing on key or not. But their sincerity made up for any lack of timbre. And considering that all had worked all day and then went to church did not quell their energies one bit.

The last service had been a special farewell service for my wife and I. We got to choose all our favorite hymns, our favorite anthem was sung, and our favorites on the electronic organ were played (pipe organs are out due to the constant 90-95% humidity!). As all our Christian friends said goodbye, I realized how close I felt to them and how much they had taught me about the real meaning of religion, faith, and fellowship. How grateful I was to them for teaching me.

We had left Bahrain early Saturday morning. Since Friday is a Holy Day, Thursday was my last day at the university and a very special day it turned out to be! The College of Health Sciences (where I taught first semester), the College of Medicine (where I taught second semester), and the Ministry of Health (which ran the Medical Center) all hosted the farewell dinner since Arabs use almost any excuse for a feast!

Although I must admit I love ceremony and I especially like any occasion where I'm the guest of honor, I was really "into" this occasion. I wondered why I cared so much and felt so strongly about this particular occasion. Then I realized that I had never felt so close to any group before. I'd never met people so totally unselfish, so giving, so open, so gracious, so hospitable.

First, Dean Faisal Al-Hammer spoke. This native-born Bahraini, currently working on his doctoral dissertation research out of Manchester University in England, was, as usual, poised, articulate, and urbane. His natural good looks blended with a personal charm that well represented the University's best interests in Bahrain society. I'd been a personal guest in his home and knew first-hand how "well connected" he was with the people that make the important decisions in Bahrain. The university rested in good hands, I thought, as he continued his speech.

My eyes next fell on Maha, the Associate Dean of the College of Health Sciences. What a fabulous woman! Brilliant, hard-working, a mother of four small children, she was a Palestinian refugee who had clawed out an education for herself in Jordan. After teaching herself fluent English, she had eventually ended up as an educational administrator in Bahrain. I first liked Maha for all the wrong reasons. Always on a diet, she was still pushing 200. But this didn't stop her from wearing the most outlandish dresses—bright, huge prints with large bows across the back. And always lots and lots of flashy jewelry—in her hair, on her fingers, around her throat. But beneath all the glitz and glamour was the soul of a Pope, the cunning of a Margaret Thatcher, and the brain of an Einstein. I loved talking to her. She was the antithesis of Americans' stereotypes of Arab women: she had authority, she made the hard decisions, she was well educated, she adored her religion (Islam), she loved both her career and her marriage, and she loved education for its own sake. A real intellectual draped in yards of gaudy material!

By now the Assistant Minister of Health was talking about Fulbright Scholars, me, Americans, and God know what else. My eyes rested on Densiba and Priya—two women from south India who'd taught me so much. Both were the first professional women migrant workers I'd met—both had left their unemployed husbands and their teenage children to come to Bahrain to support their families back home. They had been able to get teaching jobs in Bahrain simply because of the great shortage in upper-level nursing instructors. They sent everything they earned back to their families, keeping just the tiniest amount to eke out a living in Bahrain. They lived for their two months leave each summer which would be spent with their families in India. Without this great sacrifice, their families were doomed to live in dire poverty with no hope of advancement. They had to make the heart-wrenching decision we all make in far lesser degrees: what we do FOR our children often means we can't be WITH our children. Both were beautiful people and my heart ached for their dilemma.

The Head of the Research Committee of the College of Medicine was now talking about the two articles I had gotten published in Arabic medical journals since I'd been in Bahrain. My eyes fell on Jamail Al-Almoyed, Chairman of the Allied Health Professions Department, sitting quietly in his elegant white "thobe" (robe) and flowing Arabic headdress. Handsome beyond description, I knew of his inner turmoil. Educated in England and America, he had returned with many Western ideas which conflicted with his rather traditional Bahraini family. Returning to Bahrain in Western clothing, he faced a future wife he didn't know selected by his father, an expectation of doing what his family wanted as having priority over his own aspirations and goals, and a demand that he "tow the line" in terms of traditional values. None of this conflict appeared on his serene face. But he did embody all the problems the modern Arab faces: East vs. West; traditional vs. modern; technology vs. culture; Islamic fundamentalism vs. radical change.

Sitting right next to him was Nasrat Esbai, one of my favorite people. The middle daughter of a remarkable large Bahraini family, she too had been educated in the West: Canada, then the University of Illinois. She'd been so busy getting educated there had been no time for marriage or children. Now 36 years old but still glamorous, she returned to Bahrain to a job for which she was vastly overqualified with no job openings in sight that would really utilize what she knew, the prospect of marriage getting bleaker and bleaker, and living with her parents since a single Bahraini woman would never feel free to live outside their parental home. She couldn't even drive with a man in her BMW car without raising a lot of eyebrows! And although she truly loved her large extended family and her parents were most precious to her, she still felt stifled at times by all the conforming pressures and demands. She will eventually end up as one of the outstanding women leaders in Bahrain, but the position will be hard-earned through personal sacrifice and tremendous frustration. That she could remain so consistently cheerful through it all made her one of my favorite persons and spoke well of the strengths within Arab women.

At last the speeches were over. It was time for me to talk—and talk I did, of course. I told of my gratitude and my learning but my emotions got the best of me because I truly had learned to love Bahrain and especially its people.

The Dean then presented me with a red velvet case emblazoned with a silver enameled shield of Bahrain. Inside, was a custom-made solid gold plaque engraved with personalized symbols of Bahrain and some words of parting in my native English. And the most beautiful crystal vase I 've every seen for my wife. (A few days later, even U.S. customs was overwhelmed and spent a long time studying these gifts!)

In America, we typically eat first, then have the program. In Bahrain, it's just the opposite. So as soon as the program ended, the food started flowing.

All my Bahraini favorites were quickly before me: chopped parsley and Arabic millet salad, lamb shish kebab, yellow rice mixed with white currents and cashew nuts, rice custard for dessert. All washed down with Arabic tea—a steaming concoction of coriander and rose water. As usual, everyone ate with great relish. The jokes flew back and forth and a lot of Arabic hugs and farewells were exchanged. I was proud I had learned enough Arabic to say goodbye properly.

It was time to go home!

INDIA

"THE PALACE ON WHEELS"

"Do you think the 'Palace on Wheels' train will isolate us from the real India?" my wife worried aloud to a close friend from Madras.

"There's no way one can escape India," she gently replied, "no matter how you go. The swarms of people everywhere, the poverty, the smells of the crowded cities, the opulence of the palaces, the religions—they'll all be there."

We had managed to book the famous "Palace on Wheels" tour of India—the private train made up of 14 of the old maharajahs' private railroad cars. It's now run by the government of Rajasthan, one of the largest "states" of India. Although we'd heard the waiting list here for the tour is three years, by booking abroad we were able to only wait a few months and our time had come.

Our plane struggled through the omnipresent smog of New Delhi and we emerged in an airport so crowded one could hardly breathe. An ancient cab got us through the swarming streets to our hotel, where we were introduced to the idiosyncrasies of New Delhi itself: the smell of kerosene cooking stoves everywhere as the people prepared their supper; the dimming of the lights as the electric system strained with the chronic overload (the bathroom was equipped with candle and matches just in case); and water pressure that reached zero as people began drawing water for the evening.

The next few day's tour of both old and new Delhi was worth any inconveniences, however. New Delhi, built by the British in the 1930's as a whole new capitol for their showcase colony, featured grandiose government buildings, wide boulevards, and a Parliament building that would make any country envious. Old Delhi was the best of the India we see in calendar pictures with its red stone buildings and exotic architecture. Mixed in with both the new and old city were an estimated 10 million people. Although most had apartments or even houses, many families were reduced to literally living in the streets, with the lucky among them having ragged tents pitched up on railroad right of way, public parks, and even sidewalks. In many sections of the city, it was hard to walk half a block without having a thin, hungry mother approach you with tears in her eyes begging food for the baby she carried in her arms. The showplace city the British had built had been molded to the realities of India.

At 5 A.M. the next morning, we found the remote station for the medium-gauge railway line of India: the only gauge the "Palace on Wheels" train could operate on. Sure enough, the splendid train was there as promised and beautifully liveried servants were everywhere to help with the luggage, offer us refreshments, and get us to our reserved car. Each of the 14 private cars, which would serve as our "home" for our remaining time in India, were distinctly different as befit the personal taste of the maharajah who had originally had it built. But all slept eight passengers (and two young man-servants who went with the car), all featured a private "lounge" and adjacent "porch" at the end of each car; all had a small cooking facility where breakfast for the occupants was prepared, and all featured a central bathing facility of sorts. Two cars were for English-speaking, two were for German-speaking; two were for French-speaking, one for Spanish-speaking, one for Japanese, etc., while one car had been converted into a luxurious diner while yet another had been converted into a bar/lounge car for all nationalities.

Our English-speaking car had a pair of single young British women from Hong Kong, a retired Eastman Kodak couple from Rochester, New York, a Scottish army officer, complete with kilts and his alcoholic wife left over from the Raj who now lived in

Australia, and my wife and I from Madison. Plus two of the most handsome Indian men I've ever seen, dressed to perfection in the fineries of a Maharajah's livery, whose job it was to care for the car and its occupants throughout the journey.

The steam-powered train left Delhi as scheduled and the train passengers were treated to breathtaking views of the Indian countryside, complete with tidy little farms and, every few miles or so, small rural villages. We alternated from the comfortable lounge to the private "porch" where we could sit outside and watch the countryside roll by as we met those sharing our private car.

Since the cars all had porches at the end and were built to be pulled singly, unlike a regular train, there was no way to go from one car to another. So a trip to the lounge or dining car was only possible when the train stopped in the middle of nowhere at suppertime and half the cars's passengers got off, walked along the track to the dining car, while the other half got off and walked to the lounge car, whereupon the whole train would start up for an hour and stop again in exactly one hour. Those who had eaten, got off the dining car, and moved to the lounge car or their own car; those who hadn't eaten, got off the lounge car and moved to the dining car; and, after another hour of travel, the train stopped again and everyone walked track-side back to their own 'private' car. You stayed in the lounge or diner exactly one hour whether you had one drink or two, or whether you ate fast or slow!

A little strange, but fun, and it gave you a good chance to met passengers from other countries, although sometimes misunderstandings occurred. For example, one day I decided to wear my formal Arab attire which is good for traveling: a long thobe of a very dark blue wool with a closed one-inch formal collar closing around the neck. I found out a German women in the bar was asking about a fat Catholic priest who was traveling with a mistress! It was the last time I wore that outfit.

Jaipur, the fabled city of Northern India, was our first major stop and we were greeted by a uniformed band, a herd of huge elephants colorfully attired, and a fleet of buses who whisked us to the many palaces built in that city over the centuries. The Amber Palace I remember the best. It had been built on top of a mountain and we were to ride a huge elephant up the cobblestone road to the palace gates. Each elephant was to carry four but unfortunately, the four herded onto the biggest elephant were all really heavy people and I figured it was a half-ton load easy. I felt sorry for the animal and asked repeatedly to get off and walk, but no one spoke English and I was ignored. When the poor animal started wheezing like it had asthma as the grade increased, my wife and I both began pleading to get off and walk, but the tiny Indian boy riding on the elephants neck misinterpreted our pleas and prompted the animal on to even greater speed and huge gasps for breath. By the time we got to the palace gates, I was so guilt-ridden I swore I'd never ride an elephant again.

But after climbing down from the back of the huge beast with the ladder provided, and having a garland of marigolds placed around my neck as a sign of welcome, I scurried away to the Palace entrance where a new hazard introduced itself—the baboons of India were everywhere, it seemed. I blithely ignored them, since I didn't see them as beautiful animals anyway, but when one jumped right onto my head and tore the marigold garland off my neck, knocking my glasses to the ground in the assault, my ignoral technique seemed stupid. I retrieved the glasses fine, but kept a close eye out for the baboons after that. Turned out they didn't love me—they loved marigolds, and would go to any length to get them! Without the flowers, we were tuned out to each other.

This palace, as were all the others in India, was unbelievable in its awesome size (many could be measured in acres rather than square feet), its luxurious appointments (gold and silver were as common as glass in a land where people have starved to death for centuries), and its design (most were built with a large variety of geometric shapes, not just rectangles as is so common in our culture). It was obvious most would require staffs of hundreds of servants to keep them operational.

India provides work for its millions of people in ways I suspect have been perfected over centuries. I watched a small cement patch job taking place at the palace. One man was in charge of the water; one man had the cement mix; another actually mixed the water with the cement; nine carried tiny amounts of the cement to the work site; three poured the cement; and another three smoothed the cement into place. All this was supervised by no less than six overseers who did nothing but watch the other 18 men and look important. At another palace, I watched workmen cutting the well-trimmed small lawn off an interior patio. A well-built lad pulled an old 14" reel mower by a rope attached to a harness around his bare chest; another much smaller man guided the small mower; and a third supervised the first two and told them with a twitch of his finger when to cut the next narrow row.

At Jasalmere, I saw a sight I'll never forget while viewing the "Golden City." Our ancient bus had two people attached to it: a haughty driver who did nothing but that, and a young boy who handled the luggage and swept out and washed the bus as needed, usually under the harsh commands of the arrogant driver. The boy also served as the security alarm system for the bus in that he actually lived in the bus itself with a small pallet on the floor near the driver. The lad wore only a dirty loincloth and judging from the small sack of personal possessions he had on the bus, that seemed to constitute his total wardrobe. Wherever the driver went, the boy faithfully accompanied him and squatted on his haunches near the driver's feet. At one stop to see the fabulous water fountains of a long deserted palace, I noticed the bus driver talking to some other drivers under the shade of a tree. The boy was at his feet, as usual, and the driver casually reached down while he was talking and petted him on his mop of matted hair as if one would pet a dog or stroke a favorite horse. The boy looked up at the driver with a look of unabashed gratefulness in his dark eyes. A shiver went through me!

Udaipur was a place James Bond movie fans have already seen—one of the films utilized the "Lake Palace" in the story itself. Built as a cool summer retreat in the middle of a lake for the ruler, the palace appears to float on the surface of the lake itself and you leave the boat with about a one-inch step onto the main floor of the palace. Even more wondrous was the City Palace with its 400 bedrooms, its harems, its stables, its swimming pools, and its awesome reception rooms. Part of it has recently been converted into a five-star hotel, but its so vast, even a hotel only occupies a small part of the total palace.

At Jodhpur, we had a formal dinner at one of the newly restored palaces where the polo grounds made the word "jodhpur" famous for riding clothes. The dinner was staged as if we were visiting dignitaries and the wide high back chairs, the servant for each diner, and the gold and silver dinnerware was a once-in-a lifetime experience that gave one the feeling of royalty despite our inappropriate casual dress. I later sneaked out to look at the garages attached to the palace and marveled at the many old Rolls-Royces and even an old Packard in almost perfect shape.

Chittaurgarh, a city seemingly locked in a time-warp near the desert, was delightful with its unique brightly painted houses and Fatchpur Sikri, a complete royal city built hundreds of years ago, only to be quickly totally abandoned due to chronic lack of water, was now the home of monkeys, pigeons, and thousands of rats who swarmed across the city squares with nary a fear of humans evident. For some unknown reason, it was at this city that the kilted Scot Army man decided to get out his bagpipe and serenade all the unappreciative Indians in the train station while his wife hit the bottle once again. Perhaps it was all those rats!

Surprisingly, one of the largest bird sanctuaries in the world is located in India. The Bharatpur Bird Sanctuary took a whole day of viewing and even then one doesn't do it justice. The sanctuary contains a lot more than birds, however, and is filled with almost all the animals unique to the Indian subcontinent. You have to admire a country so crowded having the foresight to preserve their wildlife so carefully.

The bus ride to and from the sanctuary was never to be forgotten. The dirt road was two lane, but all the pedestrians and bikers along both sides made it effectively a one-way proposition. Our driver, like all the others, insisted on driving as fast as the overcrowded bus would go, with one hand on the wheel while the other pounded the horn incessantly. Several times I thought impending doom was at hand, but somehow we escaped by a hair's-breadth. Although you frequently read of bus crashes in India, I'm surprised they're aren't more.

When we neared Agra in late afternoon, I told my wife, "Now don't be disappointed when we see the Taj Mahal. We've seen it so many times in films and advertisements where it's been photographed under perfect conditions, we're bound to be let down."

We arrived at the outer gates of the Taj Mahal just as the sun was setting and we both simultaneously exclaimed, "My God, it's even more beautiful than we imagined." Truly, it is the most beautiful building in the world and the setting is perfect. Actually a shrine to a beloved wife, the building seems to capture the depths of human emotions.

Within two weeks, which seemed like a lifetime of adventure, the "Palace on Wheels" train tour was back in Delhi and before long we were on our way home. The long flight home quickly elapsed as we were busy planning a return trip, this time to Southern India which promises to be another whole wondrous world.

YEMEN

"A LIVING MUSEUM"

As the once-a-week flight arrived in Sana'a, I was a little apprehensive in that I really didn't know what to expect. I knew it had been difficult getting a visa to visit Yemen. I knew Yemen had been closed to foreigners from the last century until recently. I knew that few Americans had ever visited Yemen. I had heard it described as "stepping into the past." As the taxi sped into Sana'a, I looked at surely the most unique architecture in the world. I also saw short little men, all proudly wearing ornate daggers around their waists, and women dressed in brilliant reds, oranges and greens. At that point, I felt this was going to be one of the "great" trips.

How right I was! My wife and I agree that Yemen was one of the best, most exotic, and most interesting trips we had ever made. After two weeks in India in February, we thought we'd seen everything—different religious beliefs, different cultures, different life styles and values. But India was twentieth century. Yemen turned out to be a living museum.

Most Americans aren't too familiar with Yemen due to its insularity. Land of Bilquis, the Queen of Sheba, it's at the bottom of the Arabian Peninsula bordering the Red Sea. It's been the center of many great ancient civilizations, was conquered at one time by the Romans and the Turks, but during the past century has been ruled by "imams," religious leaders who kept the country sealed off from the outside world. In fact, the last imam stated: "We would rather eat grass and starve than be exposed to outsiders."

He did not allow electricity, road building, schools or even hospitals. There were no motion pictures, no television-nothing of the modern world. Apparently, there were a considerable number of Yemenis who did not agree with this as he was beheaded in the late sixties and the rule of the religious imams changed to a more participatory form of government.

But even then, change has come slowly, because Yemen is a very poor country. Small amounts of oil have only recently been discovered. As a result, in many ways Yemen gives you a glimpse into the traditional past.

North Yemen is for the most part very mountainous, making it unlike much of Arabia. It's even more rugged and craggy than the Rockies. Arable land is terraced to the very top of every mountain, so the visitor feels they are in Nepal, Tibet, or Cambodia at times. The scenery from the narrow mountain roads is simply spectacular. These terraced and irrigated fields have been in continuous use for over 3000 years and are kept in top repair. And the weather is great. Since it's a high altitude for this part of the world, it's pleasantly cool, but with bright, intense sun. Sweaters at night and very cool thin clothes during the day are indicated. I didn't take any sunscreen lotion and paid dearly. I was so comfortable I didn't realize I was burning badly the first day. After that, I always wore long sleeves and a hat for protection! If you like breath-taking scenery in brilliant light, Yemen is certainly a must.

But the real treasure of Yemen is its people and their customs. Since few people ever really migrated to Yemen, the first thing that strikes you is the genetic similarity of Yemeni—there seems to be much less physical variation among the people than you see in most countries. They tend toward a short, very thin, but wiry physique with oval faces, long straight noses, thick black hair, almond shaped eyes, and creamy brown complexions. Since foreign visitors are a recent phenomenon, Yemenis, haven't learned to dislike, avoid, exploit, or play up to them yet. In other words, foreigners haven't "ruined" it yet.

Yemeni are very curious about Westerners, but not envious or distrusting. One man popped up in front of my wife and me and asked, "What country?" When we replied "America," he giggled, danced around us three times, and disappeared into the crowd. The men and children often ask to have their pictures taken and when you agree, they sometimes jerk into military attention. But women tend to flee out of sight when they spot a camera. You are usually asked your name in broken English and, as they struggle to repeat it, they seemed most pleased if you ask their name and struggle to repeat it in Arabic. Even their Arabic is different—they don't seem to have the harsh "H" and "B" sounds of the Gulf regions.

The men all wear an elaborate curved dagger fastened to a beautiful embroidered belt around the usual Arab robe, but most Yemeni men also wear a short tailored jacket over the robe making them appear very distinct from other Arabs. These daggers are seen as symbols of virility as is the wearing of guns. We saw several men out in the mountains who had the traditional dagger around their waists, rifles slung over one shoulder, and submachine guns slung over the other shoulder—how virile can you get? Despite this rather fierce warlike appearance, all the Yemeni men we met were a gentle people with an excellent sense of humor who seemed happy and at peace with themselves. They liked nothing better than a good joke!

Around early afternoon, the "qat" market opens. Qat is a bush that is cultivated and grown in the mountains next to the famed Mocha coffee. Qat leaves contain a mild stimulant and perhaps small amounts of a distinct hallucinogen. Most Yemeni men are habitual qat chewers, and after purchasing their bundle of qat leaves, they proceed to pack their cheeks with the small tender leaves in big wads which makes them appear as if they have a golf ball between their teeth and their cheek lining. This wad lasts for hours and leads to some noticeable behavior changes like long periods of silence followed by very rapid non-stop talking followed by silence again. Some seem to go a little slower on qat, others a little faster. But the habit, which seemed almost universal, certainly strikes Americans as weird. One afternoon, a motorcade with some high government officials passed us in a large fleet of black Mercedes. Every driver's left cheek was packed with qat leaves as were the official's who were sitting in the back of the cars! I played around with just a couple of leaves and noticed no taste, but I did experience a deadened feeling in my jaw somewhat like a shot of Novocain gives you. To show you Yemeni take their qat seriously, it's interesting to note that one-third of all arable land is devoted to qat production (none is exported, of course) and that a day's supply of qat cost US$10-12—a very expensive habit! The men are careful to eat before chewing qat. That's because it is such a strong appetite suppressant that you forget to eat. If you don't eat beforehand, you quickly move into a state of malnutrition. With American's penchant for drugs combined with our weight problems, God forbid we ever discover qat!

Yemeni women seem to do most of the actual work. You see them out working in the fields, herding the sheep and goats, baking the bread, and caring for the children. Even Yemeni men admit the work load is very unequal, but women's liberation seems generations away. Yemeni women are frequently not veiled, dress in very bright colorful full-length dresses with even brighter scarves on their heads, and are exceptionally beautiful women. Although camera-shy, they certainly aren't people-shy as my wife will attest. She was invited and went to a bathhouse with some Yemeni village women and reported she had seldom met more gracious, hospitable, and pleasant women—she had a wonderful time with them. But Yemen is a very traditional country, and part of that tradition dictates rigid separation of the sexes in most social activities. So men socialize with men, and women with women.

School is voluntary at this point in the country's development. There were no schools at all until the 1970's! Parents are supportive of their children's education, but at this point, many more boys than girls are being schooled. Since most parents are illiterate, the children end up teaching their parents the basic rudiments. We were surprised how many girls were in school, however, and almost every village now has at least one girls' school (remember that even elementary school is sex-segregated). Sana'a, the capital, is now the center of a rapidly growing university offering mainly agriculture, medicine, health sciences, education, and other applied topics.

Now, there are five main paved roads in the country connecting the main cities over the high mountain passes. Due to Yemen's poverty, most of these roads have been gifts from other countries: the People's Republic of China, North Korea, Saudi Arabia, the United States, and France. These roads were difficult to construct, hang on the edge of cliffs with no guard rails, but do allow a reasonable transportation system for the country. We never saw a single railroad and there are only two regular airports in the whole country. Once you venture off these few main roads, you're into four-wheel-drive real fast. Almost all vehicles are of the 4WD variety and almost all are Toyota. I asked why Toyota since they do import other makes, and was told they are "good cars," as if that explained everything. Whoever has the Toyota franchise must be a rich man! I would guess at least half of all vehicles in the country are Toyota Landcruisers—a relatively expensive model. Twice, I was aghast that anyone would even consider driving any vehicle on the so-called trail we were on, but we always made it and never got stuck, tipped over, or simply sunk as I had originally envisioned.

Our guide and our driver always stopped for afternoon prayer in accordance with Islamic tradition, no matter where we were. One time, we stopped by a Chinese Pagoda commemorating the country that gave and built the road. As we waited in the Pagoda, my wife worked on her cross-stitch of historic buildings in Madison (Indiana). A large crowd gathered to watch her explain about Madison: a Sudanese who spoke English, an English couple touring with us, a deaf local boy, a traveler from South Yemen, an old lady from France, and a gaggle of local children—all drawn together by their fascination with Madison, Indiana. I did smile, though, when I heard her explaining the "mosques" of Madison!

Our tour circled in and out of Sana'a so that we could enjoy the comforts of one of the two modern Western-style hotels in that country. Once, our destination was too far to do this and we had to stay in a more typical hotel. A simple fan instead of air conditioning, a small cot-like bed, and a bathroom that didn't encourage lingering made up the facilities, although the restaurant was surprisingly good as long as you didn't expect to closely choose what you would eat.

Never had we had an eight-day adventure with so many rich memories and with such a sweet aftertaste. Nowhere else had we quite been face to face with life as it was—a simpler, less complicated period in human history where life is predictable and unchanging. No wonder the Queen of Sheba was anxious to get back from her visit to King Solomon—she probably missed the beautiful scenery, the colorful lifestyle, and I'm sure the men in her retinue missed their qat!

THAILAND

"A CITY OF TEMPLES"

I had wanted to visit Thailand ever since I'd heard some school teachers in Madison tell me about their visit several years ago to this ancient country in Southeast Asia.

My knowledge of Thailand was pretty limited. Until the mid-twentieth century, it had been called Siam. It was the only southeast Asian country that had never been colonized by a Western power at some point or another—in large part due to the cleverness of King Mongkut Rama IV, who was featured in the Hollywood film "Anna and the King of Siam" and later the hit musical "The King and I." I knew that Thai meant "free" and I knew that they had experienced an economic boom in the 1970's unrivaled in the Far East.

As we stepped off the long flight from Bahrain, we were engulfed by heat and humidity even hot by Bahraini standards for this time of year. The taxi ride into Bangkok, the capitol city of over six million people, was hot (it was 106 degrees F. and 98 percent humidity), wet (the "rain" came and went as the humidity would reach 100 percent), and very slow (Bangkok has some of the worst traffic jams in the world).

But all this was well worth it as the scenery began to unfold. Bangkok is literally a city of temples: old, new, refurbished—you name it, there are temples everywhere.

The recently restored Grand Palace was worth the trip alone. It has more than 20 different buildings within a beautifully landscaped compound which rivals France's Versailles or the Czars' palaces in Russia for pure opulence, architectural wonderment, and just plain glitz.

Our boat trips up and down the miles and miles of canals which form an elaborate network within the city brought us close to where Thais actually lived and worked.

Bangkok is somewhat like Los Angeles: it's hard to really find a "downtown" but the city goes on and on and on. Each new turn brings new surprises and new adventures. The city is so vast you can go in a matter of minutes from a dinner theater featuring classical Siamese dancing to Bangkok's famed brothel area to the canal's "floating markets" where flowers and vegetables are sold from small boats.

Our hotel was the tallest building in Bangkok, and from our fortieth-floor window we could never see the end of the city in any direction. But our view, especially of Thailand's beautiful sunsets, were somewhat besmirched by Bangkok's rapidly growing pollution problems.

The hotel desk had lost its only copy of an English-language telephone directory, but I was able to buy an English-language newspaper and, most fortunately, there on the back page was a small ad for the very thing I was looking for—the name and phone number of the church of Bill Rogers, a missionary in Bangkok who is the son of a close friend of ours. A quick call and minutes later we were in a "took-took" (a motorized rickshaw) speeding toward their home for dinner.

Bill is minister of the only English-language Protestant congregation in Bangkok (there are less than two percent Christians in this overwhelmingly Buddhist land). His wife June heads a task force for the World Council of Churches which studies all aspects of child prostitution—a real social problem in this part of the world. It was great to visit Americans who'd had the perspective of living in Thailand for a couple of years, and their hospitality made our visit to Bangkok especially meaningful.

Thai food was interesting: not terribly hot, but reasonably spicy for the main part. There was lots of fish and rice as one would suspect, but also surprising amounts of chicken, pork, and loads of fresh fruits including at least ten varieties I'd never seen or even heard of. It was fun to eat pork again after being so long in a Muslim country. And since we left Bahrain during Ramadan, the Islamic month of daytime fasting, we felt almost wicked eating and drinking whenever we liked.

We were able to visit several factories, much to my delight. The "sweat-shops of Asia" didn't materialize. Instead, we saw Thais working under thatched roofs where the walls were open for ventilation, lots and lots of electric fans going (but no air conditioning), plenty of first aid kits obvious, and a lot of continuous cheerful social interaction among those working. Ice water coolers were abundant, and occasionally young mothers would nurse their tiny infants that lay beside them. Most of the workers had fairly new motor-scooters or mopeds parked right up beside them. Men and women were doing the same work side-by-side. Everyone seemed very interested in what they were doing and were most eager to explain it to you—pride of workmanship was most evident. But, of course, these factories were involved in the manufacturing of quality products. Perhaps if I had visited a factory producing low-quality cheap goods, I would have discovered quite different conditions.

Too quickly, our time in Bangkok was up, and we were flying luxurious Thai Airways to Chiang Mai, capital of the northern mountain provinces. Charming is the only word to describe this city where tourism is the largest industry.

Brimming with native handicrafts, it boosts it is the largest "cottage industry" center in the world. Fascinating "night bazaars" are located in mile after mile of small, lighted booths where every type of jewelry, clothing, or home decoration conceivable could be purchased.

Chiang Mai also branches out into the surrounding forests where elephants are trained for logging and isolated hill tribes reflect primitive, remote life styles. I was astonished at how many Americans were in the place, but apparently many Far Eastern tours of Hong Kong, Singapore, Malaysia and other touristy places are now including Chiang Mai as part of the standard itinerary.

We paired up with a British couple from London to hire a van for a long trip to the famed "Golden Triangle"—the spot on the Mekong River where Myanmar (Burma), Laos, and Thailand meet. The trip there was engrossing. Good roads took us through high mountain ranges growing tobacco, opium poppies and teak trees. In between were fertile valleys where water buffalo were being used to harvest the rice crops, complete with farmers dressed in pajama-like brightly colored shirts and trousers decked off with the straw "coolie" hat.

After four hours we were on the Thai bluffs looking across the Mekong River at Laos straight ahead and Burma to our left. We arranged a boat trip on the Mekong so we could get a closer look at Laos (forbidden to Westerners at this point!). The boat we hired reminded me of the gunboats shown in movies about Vietnam. Since it was powered by an V-8 engine straight out of a Toyota truck, it could move with alarming, even frightening speed. The seating accommodations were non-existent, and as I sat on my feet in the keel of the boat, I had the distinct impression the boat was used primarily for smuggling, and only saw occasional passenger use. The opium trade in this part of the world is the number one business and certainly the most profitable, so I imagine my hunch was probably correct.

As we zoomed down the river toward Vietnam with a hostile country on one shore, steaming, incessant heat all around us, and the natural beauty and fascination of the jungle lulling you to the fact that if the boat got into trouble, no one would ever know what really happened, I was overwhelmed with the tragedy of the Vietnam War.

I couldn't stop thinking about all the wonderful young men I'd had as students at Hanover College who'd been shipped to Vietnam just as soon as the term was over, and how so many of them were sadly changed when they got back home several years later. After that boat trip, I thought I had a slight glimmer of understanding of what they'd gone through.

For Americans planning to visit Southeast Asia, I wouldn't recommend April unless you really like heat and humidity. I understand the winter months are delightful—like our spring. And don't just visit Bangkok—there's so much more to Thailand than its culturally rich capital. I'm sure you'll find the rather diminutive-sized Thais consistently charming, usually polite, and always hard working.

As our plane took off for Oman (that's another whole trip!), we reflected how we came from a Christian country, lived in a Muslim society, and had visited the most Buddhist nation on earth—a nice contrast with interesting perspectives!

THE SOVIET UNION TWENTY YEARS LATER

"AN EMPIRE IN COLLAPSE"

I had a chance to go back to the Soviet Union in 1991, exactly 20 years after my first visit. This time, though, I was traveling with a small group of fellow professors from Hanover College who were on a subsidized "study tour" courtesy of the Eli Lilly Foundation. This two week venture was led by a professor of history from a small Catholic college in Pennsylvania whose total experience with serious travel had been leading a couple of one-week tours of Russia for undergraduates from his college. Unfortunately, he used the same booking agent he'd used with those tours to arrange ours, and its undergraduate origins showed throughout the trip.

One bonus was that we first flew to Warsaw and had a couple of days before proceeding by train on to the Soviet Union. This allowed us see Warsaw, almost totally rebuilt since the heavy devastation of World War II. Thanks to the insistent intervention of a Hanover sociology professor, some of our group were able to hire a taxi and take the two hour drive to a Nazi concentration camp preserved just as it was found by a liberating Soviet Army in 1945. This all day venture allowed us to not only see the many small farms and villages dotting the Polish countryside to and from the camp, but allowed a thorough visit of all aspects of one of over 28 camps of wholesale death efficiently and methodically run by the Nazi S.S. from 1942-45 which yielded a total of over six million deaths of "undesirables."

That visit revealed there was a lot I hadn't realized about the Holocaust. When I saw the fingernail scratches on the doors of the death chambers, I realized the gassing wasn't painless. When I saw over 20,000 pairs of children's shoes carefully warehoused for shipment to Germany, I realized how many children were murdered along with the adults. When I saw human bone meal packaged in 50 pound sacks as fertilizer for the German gardener, I realized no aspect of human slaughter had been wasted. When I saw how the gold teeth fillings were extracted from the corpses prior to cremation, I realized "harvesting" took on a new meaning. When I saw bones still in the cremation ovens, I realized they continued this heinous orgy right up to the point where the Russians were knocking at the gates. When I saw how the crematory and all aspects of the brutal camp life was located in a valley directly in view of practically everyone in the Polish town right next to it, I realized what a mockery it was for townspeople to claim they had no idea of what was going on. And when I saw a literal mountain of human ashes still there because they hadn't had time to load the last batches into railroad cars to ship back to Germany as a source of phosphate, I realized the enormity of the operation.

The camp we were in "processed" all types: Gypsies, mental defectives, psychotics, German who didn't embrace "national socialism," homosexuals, criminals, and, of course, "Juden." What we sometimes forget is that remaining Polish and other Slavic peoples were treated as an inferior human species by their German conquerors, and the postwar victory plan called for Slavs (from where we get the word "slave") to be molded into a "servant race" as was their genetic destiny according to Nazi scientists. We had a lot to think about on our trip back to Warsaw.

The Russian train arrived hours late to take us from Warsaw to Kiev and was our first hint of the Soviet empire's breakdown, already well in progress in 1991, but not yet official. The train staff hadn't been paid in months and they had taken over the train gang-style. Seats had been oversold, with the extra money pocketed by the sales agents. Water, food, toilet privileges, and an actual seat went to the highest bidder instead of being a standard service. Everyone seemed to know this except our little group of American professors. When the train came in, we witnessed people climbing in and out of windows, stampeding the doorways, and confusion everywhere amid a great deal of shouting, screaming, and fisting your way through the crowds.

All of us got on the train within the very short time it was in the station, but we ended up sitting on our suitcases in the aisles when we had purchased a sleeper roomette. "Our" reserved room was locked and occupied by those who had climbed in the window and locked the door from the inside. Worst yet, I had been trampled in getting on and had my jaw stepped on by a heavy boot. The pain and rapid swelling spelled trouble.

After many hours, we were finally able to seize a small roomette of our own, but were without food or water. When we pooled our own personal food supply, we found we had a number of candy bars, snack crackers, and even a jar of peanut butter—enough so we would be far from starving during the 15 hour ride to Kiev. But thirst was going to be a constant companion on this trip.

The next crises was at the Soviet border where passports and visas were carefully checked. Our tour guide, the little professor from the Catholic college, had been fleeced by pickpockets in the Warsaw train station and had lost his cash, credit cards, all identity papers, and worse yet, his Russian visa and his American passport. Despite his endless explanations in broken Russian, the soldiers put him off the train along with an economics professor from Hanover who volunteered to accompany him. As the train pulled away from the border in the middle of the night, we saw the two of them standing there in the middle of nowhere where they would have to wait for the next train coming from the Soviet Union to Warsaw. Their two wives remained with our little group, hoping the two would eventually catch up with us.

Not long after, the track changed to the extra-wide track common only to the Soviet Union and the wheels had to be changed on each car before proceeding. This was done with huge cranes, which simply picked up each car with passengers intact as soon as the sets of wheels were disconnected. Then we were set down on a new carriage of wheels. This procedure was so refined it only took a minute or so for each car to be fitted with the new wide-track wheels. But it was a strange feeling swinging away in the air suddenly with no advance explanation or warning of what was taking place.

A few hours after that, it was early morning and we gazed out the windows at the infamous Chernobyl power plant with its hastily concreted domes, barb-wired fences, and utter desolation. I was astonished they hadn't moved the tracks away from the power plant in that the train went so close to the plant I practically felt I was glowing with radiation and tried not to breathe too deeply until we had passed.

It was time for breakfast, and the five of us remaining spread out the goodies we were going to share. As I made peanut butter crackers to pass out, the wife of the expelled tour guide asked, "Is that crunchy or smooth peanut butter?" I stared at her in disbelief. We were most fortunate to have anything at all to eat.

"It's crunchy," I answered coldly.

"I don't like crunchy," she whined.

"Then don't eat it," I responded icily, pointedly savoring the first cracker as I popped it into my mouth.

"I certainly won't," she shot back in an irritated tone.

In Kiev, the main square was filled with demonstrators for Ukrainian separatism but the Soviet soldiers, while nervously watching them, did little to interfere. We visited a Pioneer Children's Camp that day and learned first hand the problems of an Empire falling apart. Their support funds had suddenly ceased, the teachers hadn't been paid for over a month, but the children and program were going along as well as ever. That night we were lucky enough to get into the Kiev Opera House. It was packed with Ukrainian nationalists, since the only opera ever written in the Ukrainian language was being performed. This little known Tchaikovsky masterpiece featured a cast of 300, but the crowd knew the words by heart and the beautiful opera house rang between the huge chorus and the crowd singing the arias together. When the Ukrainian flag appeared on stage toward the end of the opera, the crowd left their seats and sang the finale as they filled all available standing space. It was a impassioned display of long suppressed nationalism and an experience I'll never forget. Within two months, for better or worse, the Ukraine was a separate country.

Several days later, the "lost" tour guide and his Hanover College companion rejoined our group with tales of police stations, an uncaring American embassy, and expensive last minute plane tickets. But by that time, we were leaving for Moscow by train, so those two never did get to see much of Kiev.

Our hotel, austere in Kiev, was a dream compared to our arranged housing in Moscow. Located at the very end of the subway line, the place had been built to house Olympic athletes a decade earlier. Cheaply built to start with and without any maintenance since, the place was a dump with broken plumbing, elevators that dropped six floors at a time when overloaded, doors and windows that didn't fit, and food that was indescribable.

"Do you think this is beef?" I asked one of the women in our group as I held up a green glob.

"I'm not sure," was the polite answer but I noticed the one I questioned never touched it.

"Is this a potato?" I asked, again holding up a gray looking substance.

"Just eat it," the tour guide mumbled. "We're very lucky to be able to experience the real Russia," a line that sold well to college freshman who'd never been out of their home state perhaps, but didn't sell well with me who'd been to Russia before and knew the truth.

From then on, we experienced the "real Russia" a lot as our guide's total lack of travel knowledge and connections played out. Roach-infested hotels, bad food, and worn out smoking buses became the norm.

A side-trip to Zgorst, site of the Russian Orthodox mother

church, was very interesting in that the church was reasserting itself after decades of suppression. No longer a museum only, the mother church was actually conducting mass after 70 years of silence. The rich bass voices of the monks singing their medieval chants projected the exhilaration so obviously shared with the many Russians crowding the interior of the ornate church—they were obviously worshiping the reopening of their churches as well as their God.

Although Lenin's corpse was still in the Kremlin, Stalin's body had been moved outside the walls. But the Armitage treasures were as resplendent as ever and we got a peek at where Stalin's personal apartments were. We saw the first production of "Jesus Christ Superstar" in Russian and marveled at how the Romans had all been costumed as Soviet soldiers and Pontius Pilate looked amazingly like a Soviet bureaucrat.

We later ate at the small apartment of the musical's director who, it turned out, had been director of the "state experimental theater" for many years, while his wife was an actress in the "state children's theater." They obviously had learned to walk a political tight-rope and survive. Their apartment, a prize awarded to high ranking officials, was amazingly small. It was crammed with expensive furniture, a beautiful piano, a large TV, its own bath and kitchen, and featured two small electrical refrigerators, but the building had only one functional elevator and we smelled some sewage problems in the halls. Twenty years earlier, I had visited the apartment of a person with no political connections, and knew firsthand this was luxury by Russian standards.

In Leningrad, we learned the name had just been changed back to St. Petersburg, and I again marveled at this absolutely fabulous city located at the very end of the Baltic Sea. The Hermitage was as great as before, the restoration of Catherine's Summer Palace was almost complete, and St. Michael's Cathedral was magnificent in its new restoration. Our housing in St. Petersburg, a cheap out-of-the-way port-side hotel that somehow reminded you of Leningrad's famous 400-day siege, dampened our enthusiasm but we were told it was "the best available," an open lie as we passed the numerous fine hotels St. Petersburg has always offered travelers in the downtown areas.

Since this was our last city to visit, it was time to make the visit "scholarly" since this was a study tour after all. A visit with two social scientists working for a provincial research organization was hastily arranged, and our small group met with them. Their research, as described, seemed simplistic and meaningless; our proselytizing a liberal arts type of education within the "new Russia" fell on deaf ears, and after less than a hour we sensed the dialogue was getting nowhere and they wanted us to leave. [I was amazed to discover a few of my colleagues reporting back on the Hanover campus their "finding" that Russia craved liberal-arts educational projects. If they extracted that finding from the above conversation with the Russian researchers, I must have been brain dead at the time.]

Before long, we were on our way to Prague, where again we were housed miles and miles away from the city, but Prague's charms overcame any inconveniences. A sociologist friend and I visited the National Museum which featured a special exhibition on the "Pink Triangle," the badge of shame forced upon all known homosexuals prior to their eventual imprisonment and annihilation during the first half of the 1940's by the Nazis. We both learned a lot from that exhibition in that neither of us had ever seen much about this part of the Holocaust other than a few off-Broadway plays addressing the issue.

Prague, now independent of its Soviet captors, showed a flair and ebullience that was contagious. The people were stylishly dressed, the women adorned themselves with beautiful jewelry, and the restaurants featured dishes only the Czechs had the pizzazz to produce.

Before long we were back at Hanover College, writing reports and justifying our "study tour" in scholarly jargon. Perhaps it was because I'd had such a wonderful educational trip to the Soviet Union 20 years earlier; perhaps it was because this trip was two instead of three weeks; perhaps it was because it had been arranged on the cheap; perhaps it was because this trip had been touted so highly as a scholarly study; perhaps it was because my injured jaw hurt the whole way; I don't know. But I can't recall any travel before or since where I seemed to learn less.

Incidentally, getting my jaw fixed when I got home cost more than any trip I have taken my whole life. The blow in Warsaw had split a tooth which in turn had become abscessed and impacted. By the time the damage was repaired, it was a year and thousands and thousands of dollars later.

GREECE, EGYPT, & JORDAN

"SOJOURNING WITH THE ANCIENTS"

I'd read all the newspaper accounts of how the Parthenon was in bad shape due to all the pollution in Athens. But they were going to coat it with something and when I arrived they were right in the middle of that project with scaffolding around each and every column.

Nevertheless, I was overwhelmed. First, the location! No matter where you are in Athens, its placement on top of the stone mountain called the Acropolis assures no one is going to miss it, now or in the 4th Century B.C. Second, the walk up the rather steep stone path from the streets below leaves you breathless, and when you round the last corner and view the temple head on, realizing you are witnessing first hand one of the ancient world's most heralded monuments, you feel almost light-headed. Third, even by modern terms, the Parthenon is big—not just artistically beautiful—but big. To this day, the ancient world's best example of perfect symmetry defines the term "aesthetics," a word the Greeks invented for just such awesome beauty. How impressed foreigners (like the Persians) must have been when they viewed the Parthenon from their ships in the harbor. I know I was.

But also on the Acropolis is the Erechtheum, the smaller temple with its famous "Porch of Maidens," which is almost as impressive as the Parthenon. Whereas the Parthenon is big and symmetrical and masculine, the Erechtheum is delicate, intelligent, and, well, feminine. The two together are perfectly matched. Even the Acropolis itself made sense: it's the highest place in town, so naturally you'd want to put your best efforts on display there; you can easily view the port (and enemies) from the tall lookout; below it was a huge amphitheater for theatrical productions, and a large flat area immediately below had obviously been used as their version of a giant shopping mall. That marketplace had once been the wonder of the world itself: everything Western civilization could produce was for sale there when Athens was in its heyday—items ranging from the poison hemlock to Sicilian figs to Nubian slaves. Remember, it was the Greeks who felt sorry for anyone non-Greek and labeled them "barbarians."

A hour's drive out of Athens brings you to the ancient silver mines that produced much of the Athenian's great wealth. Studying how that silver was extracted, you reflect on the irony that the world's first democracy was based on slave labor. Plato got around this by claiming some people are just born to be slaves by natural law. Other Greek philosophers sweetened that notion up a bit by adding that "fate can be fickle," which translated into the fact that even non-barbarians, such as the Athenians themselves, could be enslaved. Our version of democracy seems considerably safer, if not saner.

Contemporary downtown Athens is crowded, polluted, and vibrant. Socrates' Library is still there, right next to modern government buildings; the first Olympics site is right around the corner; and the Greek militia, dressed in 18th century white tights with tunic-like shirts and thick soled handmade shoes, guard the head of state. It's a fascinating blend of antiquities you've read about since you were a child, juxtaposed right next to a MacDonald's or Kentucky Fried Chicken outlet.

But Athens is the new boy on the block compared with Egypt, which was an ancient culture when Athenians hadn't progressed beyond herding sheep. I wanted to see two things in Egypt above all else: the insides of a pyramid and the tombs in the Valley of the Kings.

You might as well say the most famous pyramids are located in Cairo, rather than Giza, since the huge city now extends right to, and almost around, these mammoth legacies from the past. Since each stone is about the size of a boxcar, you can't imagine the effort in building even one pyramid, let alone all of them scattered around Egypt. The ones at Giza were once completely covered with a granite facade which undoubtedly made them sparkle in the sun. Nowadays, of course, only the bare stones are left, but that's impressive enough. But there are modern distractions from the scene. Certainly one such distraction are the hundreds and hundreds of diesel powered tourist busses, each spewing out tons of black smoke and thousands and thousands of tourists jostling one another to get just the right camera angle, or worse yet, a videotaping of Aunt Margaret lumbering off the bus for her first view of the pyramids, presumably to prove to the folks back home she made it, despite her arthritis. Another big negative are the non-tourists. Even before the bus has stopped, you are surrounded with hordes of screaming Egyptians hawking everything from plaster-of-Paris pyramids to plastic rosaries featuring the symbol of Isis. Cairo's population is estimated to be around 12 million these days, but does everyone have to sell tourist junk to make a living?

I wasn't going to be content with merely viewing the outside, however. I insisted on going inside, where the Priests of Horus marched in solemn procession, where the Pharaohs themselves checked out their afterlife surrounds, and where the estimated 20,000 workmen, necessary to build a single pyramid, padded along on their bare feet. After scouting around a bit, I found a small entryway in the side of a pyramid. I expected to be checked for archeological credentials or, at least Egyptologist status, but quickly found the only criteria for getting in was U.S. dollars.

We were formed into groups and, since I was at the front of the line, was told to lead the group up a narrow, steeply inclined walkway about 2-1/2 feet wide and 4-1/2 feet tall. We were to end up in the "Queen's Chambers." The walkway was so steep they had pounded ladder-like boards into the walking surface so we could get our grip on the incline. My initial thought was how small the Egyptians must have been if this was the main thoroughfare; after about 10 steps, my thoughts changed to how sturdy they must have been; and after about 30 steps, what great shape they must have been in to survive on no air. There really wasn't any air in the small channel: no ventilation of any type, hordes of people using up what little oxygen was available, and walking uphill stooped over with your head in your lap didn't maximize a person's breathing potential. The last thing I remember seeing was a small sign in English announcing we were halfway to the Queen's Chamber. The last thing I remember hearing was a guide screaming at me that my body was blocking the walkway and I'd have to continue.

"Just walk over me," I gasped before completely passing out.

That's exactly what the rest of the group did and only the next morning did I discover how badly you bruise when 40 to 50 people blighty walk on you. When I came to, I heard the group far ahead of me in some distant part of the tunnel and I was completely alone. I knew I had to get out, but how? I was too big to turn around in the narrow channel; I refused to go forward into even less air when I hadn't made it this far without passing out; but I had to do something since I knew the group would eventually be coming back down that same tunnel and would just walk over me again. I decided to crawl backwards on my hands and knees no matter how long it took. It took a good 15 minutes and even that was accompanied with a lot of gasping for air, feeling lightheaded the entire time, and a constant fear the group would overtake me coming down and trample me yet again. When I finally emerged from the side of the pyramid, my wife was patiently waiting, but looked startled when she saw me.

"My God, what's wrong?" she exclaimed.

"No air," was all I could gasp out.

"You're pure white—in fact, I think you're blue," she said in amazement. "I knew you shouldn't have gone in there."

"No air," I gasped again as she led me shuffling to the bus.

Viewing the Sphinx after that was anticlimactic since all I had to do was walk a little and stand upright.

But I had learned two things: Egyptian workmen must have been tough as nails despite their small stature; and the Royal family must have been half-dead at least by the time they ever got to inspect their final resting place.

Considerably downstream on the Nile sits Luxor, still rather magnificent four to six thousand years later. I was astonished how many remains are left, and what good shape they are in, considering the Egyptian government doesn't seem to restrict access to the irreplaceable treasures with any alacrity. The palaces and temples on the east side of the Nile are worth the trip, but the most impressive sites are in the "Valley of the Kings," way out in the desert beyond the west banks of the Nile.

When we got to the underground tomb sites, everyone headed for King Tut's tomb which guaranteed instant crowd. Instead, I headed for an obscure king's tomb which seemed to be rarely visited. Starting down the long flights of wooden steps, it looked innocent enough. Going down is always easier, despite the blinding heat present even in their cool season of November. By the seventh floor, my wife and I had reached bottom and we were in the burial chambers themselves, enjoying the cool of the subterranean chamber. We marveled at the colorful, stylistic and totally unprotected 4000 year old paintings on the wall, the elaborate and numerous chambers carved out of solid rock, and the total lack of air since no ventilation system of any type had been installed—then or now. All alone, we prattled away about how someone should at least protect the paintings with clear plastic panels or cordoned walkways—especially when some tourist at some time had scratched their name right into one of the wall murals. But our talk got less and less as the air ran out. We had seven flights of steep steps ahead of us, so we shut up and started the assent.

It seemed like a hour later before we emerged into the 106 degree temperature of the tomb's entryway. Soaked in sweat, we squinted into the blinding sun, forgetting exactly how we had gotten there to start with. Just then a swarm of Japanese went by in a swirl of dust, busily taking pictures of the dusty trail, each other, and a few rocks here and there.

"Follow them," my wife directed. "They'll find a bus if anyone can."

Sure enough, they led us right to the score of busses parked right outside the sacred valley and even took our pictures as we struggled up the bus steps breathless trying to keep up with them.

Getting back to Luxor, we were informed that there had been some "incidents" with tourists and we were to return to our Red Sea port via a convoy of 15 busses with military escort. Fine, but we didn't realize how long it takes the Egyptian Army to get things organized. Fully loaded, we waited and waited and waited for the military go-ahead until the busses ran out of fuel before we had even started the long trek across the desert—the same bleak desert Moses wandered when he had been banished from Egypt by the Pharaoh. Next, finding a station with enough diesel fuel to refill 15 busses became a chore. Six hours later and with the black of night upon us, we left for Safaga, the Egyptian port. In the far distance, we could hear the sirens on the soldiers' motorcycles screaming as they led us across one of the most barren deserts in the world. Actually, all we saw was a suffocating cloud of dust from beginning to end. The road was unpaved and the Army vehicles, as well as the first few busses, stirred up so much dust we all looked like ghosts before too long. The Egyptian guide on our particular bus threw her head down and took to loud sobbing. When her nearest neighbor asked her why she was crying, she screamed, "the anxiety, the anxiety." I thought we were the ones that were supposed to be anxious, but then maybe she knew something we didn't.

When we got back to our ship, the captain irritably said he'd been waiting for hours, but then, of course, he couldn't leave when his entire passenger list was jammed into those 15 busses. When the delay was explained to him, he just laughed and said, "Ah, the Egyptian Army . . ."

Our next destination was Petra, Jordan. Most sensible people ride donkeys down the narrow canyon into the ancient hidden city carved out of solid stone. Joyce and I declared no donkey should suffer under our weight, and boldly walked all the way down in three inches of powdery red dust. When we rounded the last curve and saw the famed "treasury building" featured in the James Bond movie, carved out of solid red stone, we were in utter awe. To our right, another tourist, even more overcome with it all, suffered a heart attack right in front of us and we watched him being dragged over to one side as a donkey cart materialized for his ride up the steep cliff.

Undaunted by this minor inconvenience, our guide announced we looked hardy enough and insisted, since we'd gotten this far, to "see it all." See it all we did, edifice to edifice, carving to carving, civilization after civilization.

"I'm sure glad we saw this while we're still able," I extolled to my wife.

"I think we've waited too long," she muttered without further comment.

Hours later, my feet ached, I longed for a drink of water, and the heat seemed overwhelming. I was beginning to envy the man with the heart attack, since he'd had a nice ride out in a donkey cart.

"Better be heading back," I suggested to the guide.

"Yes, the busses will be leaving pretty soon," my wife picked up on the exit theme.

"But you haven't seen the Roman city," the guide exclaimed, pointing his finger even further down the endless canyon.

"My God, what were the Romans doing in this God-forsaken place?" I asked in amazement.

"Oh, they built this entire city, just around the next curve, and then, of course, the Byzantines came and . . ." the ambitious guide rambled on.

"Let's compromise," I suggested. "We'll see what the Romans did, but then we simply must get back."

"I knew you'd understand," he responded with an enthusiastic smile.

The Roman city was impressive but I doubt few people ever see it, considering how far you have to walk to get to it. When we turned to go back, our guide pointed us in the right direction, said he'd meet us "at the top," and promptly disappeared into thin air.

What seemed like hours later, we emerged at the top, soaked in sweat, breathing like an asthmatic, and completely colored a brilliant clay red. When she would begin to breathe again, my wife wiped her eyes, and squinted through the glaring sun.

"Why, your hair's red again, Harve," she exclaimed as if a miracle had occurred.

"But so is yours," I countered, "and what happened to your face? You look like a mummy!"

Our guide reappeared for his tip, offered us a warm coke for $6 U.S., and disappeared again. When we finally got back to our bus, we discovered we were the last ones to board. Most had thought we had died in the heat, but some of the more optimistic had seen us heading for the Roman City and assumed we had quietly died of exhaustion. Two hours elapsed before I had any feeling return to my legs, and it took three runs through the laundry before my pants were anything but clay red.

My wife summed it up. "You only see Petra once."

DJIBOUTI

"COLDEST DAY OF YEAR IN LAST PLACE ON EARTH"

"You're very clever to come here on our coldest day," the driver said in his halting English. I stared at him thinking I had misunderstood since it was 99 F. and the humidity seemed much worse than the Ohio Valley in August.

"I'm glad I came in the depths of Winter," I answered caustically, wiping the sweat from my brow once again. "How hot does it get here?"

"About 40 (~130 F.) in the summer," he answered with a big smile, "Warm," he added for emphasis as the old Renault car chugged along.

I had always wanted to visit the former French Somaliland in that its history was so interesting. Long a major trading center at the "Horn of Africa", Djibouti had been the largest Arabian market of Ethiopian and Sudanese slaves for centuries. Occupied by Arabs, Portuguese, Italians, and finally the French, it had always had to import all the basics: everything from food stuffs to even water.

Over the centuries, its population had become a wild mixture of black Africans, Arab traders, Portuguese hangers-on, remnants of Benito Mussolini's defeated Ethiopian invasion force of World War II, some Indian and Egyptian merchants, and a few remaining French colonials. All they had in common was their language of commerce: Swahili, itself a mixture of many tongues. Once filled with tattered remnants of the Italian Army in 1943, it was last distinguished as a "disciplinary" assignment for the French Foreign Legion due to its climate and its restive, rebellious population.

When the French left, it became the Islamic Republic of Djibouti and has remained independent ever since, despite the civil war raging in neighboring Ethiopia on three sides of its borders.

The old French colonial buildings are everywhere with their unique pink stucco and white shutters but their rundown appearance seems to say there has been little maintenance since the French left. The port area seemed prosperous though, as it continues to be a major refueling station for ships either coming down from the Suez Canal or coming up through the Red Sea.

Our ship had stopped at Djibouti for that very purpose plus the fact we had to take on water there, which was itself hauled from somewhere else (and which was noticeably quite salty!).

The central market of Djibouti, located far from the piers and probably changed little over the past thousand years, was vibrantly alive. People here dress in vivid colors and reds, purples, greens and blues contrast beautifully with skins that vary from the light tans of Ethiopians to the coal black of Nubians to the burnt reddish-white of the last Western colonists. In this part of the world, eye colors vary just as dramatically, from light blues and greens to jet black.

Djibouti has few visitors outside of a few freighter ships anymore, so tourists are a rarity and a sight-seeing novelty for the natives who openly comment on your various qualities. Most understand Arabic as well as French and once you greet them in Arabic or French and they comprehend you might understand what they're saying, the comments tend to rapidly diminish. Since I know the Arab word for "fat," I know not all the comments were necessarily positive by our standards!

Almost every product of Africa was for sale in the marketplace at one little booth or another. Bananas, rice, chickens, goats, and spices were everywhere. Alongside the food was bright patterned cloth from India, face masks and carved (illegal) ivory from Kenya, and shockingly, one could even purchase animal skins such as leopard, long forbidden in world markets for endangered species.

People with filed, pointed teeth and scarified faces grinned at us, along with others who had stretched ear lobes and coiled rings around their elongated necks. It was like witnessing, first hand, old copies of *National Geographic* magazine.

One had the feeling of stepping back in time and seeing an East African port city as it was several centuries ago. My wife said she felt if we had gone three blocks further we could run into its historically famed slave markets, active until the French came, and reactivated briefly the minute the French had left for World War II.

But exotic has its price. The smells of rotting garbage and no functional sewer systems assaulted your senses. Huge biting flies and malarial-infested mosquitos have a feast on your exposed skin. And the humid heat is everywhere until any movement whatsoever leads to riverlets of sweat oozing out of every pore. As it pours down your face, it blinds you after a while and everyone's eyes take on a reddish hue.

As we bought some silver jewelry from Ethiopia, watched the men respond to the late morning call to prayer, experienced the gentle joviality of the merchants and their native customers haggling in the musical sounds of Swahili, Djibouti replaced another African city, Marrakesh in Morocco, as my nominee for the most exotic city in the world.

ZANZIBAR

"LAND OF SPICES, SLAVES, DR. LIVINGSTONE & ARAB SULTANS"

When I was a boy, I had read the British explorer Richard Burton's book on his trip to Zanzibar in 1856 and was fascinated with his Victoria-era description of this unique island off the coast of East Africa.

When I finally got there myself 140 years after that book was written, I was not disappointed. Zanzibar is just as exotic now as it was then, and should be on every traveler's agenda.

Zanzibar is best known to most Americans through the old Bob Hope and Bing Crosby movie "Road to Zanzibar" which was filmed near Hollywood and has no relationship whatsoever with Zanzibar or its culture other than the strange name.

To historians, it is best known as the largest slave market in East Africa and the temporary home of Dr. Livingstone who was so horrified at what he saw going on in the slave markets there that he later began arousing British sentiment against the slave trade in that part of the world. In fact, Zanzibar was known throughout East Africa as "Slave Island."

To food merchants and cooks, Zanzibar is the largest producer of cloves and still produces 80 percent of all cloves in the world as well as large amounts of vanilla, nutmeg, cinnamon, coffee, cocoa, and many other spices not popular in the United States. Certainly, it could have been named "Spice Island" with accuracy.

To anthropologists, Zanzibar is unique due to its various cultural migrations. First occupied by Africans, it was supposedly once occupied by the ancient Chinese and there is some evidence the Romans traded with, but never settled, with Zanzibari. The Portuguese built a fort there, but were driven out by the Sultanate of Oman several centuries ago. The Omani brought their religion, their Arab culture, the spice plantings and seed, a plantation economy which has lasted to this day, and slaves to work the vast spice plantations. Later, shamefully, slaves became the major trade commodity in and of themselves, mainly destined for Arabia and beyond.

Few Americans realize that the slave trade was far longer lasting and actually more extensive off the East coast of Africa than the West Coast destined for the Americas. The East Africa trade lasted over a 1000 years and ended only during the second half of the 20th century. The horrific West Africa trade lasted about 400 years, ending with emancipation in Brazil and Cuba. But its brutality and horrors could easily be matched by the Arab-controlled East Africa trade.

The site of the infamous slave market in Zanzibar has been replaced by an Anglican church deliberately placed on this site with a strained glass window honoring David Livingstone. But its alter is the old whipping post of the slave market finally closed at the beginning of this century. Nearby are the old underground slave pens where those not auctioned off one day were kept for the next day's sale. One can't help pondering man's inhumanity to man when viewing them.

The British, in one of the shortest wars in history—37 minutes, 23 seconds long—took over Zanzibar in 1896. The invading fleet was commanded by Sir Harry Holdsworth (Henry) Rawson, a distant relative of mine. [Fleet Admiral Rawson decided to let his sailors play a quick game of cricket on the shores of Zanzibar after a long voyage in the Indian Ocean. This so enraged the Sultan he declared war against Great Britain, whereupon Sir Rawson bombarded the Sultan's Palace who quickly surrendered. (The old coot then went on to raise a lot of trouble in what is now the Ivory Coast and ended up serving as Governor of South Wales, Australia)].

The British takeover, started over a cricket game, did promptly end the import and export of slaves. But Admiral Rawson failed to free those already enslaved on the island or the slave status of their children. Nor did he disturb the Omani aristocracy already owning all the land. Hence, for most Zanzibari, life went on as usual despite a token British presence, obviously more devoted to cricket than emancipation.

The spice plantations, developed by the Omanis and originally worked by over 20,000 slaves, are still flourishing today, although over 1600 Arab landowners were massacred in a political uprising in 1964. A Marxist government emerged, which led to land redistributions and government ownership of the plantations. Recently, elections have led to a close affiliation with nearby mainland Tanzania and its more moderate socialist government. But the plantations are still there and produce more spices than ever before. And workers are now paid!

Our tour of rural Zanzibar was from the bed of an old British Leyland diesel truck which gasped and choked along the rutted trails erroneously labeled as roads. But the air was crisp, the people friendly and curious about the strangers visiting, and no crushing poverty seemed to be present no matter how far off the beaten path we got. Of course, housing and clothing needs are minimal in this equatorial seldom-changing climate, and most food literally grows on trees around you. Some Zanzibaris call it "Paradise," but I wouldn't go that far with its constant heat and humidity as well as its infamous history.

The central market in Zanzibar City features fruits of every size, color and description as well as every variety of fish fresh from the Indian Ocean surrounding the island. Although the fish were delicious cooked, smelling them in the intense close heat of the marketplace almost made me retch until I got used to it.

Most sellers understood Arabic as well as some English, and one fish merchant, knowing I was from the U.S., asked me about Mike Tyson, Michael Jackson and Mohammed Ali as if I knew them personally. And we found out Clinton had been reelected from a woodcarver in this same market!

The Sultan's Palace is now a museum and we were able to visit it now that the last Sultan is gone—part of the 1964 massacre. So I was able to sit at the same dining table where Sir Richard Burton had been entertained by the Sultan of Zanzibar in 1856.

But there were differences. It had taken him six months to get to Zanzibar from Bombay, India on a British steamer headed for the Suez, making the last part of his trip from Dar Es Salaam on a small Arab dhow (boat). I had arrived on the modern ship the *Marco Polo*, especially built for travel to hard-to-reach ports. And it had been a simple overnight trip in air conditioned luxury from the port city of Mombasa, Kenya. I arrived fresh and able. Richard Burton arrived haggard, dehydrated and malarial-ridden. He was wined and dined by a Sultan. I was greeted by an old truck rented from a tour company. I'd rather have it my way!

Incidentally, I was actually the third Rawson to visit Zanzibar. You would think it was right around the block rather than in an obscure corner of the Indian Ocean. At some point, Sir Rawson William Rawson (yes, his first and last name were the same), who would later become Governor of the Bahamas and the Windward Islands in the Carribean, visited Zanzibar as an Admiral for the British Fleet. He is the one for whom Rawson Square in Nassau is named. But he's a distant relative: he took his wife's name in marriage (as well as changed his first name) in order to gain her inheritance!

You can see why I never used my last name while visiting Zanzibar.

MISSISSIPPI

"LAND OF THE BULLDOGS"

"This is the only third world country we've been able to drive to," my wife said sardonically as the loaded minivan sped southward.

I had accepted a visiting professorship at Mississippi State University for the term starting right after Christmas and ending with graduation in the spring. Neither of us had been in Mississippi since the civil rights struggle of the 60's. At that time, we'd delivered school supplies to impoverished black schools and had suffered snide catcalls from a few white teenagers in pick-up trucks because of our Indiana license plates. I remembered leaving the state via a toll-bridge across the Mississippi to visit my brother in Louisiana and venting some of my frustration.

"Do you take American money?" I snottily asked the toll taker at that time. I can't repeat his answer, but he did snatch the dollar bill out of my hand.

Both my older brother and sister lived in the South and loved it. They dismissed my stories about Mississippi as distorted and exaggerated since I was "a Northern liberal."

"The South had drastically changed anyway, so you're just spouting off half-truths about past history," my Arkansas sister cut me off the minute I opened my mouth in her thickest Southern accent, although she failed to indicate which direction the change had taken. Since Senator Jesse Helms was her current hero, I was afraid to ask.

My sister was right. The South had changed dramatically. Starkville, the host city of Mississippi State and home of the

"Bulldogs," was not the tension-ridden cultural backwash we expected based on our experiences of 30 years earlier. Quite the contrary.

The university, which had started as a small state-supported technical training institute generations earlier, was now a full-fledged Ph.D. granting research university, specializing in applied fields. It had learned a lot from all the open warfare at Ol' Miss regarding integration, and had quietly integrated a few months later without incidence. Further, it had been the leader in trying to avoid the "white flight" from public schools into the old garages, abandoned churches and warehouses hastily labeled "academies," which might as well have been tagged "white-only enclaves." The university leadership had done this by visiting each faculty member and their family, pointing out that if they did this, they would: (1) turn the public schools into black-only schools; and (2) end up paying taxes AND tuition. The argument even flattered the professor's ego. People would be looking to them to see what they did before acting since they were the social leaders of the community (even the most dense college professor knows the inherent untruth of this statement), and they should try to make the public schools "the place to be" by enrolling the "brightest and best" in just those schools (implying, of course, that the "brightest and best" were somehow out of their genetic pool). The strategy worked and "white flight" was avoided except for the die-hard "red neck" who could ill afford extra tuition anyway. Public schools had all the scholarship winners, all the prominent family's children, the best sports programs, and was, indeed, "the place to be." The most ingenious part of the strategy to save public schools was how they had addressed bussing from the very beginning. Since blacks rightfully objected to always being the ones being bussed long distances to achieve racial balance in the schools, Starkville had handled it differently. Schools were segregated by grade, not race. First grade was in one building, second grade in another, third grade in yet another, etc. Everyone was bussed to the appropriate grade level and race had nothing to do with it. Even the most militant black couldn't object to that one in terms of fairness. So Starkville never experienced all the turmoil over public school integration so common during the late 60's and even into the 70's in so many communities.

Mississippi State specialized in training students in applied areas. With my liberal arts background, I was sort of floored with the types of majors offered: wood products technology, golf course administration, forest management. Most were four-year degree programs with very specific job markets in mind. When I airily asked if they offered Greek or Latin, they just sort of stared at me. Whereas I was used to students talking about the problems of gaining admission to graduate or professional schools and whether "English Lit" or "European History" was the best background for getting into law school, I now confronted students whose entire education was centered around making Masonite wallboard or whether fescue or bent grass held up to abuse longer on the fairways. I now understood the slogan "Go to college to get a job," which I had always thought was kind of a joke in that I thought you went to college in order to be knowledgeable and informed.

When eight people in one class of 80 told me they were in golf course administration, I dumbfoundedly muttered, "There must be more people studying golf course administration than there are golf courses."

"Nonsense," one of the bright eyed students vivaciously responded. "There are three new golf courses a day in the United States. And," he paused for emphasis, "they all need trained staff." Not being a golfer myself, I knew when I was out of my league, and ceased further comments on esoteric majors.

Anyone with a Mississippi secondary diploma was accepted at Mississippi State, but survival was another matter. Unfortunately, a high school diploma didn't guarantee you could even read or write and some of my freshmen students read at about a second to third grade level. The university, following state law, took them anyway. The professors teaching the lower level courses watched their struggles for a term or two and then never saw them again as yet another educational defeat was validated. Although some white students, products of hurriedly contrived "academies" suffered this total lack of educational background, the problem was most predominant among blacks, especially those from the "integrated" public schools of the Delta regions, now almost solidly black and where educational standards had largely been abandoned by uncaring administrators and teachers. These students came to Mississippi State with high hopes and unrealistic aspirations. They left a term or two later with a string of "F"'s and "D"'s, a confirmation that they were dumb, and a dogma that the white establishment wouldn't allow them in. Whereas these blacks, like most whites, originally felt that education is the route to advancement in our society, the flunked-out blacks now felt denied this opportunity and would seek out other ways to advance, perhaps in ways whites didn't approve of too much. Such a system was a waste of the university's time, was a waste of the unprepared student's time, and worse yet, hardened an already dispirited population. The saddest of all were the whites who had been told they were educated in their academies, but weren't. The blacks, at least, suspected all along they weren't learning anything.

Our neighbors in Starkville proved to be delightful. They ranged from born-and-raised in Starkville with thick Southern accents to "damn Yankees" relocated to the university or a local industry. They were proud of Starkville's progress, its response to the integration challenge, its resultant school system, and its social life.

Most of the latter was based on either family or church. Our Presbyterian church was friendly, open, tolerant, and prosperous. They made us feel welcome right away, asked our help on several projects, and was proud of its role in the town's social progress. Whereas Presbyterians nationally were rapidly losing membership and were chronically cutting back programs as a result, this church was growing, had plenty of money, and was busily setting up new programs. People were proud of their church and supported its programs enthusiastically. The church was a big part of your social life and this seemed to be true of every church in town.

Family was a big part of my student's social life. They seemed to always be going home to celebrate someone's birthday, marriage, funeral, or anniversary. When I advised a theater major that he should try to get some experience in New York City since it was the center of theatrical productions in this country, he just stared at me uncomprehendingly and finally stated, "I couldn't do that—I'd have to leave my family." How one gained professional theater experience in Mississippi was beyond me, but I ventured no further advice for fear of being a home-wrecker.

One of my students was a 430 pound guard for the Mississippi State Bulldogs. Jet black, pure muscle without an ounce of fat on him, he tried to sit in a chair right in front of the lectern. I say tried, because all he could do was sort of scoot in sideways into the tiny plastic desk chairs provided in the crowded classroom. I saw him taking copious notes, unusual in this freshmen level class where many students didn't bother to bring anything to write with, let along something to write on. Further observation revealed he actually was taking notes, not writing a letter or doodling, so naturally I took an instant liking to him. Furthermore, he showed up at every class, a relatively rare phenomenon.

"How come I got a 'D'?" he angrily asked in his deep bass voice when I handled back the first exam.

"You didn't study enough," I countered. "Surprised me, though. Since you pay such good attention and you're obviously smart, I thought you'd get at least a 'B'."

"Well, I did too," he answered, still angry, obviously not fooled by my cheerfulness. "You better call Academic Support over at the Athletic Department and get me a tutor," in a tone that clearly implied it was my fault he had done so poorly on the test.

I did call "Academic Support." They cheerfully said the student was a senior taking my freshman level course to meet a graduation requirement. But he was no longer eligible for their services since he was a graduating senior and his eligibility for football playing was over.

"So how does he get a tutor?" I countered.

"He doesn't," they stated. "Thanks for calling. Any other players we can help you with?" they brightly added.

"You're on your own, buddy," I told the football player the next morning in class.

He took the news disbelieving. "But's who's going to help me?"

"Nobody, apparently. But, you're smart. You don't need anyone to help you, anyway. Like a baby sucking on a nipple if you ask me, especially for a good man to start with. Why would you need help when you listen up, take all those good notes, and come to class every day. Nobody does all that and gets a damn 'D' in my class. Tell you what," I said enthusiastically, "if you don't get a 'B' on the next test, I'll beat you up right in front of the whole class. Think how embarrassed you'd be, having an old fat cracker like me beat the crap out of you right in front of the whole class. All you have to do to avoid it is get a 'B' on that next test."

He stared for a minute before he caught the absurdity of the proposition and his eyes sparkled. "I'll get the 'B', prof," he laughed.

On the next exam, he did get the "B."

"Well, I won't have to beat you up in front of the whole class after all," I said as I plopped the test back on his tiny little armchair. "I knew you could do it. But I don't see why you can't get an 'A' just as easy. Tell you what. If you don't get an 'A' on the next test, I'll just have to beat you up in front of the whole class. Think of the embarrassment."

"Yes sir, I'll get the 'A'," he laughed.

He got the 'A' on the next test I expected.

"Despite that first 'D', I figured up your total points and now you could get an 'A' for the whole course, you know," I mentioned. "All you have to go is get a solid 'A' on the final."

"I can't do that, prof," he said, "I'm working for a 'B'."

"Nonsense," I countered. "Nobody as smart as you are is going to insult me with a 'B'. Tell you what, You get a solid 'A' on the final and I won't have to call your mother about how disappointed I am in you."

"You wouldn't," he looked worried.

"Yes I would," I said. "I'd probably like your mother and it would give us a chance to talk."

"Don't call my mother, man," he countered. "I'll get the 'A'." He sounded defeated and I knew I'd hit a nerve.

He did get the 'A' and I didn't call his mother. He proudly told me that was the first "A" he'd ever received in a regular course (even he excluded the P.E. courses with a guaranteed "A" he'd always been automatically enrolled in, such as "Sports Management," "Kinesthetics," etc.) and his mother would be "awfully proud of him." I imagined she would be and I regretted not getting the chance to chat with her.

"Thanks, prof," the huge black said as the course ended. "I learned a lot."

"Thank YOU," I replied.

"Why so?" he smiled warmly.

"You've restored my faith in education."

COSTA RICA

"LAND OF MANY SURPRISES"

As we stepped off the ship for my first visit to Costa Rica, I realized my expectations of Central America had been formed by a lifetime of reading tragic news reports: military dictatorships, revolutions, corruption, exploitation of the peasantry, fantastic wealth of a few matched by incredible poverty of the many.

What a surprise Costa Rica was for me. Frequently called "Switzerland of the Americas," it was truly a geographically beautiful country with its many volcanic peaks and lush tropical valleys. The mountain ranges hosted the bright green coffee trees while the valleys harbored the many banana plantations everyone associates with Costa Rica.

But I was surprised at the many cashew nut farms and tropical flower plantations which seemed almost as frequent. The last time I'd seen flowers grown in such profusion was in Peru where cultivated marigolds were a primary source of chicken feed—to the degree where some of the chicken meat had a tell-tale hint of marigold orange to it!

While coffee and bananas are still the largest agricultural exports of this country no bigger than West Virginia, its 3.5 million people have wisely expanded their economy far beyond these two basic cash crops. Many of the trendy tropical plants we see displayed at large hotels, fancy weddings, and formal receptions are grown in Costa Rica. And I've seen a lot of Costa Rican textiles and crafts, especially small models of the brightly painted donkey carts of the town of Sarchi, displayed in homes throughout the United States.

Christopher Columbus himself named Costa Rica ("Rich Coast") after viewing little but its coastline. He imagined a land rich in gold, silver, and fertile plains. The fact that Costa Rica really had none of these was perhaps its saving grace. Without the precious metals, the country didn't attract the greedy exploiters from the Old World and without land suitable for large scale labor-intensive plantations, new settlers found it uneconomical to import African slaves. Hence, from the very beginning, Costa Rica escaped perhaps the worst of foreign influences. The Spanish settling the country were primarily small farmers who seldom became wealthy, but did spread their language, culture and religion to the native population.

It wasn't until 1949, though, that Costa Rica really distinguished itself from its politically unstable neighbors. As the result of a brief revolution in 1948, a new constitution was established that made an army illegal, guaranteed free elections, prohibited government leaders from succeeding themselves indefinitely, and sharply limited possibilities for corruption. Amazingly, this constitution is still in effect and proudly protected by the Costa Rican people. A recent president, Dr. Oscar Arias, won the Nobel Peace Prize for promoting active neutrality and helping other Central and South American countries attempt to reach some degree of democratic process within a climate of political stability.

Over fifty years of a stable democracy has paid off handsomely for this small country. The standard of living is noticeably higher than in most Central American countries; the distribution of wealth is noticeably more equitable; and people seem free to actively engage in those aspects of a free country we take for granted: freedom of expression including a free press, freedom of religious expression, and freedom to vote without interference. Costa Rica boasts a 93 percent literacy rate, certainly the envy of almost any other Central American country, and many of its citizens enjoy decent housing and a car in the garage. The availability of good health care has led to the highest average life span in that part of the world. Not all is perfect, of course, but comparative to its neighbors, its progress seems remarkable.

To a naturalist, the country is a marvel. Costa Rica's steep mountain ranges along with the low coastal areas insure that the animal and plant life is fantastically varied for a country so small. Over 10,000 species of higher plants (trees, flowers, ferns), 850 species of birds, 1000 species of butterflies, and 200 species of reptiles are everywhere as they flourish in the tropical climate. This forward looking country has made sure visitors will be able to see all of this in the future too! Nearly one-fourth of the land is protected from commercial development through a system of national parks and preserves. No wonder tourism is rapidly becoming its number one industry.

The Costa Ricans I met were understandably proud of their country and its accomplishments. Their eyes blazed with excitement when they described the schooling of their children, their last national election, even their current social and economic problems. They clucked with disapproval at the plight of their nearby neighboring countries.

Experienced travelers had urged me years ago to visit Costa Rica when I had a chance. They told me then I would be pleasantly surprised. How right they were!

AMTRAK IN THE U.S.

"TRAIN OF TOMORROW HERE TODAY"

As most people my age are aware, passenger trains just never quite recovered from World War II. Aging cars that led to broken seats and temperatures that hovered around 90 whether it was summer or winter became the norm. Freight trains usually took precedence, and you seemed to often end up on a sideline, watching the profitable side of trains whiz past you as the trips took longer and longer.

When the government created Amtrak to take over passenger service, the new agency inherited unprofitable routes, antiquated equipment, and too many employees. Now, years later, they still aren't making money but service on the few remaining routes has improved and most of the old broken equipment is gone.

In a bold experiment, Amtrak is trying out a whole new concept in train travel on a few medium length day routes where they are probably in the best position to compete with airlines. One demonstration, a three week trial, was between St. Louis and Kansas City, Missouri where air travel can be burdensome by the time you get to and from the airports and where car travel is a hassle on the overburdened I-70.

The "Flexliner" is a three-car self-propelled unit that carries 141 passengers in either coach or club car accommodations. Made in Denmark by a German outfit, it is already in daily use in Scandinavia, Germany, and Israel. It is a lightweight train, built somewhat like a luxury streetcar, but powered by four Mercedes diesel engines totaling 1600 horsepower and averaging 2.4 miles to the gallon—not bad considering you're carrying 141 passengers at speeds up to 110 miles per hour.

We boarded the Flexliner at the downtown St. Louis Amtrak station, a small modern prefab located on an old parking lot in back and out-of-sight of the hulking St. Louis Union Station when, in its glory in the 1940's, 60 passenger trains a day were boarded. Our coach tickets to Kansas City entitled us to two very wide, comfortable seats with a table in front on which the morning's newspaper was placed for your convenience along with an annotated map of the route, individual air conditioning and reading light controls, a huge picture window fleshly washed and even a laptop computer plug-in. The restroom featured electric doors and was sized for the handicapped—a far cry from most airplanes I've been in. The conductor and steward were cordial and in high spirits with a lot of jokes about the way trains "used to be" and how this train always ran on time. I noticed the three-unit train could be driven from either end, like a subway, so no turntables or turnarounds were required at either end.

Exactly as scheduled, the train glided into action. It was so smooth on the takeoff, you had to look out the window to realize you were moving as the diesels revved up and you could vaguely feel the five-speed automatic transmission take you through the gears. The first impression is how well it rides, and how very quiet it is, but the biggest difference was it's amazing acceleration: very smooth but very quickly you're up to speed and, before you know it, you're zooming along at 79, the maximum allowable on Missouri's aging tracks. Despite the tracks, the ride was very smooth and quiet at all times. Even going around curves seemed to be effortless in that the Flexliner seems to lean into them and I never noticed them reducing speed much for the curves.

Within 20 minutes, the "hosts" (a smartly dressed man and woman who were near retirement age) were wheeling a snack cart up the aisle offering free coffee, juice and soft drinks along with reasonably priced beer, wine, sweet roll, and sandwich options. As we sipped our hot coffee and ice-cold orange juice, the aluminum train whisked right next to the Missouri River for a 80-mile stretch that no highway could match for dramatic scenery—the tracks were right on the tiny area between the Ozark bluffs and the river itself.

As we finished our coffee, the train was already in Jefferson City affording the very best view of the capitol building and then veered off away from the river to the Missouri prairies giving us a chance to read the morning newspaper. Exactly as scheduled, the train pulled into Kansas City's new Amtrak station 5-1/2 hours later, conveniently right at the Hallmark Crown Center. I figured we'd averaged 57 miles an hour including all eight passenger stops and the one delay we had to let a freight train go by. That rate is hard to beat for medium intercity hauls no matter how you travel.

After a leisurely lunch and some quick shopping at Crown Center, we boarded the Flexliner for the return to St. Louis, this time on the premium priced Club Car. This car held only 32 people so it was even more commodious and featured a steward that attended to your drink and magazine needs on the spot, almost identical to first class plane travel. This time, the afternoon *Kansas City Star* was at our seat and in a mere 5-1/2 hours, we were gliding smoothly into downtown St. Louis.

The Flexliner was headed next for the Portland-Eugene run in Oregon where the Oregon Department of Transportation, like the Missouri Department of Transportation, has agreed to underwrite a demonstration period. From there, it will undertake similar demonstrations in medium length day routes between major cities where sufficient passenger demand is evident and where state department's of transportation are willing to underwrite modest subsidies for its operation. In my opinion, the Flexliner would be perfect for the Midwest's Cincinnati-Indianapolis-Chicago run, the West Coast's San Diego-Los Angeles-San Francisco run, as well as the East Coast's Washington-Philadelphia-New York-Boston run—comfortable, modestly priced, and just about as fast as any airplane when you include getting to and from the airports. If you get a chance, take a demonstration ride. The cost is very reasonable and you'll be in for a real eye-opener of what train travel could be in this country.

BRAZIL

"VISITING THE AMAZON RAIN FOREST"

While smiling broadly, the Indian boy looked straight at me and said in broken English, "Don't stick hand into water. Piranhas heavy today." Since the red piranhas around us were the ones that like to eat fingers, I looked dubiously at the ten-man canoes wondering if this trip into the flooded Amazonian rainforest was as good an idea as I'd originally thought.

As the canoe loaded, it kept sinking until less than half a foot separated us from the famous flesh-eating little fish, but the Indian boy looked confident and we started out through the flooded forest. Within minutes, I was totally lost and was sure we'd never find our way back through a maze of vines, tree branches and exposed roots.

But I was totally unprepared for the amazing wild life everywhere: parrots of every size, color, and description; three-toed sloth's slowly moving up the branches as they dined; tiny little monkeys chattering as they leaped from one treetop to another; spiders as big as dinner plates; and snakes larger than any I'd ever imagined. We had to constantly be alert for intruding branches and twice my hat got swept into the canoe's bottom.

"Water lilies," the Indian boy announced and there they were—a whole lake full of them. Three feet in diameter each, perfectly symmetrical, each with a white flower that lasts just the day—it was a sight I'll never forget.

Somehow the Indian boy found little channels the canoe would fit through and what seemed like a hopeless maze to me led us back to where we'd started within a couple of hours. I breathed a sigh of relief, but was sorry this spectacular close-up look at the central Brazilian rainforest was over.

Manaas, Brazil, where we had flown to start a long journey down the Amazon, was built by the rich "rubber barons" at the turn of the century, when Brazil had a monopoly on rubber production, and demand was growing due to the ever increasing number of automobiles and trucks. But a wily Englishman snuck some rubber seedlings to Malaysia where they grew even better, so the monopoly only lasted a few decades, and would have ended anyway with the development of synthetic rubber. But in that time, they built a whole city in the middle of a jungle, complete with an elaborate opera house where divas from Europe and North America performed. When we were visiting this historic but strangely situated palace of marble and gold veneer, they were busy practicing for "Carmen," the first operatic production in over 70 years.

At Manaas, two rivers meet: the Rio Negro and the Amazon. The Rio Negro, named for its black water, is heavily acidic and does not mix with the alkaline brown waters of the Amazon. Hence, for many miles, the two rivers run side by side distinct by their color. The Amazon is so deep that ocean liners have little trouble going all the way from the coast to the center of Brazil as we did on the "Pacific Princess", the ship used years ago to film the TV series "The Love Boat."

The Amazon doesn't much resemble any river in the United States. It is so broad and slow moving in most places it more resembles a 1000 mile lake. In fact, especially as we neared the delta, it was so broad neither shore could be seen from our boat. Since this was the "wet season," the water was muddy and filled with floating tree trunks and other debris. Along the sides, the rainforest canopy of green is all one can see except the few places where small Indian villages have cleared a little land.

Fortunately for the preservation of the forest, most large scale land development projects are failing financially, starting with Henry Ford's huge venture to produce his own rubber in the 1920's.

So the main threat now seems to be an exploding population and lumbering firms. A more immediate threat is the alarming increase in mercury and lead, a refining byproduct of newly discovered gold fields near the Amazon. Both poisons have spread throughout the water table and are leading to serious health problems for the peoples living in these areas.

Brazil has long suffered from extreme inflation and the end result is lack of capital for investment. Manaas, long in decline, has had a recent economic boom since it was declared a "tax-free zone" by the Brazilian government. Many assembly factories for electronic goods have sprung up and names like "Canon," "JVC," and "Sony" are common as the Japanese ship the parts all the way to Manaas to be assembled and then ship them all the way to North America to be sold. I was amazed it was profitable to ship goods from one hemisphere to another and then back again on the basis of cheap labor and tax relief. Although the workers of Manaas gained employment, the profits go elsewhere.

We stopped at Alter do Chao and Santarem, two river cities between the coast and Manaas. Along with the rest of Brazil, these cities were experiencing rapid growth as more and more people move to urban centers.

At Alter do Chao, we were able to visit the Center for the Preservation of Indigenous Art, Culture, and Sciences, where some efforts had been made to save at least a little of the original Indian cultures. Sadly, many of the tribes have already been extinguished with only a few baskets, shields, and face masks left to mark their existence. For some other tribes, only a few hundred survivors were left. As it stands, the curator of the Museum told me his biggest customers were other museums around the world, eager for something from the Amazonian Basin before it's all gone. I distinctly had the feeling I was able to see sights that would be gone by the time the next generation visits here.

Since the Amazon flows west to east, parallel but a little south of the Equator, the temperature, even in their Fall, is remarkably similar to our Midwest in the "dog days" of August. It was invariably hot and humid, and the ship's air-conditioning struggled with the heavy load. Several passengers came down with huge bug bites and other skin ailments.

As we wove our way through the silted islands of the 160-mile wide Amazon delta, it was six miles offshore from Brazil before the blue frothy waves of the Atlantic Ocean took over and we were on our way to Africa on one of the longest and most unique voyages ever attempted by the "Love Boat."

GOREE ISLAND

"THE HOUSE OF SLAVES"

The strong Atlantic waves pounded the overloaded ferry as I clung on to avoid getting tossed overboard. Any hope of remaining dry had been abandoned the minute we left Dakar's harbor and headed out into the constant spray from the ocean's towering waves.

"How'd they ever get out to Ile de Goree 200 years ago?" my wife asked.

"In large rowboats which took 16 strong men at the oars," I answered, "but even then they could only take a load of 20 at a time according to what I've read."

My wife lost her hat in the strong wind and renewed her grip on the railings.

"Can you imagine how you would feel in the bottom of a rowboat chained together by the neck with 20 others going to God knows where?" I shouted to her over the pounding of the boat's hull as it broke through the waves.

"Like all life had come to an end," she answered and looked out at the approaching island with one side sloping down to the sea and the other side faced with sheer cliffs.

We had crossed the Atlantic in the *Pacific Princess,* the original "Love Boat" of TV fame, and after visiting the Cape Verde Islands, a volcanic outcropping far out in the Atlantic between Brazil and Africa, had finally arrived at our first African port, Dakar.

Dakar, the largest city of West Africa and the capitol of Senegal, is modern, robust, and French despite its heavy African overtones of dark smiling faces, bright colored clothing on both men and women, and the lilt of French spoken with a multitude of tribal accents.

But just a 20-minute ferry ride out into the Atlantic from Dakar's port brings you to Goree Island, often called the "Island of Shame." Here, an estimated 40 million African people were graded, sorted, and forcibly shipped over a 300 year period to the eager markets of the emerging plantations of the Western Hemisphere. Anywhere from an estimated one-fifth to one-third didn't survive the horrors of the trans-Atlantic trip, and those that did survive were never to see their homeland or experience freedom again.

Goree Island was deserted at the abolition of the slave trade and much remains just as it was in its heyday—a haunting reminder of an infamous period in colonial history. The "slave houses," numbering close to 200 on this small island, housed the slaves brought over from the coast of West Africa. Since the island offers a deep port with strong currents and shark infested waters, it became the most popular spot for transshipment of slaves to the New World. Once a newly captured African reached the island, any attempt at escape almost certainly led to death.

One slave house, the "Maison des Esclaves," has been totally restored and visits are conducted by a Senegalese man whose ancestors had been sold and shipped to America in this very house. As you go through the "house," he carefully explains each room's grisly purpose.

"Upstairs the traders wined and dined, oblivious to the suffering going on beneath," he explained and indeed the upstairs was airy, well ventilated and pleasant with good ocean views, a well equipped kitchen, and a balcony to view the merchandise below without having to smell the offending bodies when sales were scheduled.

The downstairs was made up of cells holding 15 to 20 people who were shackled by the ankles to the stone walls with tiny slit windows and metal-barred doors that prevented any escape. There was a "sorting room," a "children's cell," separate cells for adult men and women, and cells for recalcitrants who hadn't been "broken" yet where arm and leg wall restraints were both utilized along with starvation and branding. A large scale weighed those up for sale and those weighing less than "shipping weight" (approximately a minimum of 150 pounds for a grown man) were placed in a "fattening room" before being offered for sale. Those crippled, diseased, or too sick for shipment were fed to the sharks through a convenient door at the end of a hall which led to a quick drop to the sea, and which was visible to all cell occupants so they understood by sight alone the consequences of self-mutilation or suicide attempts. This same door ("The Door of No Return") was used with a long gangplank to load the slave ships which could anchor adjacent to the slave house due to its deep harbor.

The sales involved the traders viewing the unclothed slaves from the upstairs balcony and bargaining over the price as physique, musculature, age, and sex were assessed. Once sold, the slave was led out the "sea door" in chains to be "stacked" between the narrow decks of the slave ships where he or she would remain much of the time during the three to five week journey. Once shackled in place, it was impossible for them to stand up or even roll over much of the time due to the cramped confines of these specially built ships.

"They had to be chained together on the gangplank to prevent them jumping overboard to the sharks," the curator of the slave house explained rather matter of factly. "Suicide prevention was one of the major tasks of the houses," he added, "that and getting them used to being just bought property."

By the time we left the slave house, the enormity of the anguish and suffering that had taken place was indelibly imprinted. I had the exact same feeling I had viewing a preserved Nazi concentration camp in Poland. Man's capacity to do harm to each other is often unimaginable.

The rest of Goree Island is also interesting. The descendants of the original African inhabitants are still there and are trading in cloth and leather as they probably were in the heyday of the slave trade. Someone mentioned the Hollywood film "The Guns of

Navarone" used the island, especially the cliffs, as the setting for that famous Gregory Peck movie but I could never confirm that. And, we were told, Afro-Americans from both South and North America are frequent visitors to the island, often taking their children with them, to explain their ancestor's origins and horrific migration to the New World.

The ferry trip back to the exciting city of Dakar was somber as most visitors were deep in thought. Dakar, populated by the same peoples once shipped out of Goree Island, was vibrant, alive, prospering, proud, and free. The brilliant colors, flashing smiles, and constant energy restored your spirit. Before long I was busy joking alongside the persistent salespeople lined up on both sides of my ship's dock. But I shall never forget my visit to Goree Island. It's part of our cultural heritage.

MAURITANIA

"A FORGOTTEN LAND"

The sirens on the two motorcycles were screaming as our motorcade of six buses and a truck full of local student "guides" were escorted into Nouakchott, the capitol of one of the most remote countries on earth.

I was in the lead bus of the first group of Westerners to ever be allowed into this little known but ancient Berber country in Northwestern Africa, now known as the Islamic Republic of Mauritania. The people lined the roadway the entire four mile drive from the coast so see what all the excitement was about. Even the six buses were a new sight to them—all of them had been shipped from Senegal especially for this occasion in that in all of the vast Saharan areas of the entire country, no transportation larger than a minivan exists!

Mauritania's Minister of Culture, the Minister of Education, and the capitol's mayor were on hand to greet us in an elaborate Arabian canopy set up on Nouakchott's main market square. The vast tent was furnished with hanging brass lamps, incense burners, and completely carpeted with beautiful red, blue and green Arabian rugs. The state's television was broadcasting live the arrival of the Western visitors as we exchanged greetings with the country's officials.

"Sa-laam-a-la-e-kum," my wife said in Arabic to the ministers as she greeted them in her Persian Gulf Arabic dialect.

"Wa-ala-e-kum sa-laam," they responded indicating instantly they understood her Arabic and looked surprised and pleased at her use of their language.

As soon as the ceremony was over, I plunged into the huge crowds surrounding the roped-off and police-cordoned areas meant to separate the two worlds. This act made the police very nervous, but they didn't stop me, and instantly I was surrounded by the curious Mauritanians who I greeted in Arabic. This delighted them and I was able to exchange a few religious slogans with them in my limited knowledge of this language. Within a minute, a young man who spoke perfect English was pushed forward by the crowd. "I'm a graduate of Mauritania's university," he said proudly. "I speak five languages—Wolof, Arabic, French, Spanish, and English—as you can see for yourself. I will translate for you in that most people here speak only Wolof and just a little Arabic and French." I explained I too spoke only a little Arabic and had no understanding of Wolof.

"Who are these strange people?" was the first question and I answered we were the first group of North Americans allowed to visit their country since before they were born.

"Why are the police leading you, and high government officials greeting you? Are you very important?"

"No, we're not important—just new," I responded although I really couldn't recall ever rating a police escort for anything legal.

"Why bother to visit us? We have nothing in Mauritania except the desert," the questions continued.

I paused. "Because we're interested in your country and respectfully curious about your ways of life," I carefully answered.

After this was translated to the surrounding crowd of eager brown and black faces swathed in the blue, brown and white headdresses of the Berbers, Moors, and Black Africans, shouts of approval matched with hand clapping rent the air, and the police circling the edge gripped their rubber truncheons as if a riot were about to break out.

Mauritania was enough to whet anyone's curiosity. A land nobody really ever wanted due to its lack of water and minerals, it has been made even less appealing by the steady intrusion of the Sahara Desert to the very edge of the ocean. Nouakchott, a city newly constructed in 1960 to serve as the capitol of this country, has wide streets and a well organized street grid where the Sahara sand runs amok over the few paved roads.

Since 1980, a new city of shacks crudely made of old signs, pieces of plastic sheeting, and palm leaf roofs surround the modern concrete capitol. This "suburb" is locally called "town of the freed slaves" in Arabic, because that's exactly what it is. Mauritania was the last country on earth to abolish slavery in 1980. It has been condemned every year since then by the New York based *Human Rights Watch* for tolerating continuation of slavery in remote areas of the country (which is practically anywhere but the capitol). But even newly freed slaves, whose ancestors had been held in bondage for hundreds of years, have no property, no job skill training, no place to live and no families. Consequently, they drift to the city, scrounge together some shelter and strive to support themselves through the sale of their manual labor. It will take years for them to lay claim to an equitable share of their country.

With little exposure to the outside world, attitudes and customs have seen little change for hundreds of years either in religious beliefs; their traditional nomadic disdain for land rights; their rigid social stratification of white Moors (descendents of Berbers and Arabs), Africans, and Harratines (Arabized black slaves) in that order; or their economic system of goods exchange through barter. Some iron ore was discovered and is being mined, but through a foreign concession which built Mauritania's only train to haul the ore to the coast. Fishing, once Mauritania's main export, has reportedly been severely damaged by over-fishing. Most of the 2.2 million people maintain life by moving their huge herds of sheep and goats over vast areas where enough food and water can guarantee sustenance and where life can go on undisturbed by the modern influences of Mauritania's only city, Nouakchott, with its 250,000 people.

Nowhere was this better illustrated than in our visit to the sheep market on the outskirts of the city. Filling at least an eight block area, all one can see are the multicolored sheep and goats accentuated by the flowing bright blue robes of the Berbers and the white robes of the Arabs often decorated with some touches of red. The constant baaing of the sheep do not drown out the lilting tones of Arabic and Wolof as the traders do business. Children dressed in the brightest colors imaginable are everywhere playing in the midst of the crowds and women around the edge are busy selling fabrics and handmade jewelry along with snacks hot out of their portable ovens. These people are, of course, the prosperous ones in that they have something to sell. Those who didn't, many themselves owned not too many years ago, were sprinkled around the edges hoping the prosperous would remember that Allah blesses those who give alms to the needy.

The local fish market is located next to the sea in a brand new concrete open air shelter which was inaugurated the very day we visited. The market it replaced was a mile or so down the beach and was long overdue for a new site. It seemed to me it would take a hundred years to clear out the smell of rotting fish despite the constant ocean breeze and tidal cleansing. At least the new place could be hosed down daily and had some protection from the glaring sun. A very brief visit to the old market was all I could stomach. Despite the smells, my wife thought the white sand of the Sahara going right into the blue waters of the Atlantic dotted with the dark woods and bright sails of hundreds of fishing boats being manned by men with glistening black skins hauling in their nets was one of the most beautiful sights she had ever seen. "Truly a Kodak moment," she exclaimed.

[Authors note: According to *Human Rights Watch*, people are still being bought and sold in 21st century Mauritania. The Government of Mauritania steadfastly refutes their claims.]

PRINCE EDWARD ISLAND

"ANNE OF GREEN GABLES ALIVE AND WELL"

My wife and I watched as two huge Japanese tourist buses filled to capacity were driven off the ferry to Prince Edward Island after an uneventful crossing from Nova Scotia in Maritime Canada.

"What are the Japanese doing way up here?" my wife asked in utter amazement as swarms of other Japanese began leaving the ferry.

"I haven't a clue," I responded, "but I'm sure we'll find out soon enough. For a moment, I thought we were in Tokyo, not way up here in Maritime Canada."

When we arrived at Charlottetown, the capital of Prince Edward Island, we did indeed find out the attraction of the island to the Japanese. The famous novel, "Anne of Green Gables" by Lucy Maud Montgomery, a fictional account of a bright, saucy and audacious orphan girl mistakenly placed in the home of a Scottish farmer living with his unmarried sister, is part of the required reading for the English language curriculum in Japan. "Anne," the orphan in the story, is reportedly highly appealing to Japanese girls reading the story of this independent, adventuresome, and even stubborn young girl as she grows through adolescence. So much so that many of them decide to get married in this fictional homestead of their heroine.

A whole industry has grown up around this desire. Charlottetown shops have signs in Japanese in almost every window and many boost Japanese interpreters are available among the sales staff. The hotel we stayed in advertised the availability of wedding receptions complete with Shinto priests, Japanese food and interpreters, and "traditional Japanese wedding gowns." It was fun to see the young Japanese couples and their wedding party excitedly making the arrangements alongside their parents, who, like most parents around the world as marriages approach, looked at times apprehensive and worried.

Our knowledge of "Anne of Green Gables" was based mainly on the PBS award-winning television production of some years ago. This teleplay was actually filmed on Prince Edward Island and when we first watched it, we marveled at the awesome beauty of the Island and decided to go there when we got a chance.

We weren't disappointed. The island is even prettier than the television show portrayed it, especially since the first hints of autumn were already in the foliage. It was certainly as good a place to get married as any other, we decided, and if the fictionalized "Anne" was really appealing to you, a trip half way around the world to get married there may make sense.

When we got to Lucy Maud Montgomery's home, we actually witnessed a Japanese wedding in progress complete with traditional costumes, a radiant bride, a proud bridegroom, a Shinto priest, and a Protestant clergy. Getting there toward the end, I couldn't figure out which religion was involved in the wedding or if both were.

Prince Edward Island itself was also charming. Small, well-kept farms dot the rolling landscape and the potatoes, noted for their excellent taste and texture and one of the Island's largest export crops, were beautifully green on the ground surface. Even the farm houses were neat as a button with nary an abandoned car, old farm implements, or rusty old appliances in sight anywhere. When I queried our local guide about this, she said any refuge in the yard raised your taxes so no one allowed that. An interesting proposition, but she offered no explanation of exactly how such a tax law was implemented.

Back at Charlottetown, we saw a musical based on the novel "Anne of Green Gables" which was well produced in a very large municipal auditorium. As is true throughout Canada, the opening remarks were in both French and English. I thought it would have been much more appropriate to have the remarks delivered in Japanese since the sell-out crowd was at least 70 percent Japanese and practically no one in that particular audience was French-speaking.

Prince Edward Island was larger than I thought and there were many things to do beyond the famous "Green Gables" novel. Provincial parks were outstanding, the beaches were appealing, and the small towns dotting the island had unique appeal to historians and antiquers. The "Loyalist" movement, where many American colonists moved to Maritime Canada during the Revolutionary War era to remain loyal to the Crown; the long struggle between France and England over North American territory; and the American War of 1812 all come alive when you visit this part of East Coast Canada.

Fortunately, the weather was with us the entire way—unusual for this time of year according to the natives. We left the island by the brand new Northumberland Strait Bridge, currently claiming to be the longest bridge in the world—8.0 miles long with a horrific toll ($35 per car). The Islanders are worried that the completion of the bridge will ruin their way of life by making it "too easy" to get to the island. Perhaps, but isolation is hard to maintain in today's world.

Prince Edward Island is charming and it would be a shame to have it spoiled by huge influxes of tourists. But it makes for interesting travel and, I must agree with the Japanese, a neat place to get married.

ALASKA

"THE LAST VOYAGE OF THE S.S. ROTTERDAM"

"Wow!" was all we could say when we first sat eyes on this magnificent ship resting in the Vancouver, British Columbia harbor.

When the new International Maritime Safety laws went into effect recently, one of the best known casualties was the S.S. Rotterdam V, one of the few remaining great steam-powered ocean luxury liners of a bygone era. There were special celebrations in Vancouver as the S.S. Rotterdam V prepared for its very last voyage north to Alaska. The passengers, many of them alumni of previous Rotterdam cruises, were somber but happy they had booked for this historic last voyage.

When my wife and I first heard of this historic last voyage, we booked as soon as we could along with our younger son and his wife. What attracted us was the opportunity to cruise on an actual operational steamship, an ocean liner of renowned old-fashioned opulence not seen in modern cruise ships, and the itinerary itself: a leisurely trip of unparalleled scenery up the Inside Passage to Alaska. It was a trip we'd taken some years before on another ship, but well worth a repeat.

This huge ship, completed in 1959 to carry passengers in great style between Europe and New York, was originally designed to carry "first" and "tourist" class passengers and the ship was cleverly designed so the two classes never laid eyes on each other.

But as jets rapidly replaced ocean liners in the 1960's, the

Rotterdam found itself antiquated before its time, and the Holland-America Line quickly renovated the ship to physically eliminate the snotty two-class system and equip it for the more profitable and certainly more democratic cruise business. Since the renovation, the S.S. Rotterdam has primarily been noted for super-luxurious "around the world cruises" starting every January for the past quarter of a century and invariably fully booked despite the hefty fees for such an adventure.

"I've never seen so much mahogany, beech, and teak in my life," my wife commented as we dutifully took the Rotterdam's "art tour" designed to show off the many paintings, sculptures, and art deco fittings especially commissioned for the ship over the years. The intricate wood floors of the ballrooms, the beautiful brass, nickel, silver and even gold fittings, and the specially made china and stem ware all added to the unabashed and probably excessive elegance of years past.

Many of the ship's activities were designed around the nostalgia of the Rotterdam's "last voyage" and souvenirs of the event were frequently handed out. Where we had expected things to be sort of run down if the ship was to be scrapped at the end of the voyage, we found it anything but. Even the last day of the cruise, they were painting away on the outside as it headed for oblivion, whiter and more pristine than ever.

The real attraction, of course, was the Inside Passage and the natural wonders of our 49th state, Alaska. As we headed up the Passage, the glaciers, the rugged mountains running right into the ocean, and the trees just beginning to turn color as winter approached were all breathtaking in their beauty.

The stops along the way also proved interesting—the salmon factories, the remnants of the "gold rushes", and Sheldon-Jackson College in Sitka with its unique mission to the Indian population. Perhaps most inspiring was witnessing the renewed interest and pride in their Indian heritage demonstrated by many young people in that area, who clearly were reclaiming and preserving the best of their native culture. This latter phenomenon's timing is just right:

if the young had disregarded or ignored their Indian culture one more generation, it would all be gone. As it is, it is being carefully preserved and meaningfully integrated into their everyday life.

As we neared Anchorage, where half of Alaska's population now resides, the huge S.S. Rotterdam managed to sidle up remarkably close to the Hubbard Glacier and a huge portion of the glacier fell off with a mighty roar just as I had my camera poised for a true "Kodak moment." What was even more remarkable was that the weather each day was crystal clear, totally unlike our previous trip taken in July of 1983 where fog and rain obscured much of the scenery.

Anchorage, almost completely rebuilt from its devastating earthquake of 1964, still retains a frontier flavor somehow, despite boosting a Nordstrom's Department Store and some very fancy and tall hotels.

As to the S.S. Rotterdam: when we disembarked in Seward for the bus trip to Anchorage, it was headed to the Panama Canal and then to Fort Lauderdale before October 1 and its banishment from international waters. It's fate was uncertain even as we left it. Rumors flew that it was being sold as an off-shore hotel in Rotterdam, the Netherlands. Another rumor claimed it was being bought by Saudis for a local cruise ship not venturing into international waters. But the most persistent rumor was that it would be auctioned off for scrap at Fort Lauderdale and all that beautiful wood, metal trim, and fine china would go to the highest bidder before the hull itself was chopped up and melted down for its valuable steel.

The Holland-America Line is well prepared for the loss, however. The brand new M.V. Rotterdam VI, being built in Holland as a huge cruise ship to start with, is almost finished and fully booked for its inaugural cruise. Nice as it promises to be, it won't have the genuine teak and mahogany, the silver fittings, and the old fashioned steam power of a elegant era now slipping into the past.

CROSSING THE ATLANTIC IN THE LARGEST SHIP IN THE WORLD

"PASSING THE TITANIC"

Only 36 miles from the site on the ocean floor where the famed Titanic now rests, the alarms sounded on the inaugural transatlantic crossing of the largest passenger ship in the world. The engine room was on fire at 8 A.M., just two days from New York.

All 3750 people on the giant ship tensed. The Grand Princess became eerily silent as the huge generators running the electric engines slowed down and then stopped, the air conditioning ceased its endless swishing, and the enormous ship quickly slowed.

As everyone now knows from the most popular movie ever, "Titanic," stopping mid-ocean is a strange phenomenon. But, at the time, comparing ourselves to the Titanic 86 years earlier was inevitable. Like the Titanic, our ship was on its inaugural transatlantic crossing. Like the Titanic, the Grand Princess was the largest passenger ship in the world at its time, and, like the Titanic, it was the latest marvel of engineering technology.

The Titanic weighed 45,000 tons, the Grand Princess 2.4 times more at 109,000 tons. The Grand Princess carries twice as many passengers, is twice as wide, and is considerably longer—the ship is longer than three football fields end-to-end—and towers 17 decks high. It's too large to fit into the Panama Canal and to fill its tanks, it takes 5.3 million pounds of fuel. It cost over a half billion dollars to build. And here we were at a dead stop with crew scurrying everywhere with their life-jackets on.

I suppose rumors about the new and untried are inevitable. We had heard our fill of them since first boarding this floating city in Barcelona ten days earlier. The ship, towering 18 stories (17 decks) above the water, would tip over in the rough waters of the Atlantic, especially with its relatively flat bottom; the ship was too dependent on all of its heavily computerized navigational and drive management systems; the ship was simply too big to navigate outside of relatively smooth waters.

Perhaps to dispel such talk, the cruise line audaciously showed the movie "Titanic" as we neared the famed ship's final resting place and, in a note of hubris, pointed out that the Grand Princess was actually the only ship in the world where you really could legally stand at the very front of the ship as Leonardo DiCappio and his love, Kate Winslet, had done in the movie where they flew in the breeze with abandon.

The captain came on the intercom and explained there was a fire in the engine room, there was considerable smoke in that area, and to remain calm—we were not in alert at that point. Within a half hour, the fire had been extinguished, the smoke cleared out, and the generators started up again. The familiar churning of the two electrically-driven 46-ton propellers started up and the swish of the air conditioning returned. All was back to normal. Relief swept through all 3750 people and life quickly returned to normal in the seven restaurants, huge shopping arcades, pizza and ice cream parlors, the 24-hour buffet, the three swimming pools, the disco on the seventeenth deck reached by a laser-lighted moving sidewalk (labeled the "Skywalk"), and the fully equipped hospital connected directly with Cedars-Sinai Medical Center in Los Angeles by satellite. The frivolities of virtual reality games, onboard business centers, computer animated photos (where you could be photographed shaking hands with the President, water-skiing behind the ship, or even tackling a tiger), or playing in a sports center equipped even with a full-size basketball court, all resumed.

My wife and I tried to walk off the endless eating with laps—twice around the deck was almost a mile unlike the four or five times it takes on a normal sized ship. And we enjoyed the many Las Vegas-style shows in the 1200 seat theater—the largest of three on the supership.

We had been on this magnificent ship through many Mediterranean ports prior to crossing the Atlantic. But the greatest thrill of all was entering New York harbor one early morning and seeing the Statue of Liberty greeting this new technological wonder as it had greeted millions of new immigrants in smaller and surely lesser ships over the past two centuries. Unlike the lengthy trials and tribulations of the immigrants entering Ellis Island, six U.S. customs officials boarded the ship in Europe and cleared us onboard prior to our arrival to avoid any hassles due to the huge numbers involved. As the sunrise rose behind us and the light outlined the skyscrapers of Manhattan, I thought of those millions of hopeful immigrants and the thoughts they must have had viewing that very same sight for the first time. For us, it was coming home. For them, it was a new life.

The largest passenger ship in the world nestled right next to the same slip the Titanic would had berthed in 86 years earlier if she had made it. The fireboats streamed their water nozzles upward as New Yorkers lined the peers gawking at the huge ship for the first time.

The maiden voyage was over, but even bigger ships are on the way. Four more will be launched by the end of 2001, and several more are on the drawing boards, each bigger than the one preceding it. The era of mega-sized passenger ships, so big they are useful only in the hemisphere in which are built, is here.

ITALY

"ANCIENT ROME AND THE RENAISSANCE"

"I swear the tower leans a foot further," my wife said as we passed the famed Leaning Tower of Pisa. She hadn't seen it in 30 years and indeed it was leaning considerably more—so much so people can no longer climb up its many balconies. Fifty years from now, I wonder if people will be viewing much more than scaffolding and supports.

By the time we got to Florence, the weather had changed from the usual clarity of the bright Italian sun to the gloom of an Italian squall, and we looked like two drowned chickens by the time our walk led us to the National Academy, where the most famous statue in the world is housed: Michelangelo's "David." Its reputation is well earned: it is surprisingly tall (17 feet), beautifully proportioned, and sculpted from a lustrous white marble. I was surprised how relatively unprotected it was and how close you can get to it. Seven other Michelangelo sculptures are nearby, almost as famous. The whole array of Michelangelo's work overwhelms you and you're left with a feeling of utter awe—so much so we totally forgot we were soaking wet.

The other sights of Florence—the cathedrals, the baptistries, the bell towers, the many shops, the charming old restaurants, the cobblestone streets, the sleek Italian motorscooters zooming everywhere, the rich aromas streaming out of the many bakeries—tell any visitor they need to spend far more time than a single visit will allow. It amused me that the many cheap plaster copies of the statue "David" for sale all over the street stands of Florence exaggerated David's anatomy considerably from the original. I suppose modern Italians think bigger is better or that they need to "improve" on the world's greatest sculptor somehow.

But Florence was Renaissance in all its vitality. Pompeii, located at the base of Mt. Vesuvius near Naples in southern Italy, is pure Ancient Rome in all its glory and decadence. Pompeii, as every school child knows, was buried intact in 79 A.D. by a huge volcanic eruption from Mt. Vesuvius, still sitting there smugly with a slight hiss of steam coming out of its top. Last erupting in 1944, it's about due for another discharge if historical rhythms prove true. The eruption covering the resort city of Pompeii was so quick and sudden both people and buildings were buried under tons of volcanic ash, freezing them forever in time. Each year since the late 1700's, excavations have unearthed more and more until now a whole city is exposed to historians, archeologists, and millions of curious tourists.

You enter the city through a gate just as you did in the very first century and quickly try to acclimate your trifocals to the rough cobblestone streets complete with gutters, raised street crossings so Pompeiians didn't get their feet wet, and directions to major buildings built right into the stone streets.

Our Italian guide seemed to have a low opinion of American visitors. "Americano's always interested in Pompeii's brot-thels," he said in a high pitched whine with his eyes rolled to the back of his head in some sort of affected stance, "so we visit the brot-thels first," he giggled. "Pompeii had 15 brot-thels," he droned on. But we discovered the amphitheater, the forum, the markets, the bakeries, the residential sections, the fabulous villas, the elaborate public baths, and the well-placed grid of streets far more fascinating and before the day was over, we felt like Romans ourselves as we mastered walking on cobblestone, began to feel familiar with the layout of Roman houses, and even knew where the kitchens and slave quarters were likely to be within those homes.

Pompeii's homes were no different from most homes of well-to-do Romans of the time. Only a wall faced the street, but once inside, you find yourself in an atrium with dining rooms, libraries, and some sleeping quarters, all facing the flowered and fountained atrium. Beautiful painted frescos adorned the walls of the main rooms and marble was used lavishly on both floors and walls. By contrast, the slave's quarters were airless, dark rooms little bigger than closets. One should never forget that it was the occupants of these airless holes who made such lavish lifestyles possible and who did almost all of the real work done in this lovely resort town of so long ago. The stones in the carefully paved streets, the hot water in the beautiful baths, the entertainment at the amphitheater—all were slave generated.

Bakery ovens, flour mills, and shop stalls are all there almost as if they had been used just yesterday. Perhaps the best preserved buildings were the baths with their gymnasiums and pools of hot, warm and cold waters so elaborate it makes most modern health spas look cheap and tawdry. You could easily imagine a chariot rattling down the street or the patter of litter-bearer's feet as they hoisted a luxurious litter's occupant from one section of town to another. Pompeii's amphitheater, still in remarkably great shape, reminded one of the ancient Roman's fascination with watching the agony of death first hand. Indeed, one of the most recent excavations has revealed a gladiator slave still chained by his ankles to the walls of his cell as the ash covered him for posterity. It's a shame every student of history can't view the city as they study Roman culture. It would teach them things they'd never learn out of a book alone.

Not far from Pompeii lies the Isle of Capri where Augustus Caesar built a huge vacation retreat for himself and which his successor Tiberius Caesar liked so well he spent the last decade of his reign there. It is surrounded by high bluffs so the lack of easy access assured privacy for the emperors just as it does today for the rich and famous who vigorously outbid each other to own a villa there just like the Romans 2000 years earlier. It's green, lush, private, expensive, and enjoys almost perfect weather—enduring traits which have kept real estate prices up for 20 centuries.

Nearby Naples, which derives its name from Neopolis meaning "new city" to its Greek founders, was a large port city for the Romans as it is today. But Naples is now a huge industrial complex a hundred times bigger than when any Roman Caesar ruled. I'm sure the Romans didn't have the unbelievable traffic snarls and the smog we encountered. But, even in Roman times, it's been described as lively, temperamental, and brash—all characteristics which have endured the centuries.

These lands produced one of the world's greatest empires and a thousand years later birthed the Renaissance. During this century, it's been noted for fascism, ruthless colonialism, inglorious military defeats, and most recently, design flair, industrial vigor, and sharing its treasures with millions of tourists.

SPAIN AND PORTUGAL

"BARCELONA, LISBON AND THE ALLURING AZORES"

"Is that building for real or are my eyes giving out?" I asked my wife as we stopped to stare at a bank building in downtown Barcelona designed by their famous architect Gaudi. Indeed, the building seemed to be melting, as if it were made of wax left out in a hot sun.

"It's for real," she answered, "and it's all concrete," she added with a certain note of astonishment. After staring some more, she added "I like it somehow."

A visit to northeast Spain's great city of Barcelona leaves one with a new understanding of Picasso, Muro, Gaudi, and other modern artists. Picasso did many other styles of painting other than the abstracts we generally associate with him—his traditional portraits were particularly compelling; Muro's use of primary colors are splashed all over the city like we spray paint subway cars; and Gaudi's architectural style of "weeping Gothic" adorned apartment houses, restaurants and banks as well as his famous landmark, the Church of the Holy Family, less than half done after 12 decades of work. Although it's been over six years since the Summer Olympics were in Barcelona, all the facilities built for the occasion seem to be put to good use since.

It was obvious this was not the old, repressive Spain of General Franco I had visited in 1969. Franco had ruled with an iron hand since the Spanish Civil War preceding World War II, until a much more liberal government took over in the late seventies. Barcelona's night life made New York or Paris look staid and traditional and the vibrant city seemed to revel in its newfound freedom.

Our next stop, Portugal's capitol of Lisbon, now also part of the European Union and, like Barcelona, recovering from a 40-year repressive dictatorship, was also definitely a city of dynamic progress. Outlined against the third largest suspension bridge in the world (built by the same people building our Golden Gate Bridge), it combines medieval style with the most modern arcades and parks, pinpointed by quaint little architectural gems reminding you Portugal was the birthplace of some of the world's most daring explorers. Their efforts ultimately resulted in a huge colonial empire, which is only now ending in far-flung parts of the world.

One of those tiny possessions is the archipelago called the Azores, 600 miles west of Lisbon way out in the Atlantic Ocean. A volcanic outcropping geologically youthful, the Azores were originally found barren of most mammals, most species of birds, and no humans whatsoever. The Portuguese, upon discovering the islands, named it with the Portuguese word for "hawks," which was the only bird they saw there. Actually, the birds weren't hawks at all, but kites, so the islands should be known by the Portuguese word for "kites." But it's hard to correct history and, in this case, no one seems to care. So Azores it is to this day.

Our guide was a college professor from the teacher's college located in Puerto Delgada, probably the most prominent city in the Azores. He proved to be a font of knowledge and was old enough to remember the many American servicemen visiting the islands as they utilized this strategic refueling depot during World War II.

The history of the nine islands making up the Azores was interesting. Since each island is widely separated, species of animals have evolved distinctly on each island, as has the vegetation. Even the Portuguese universally spoken has taken on such distinct accents within each of the islands some argue they have evolved into new languages rather than regional accents. It's like saying people from the Deep South don't speak English! Easier access between the islands by plane and ferries, as well as Portuguese television available to all, will no doubt remove that problem (and charm) in a few years.

Many Azorians have migrated to the United States over the past 200 years since the islands, until the most recent of times, has remained poor and backward. The old timers remind you at every opportunity of how the 40-year Portuguese dictatorship exploited the Azores at every opportunity with severe import-export restrictions, oppressive taxation, and unceasing restriction on freedom of speech.

But a revolution, this time economic as well as political, has overtaken the islands. Everywhere new quaint white stucco housing with red tile roofs and black outlined windows is being constructed, financed by 30-year government-subsidized loans requiring minimal down payments. New cars from France, Spain, Germany, England, and Italy are everywhere, and shops feature goods from all of Europe, not just the Portuguese mainland which was true only a few years ago.

Azorian fish, cattle, and pineapples are now sold throughout Europe and milk and meat products form the foundation of a huge export business. When asked why such vitality, all Azorians we asked answered alike: "the European Union." I never dreamed a group of sedate bankers meeting in Paris or the Hague or Berlin could have such an effect on a tiny set of islands located way out all by itself in the Atlantic Ocean. But it's opened up markets they never knew existed and the money they earn buys all those cheap duty-free cars and appliances they so enjoy.

Despite all this, the islands retain their historic charm unfamiliar to almost all foreigners, with the exception of a few British and later American Air Force personnel stationed there in varying numbers clear up to the present time. When was the last time you heard someone planning to visit the Azores?

Cattle, predominantly Holsteins, dot every mountainside, complete with cattle bells and mobile milking machines powered by tiny little diesel engines. The milking machines come to the cows rather than the other way around as we're used to. The very mild, even climate means no barns are necessary, so the cows produce large amounts of milk at relative little cost since their feed is easily grown here.

But other crops also flourish in the rich volcanic soil. Squat little pineapples, noted for their rich sweetness, is primarily funneled into the production of pineapple liqueur—a product which has proven to be a big hit with Europeans. Unlike Hawaii, these pineapples must be protected from the scorching sunlight, and are grown from seedlings to harvest inside white-washed greenhouses. Tobacco, almost identical to that grown in Kentucky, sugar beets, and tomatoes round out the agricultural picture.

The Portuguese love birds and so many, many species have been introduced over the years to supplement those misnamed kites. So much so the Azores is now a bird lover's paradise. And in their zeal to add to the variety of vegetation, they brought a yellow ginger lily from the Orient which has turned into a scourge—no one knows how to stop its exuberant growth. It was interesting some other place has their "kudzu" problem, but at least theirs is a beautiful flowering plant.

The Azores suffer from their heritage—every 20 years or so produces earthquakes, new volcanic eruptions are predicted within the next five years, and sulfurous steam hisses out of the ground unceasingly in certain spots. But the Azorians now produce over 20 percent of their electricity from the free geothermal springs.

The Azores are so lovely you leave reluctantly, hoping no volcano gets too lively in that area and it'll still be there for others to enjoy as much as we did.

AFRICA'S SLAVE COAST

"COTE D'IVOIRE, GHANA, TOGO, AND BENIN"

[Authors note: We had originally been scheduled to first visit the westernmost country occupying the old "slave coast" of Africa, Sierra Leone. But the civil disturbances there had canceled that part of the trip long before we left the U.S. On the very day our ship passed Freetown, the main port and capital of Sierra Leone from a safe 12 miles offshore, 212 civilians were literally hacked to death and then ritualistically dismembered in the streets of Freetown so brutally that the bodies were beyond recognition. It was a sobering reminder of the untellable violence underlying the chronic unrest that permeates much of African society today.]

One of our ship's lecturers, a rather tired old history professor from South Dakota State whose only claim to fame seemed to be that his brother had been a Lutheran missionary to the Cameroons in happier times, did point out Africa's two greatest problems: (1) national boundaries, still predominant today, had been set in 1880 by the European colonial powers at the height of their influence in the presumptuous and ill-fated "Congress of Berlin" where African real estate was greedily carved up without regard to ethic, tribal, language, or religious groupings and hence political entities were totally artificial from an indigenous cultural viewpoint; and (2) the AIDS epidemic, which started in Africa, was now completely overwhelming all available resources in many African countries. Nowhere was this more true that the four small countries we visited next.

The first small country on the "underlip" of Africa had been a French "possession" for over a century and it showed. French was heard much more than any tribal languages, all the cars and industrial machinery were still French in origin, and French colonial architecture prevailed over anything African. Despite that, the people and their culture were definitely African and the last remaining Frenchmen had left years ago. I had naively thought the Ivory Coast (as Americans call it), or Cote d'Ivoire (as the sophisticated call it), was named for its export of elephant tusks back when ivory was in such demand in Western countries. Sadly it was named for "black ivory," the nickname given the even more profitable export of black slaves to the New World and the good harbors and natural inlets here was where thousands of slave ships loaded their doomed cargos for the Americas.

Abidjan, the capital and main city is some distance from the infamous ports the slave ships used, which are marshy and malarial-ridden to this day, and resides on higher, healthier ground. The city is vibrant, colorful, and exciting with its huge open bazaars, the glowing bright combinations of red, green, orange and yellow clothing worn by both men and women, swarms of putt-putting French mopeds which are the main means of transportation, and the street vendors who carry unbelievably huge loads balanced on their head (including spare tires, car batteries, gasoline repackaged in old liquor bottles, stacks of tee shirts, and even a crate of chickens). Ivory is sold in the markets in that the import of ivory still isn't illegal in some countries, bright African prints are available by the bolt, and wooden carvings of anything you can think of are sold everywhere. Everyone seems to be selling something. On the streets, dodging the many taxicabs and mopeds, one person sells only toothpaste, another sunglasses, another soda pop, another mangoes—each seems to have specialized in something they can carry, can sell through a car window, and still make a tiny profit. Mixed between them are naked children, themselves trying to sell a bar of soap, a handful of nails, or just begging. In a nearby river bed, hundreds upon hundreds of grown men were washing clothes by pounding them onto rocks, scrubbing them with soap, rinsing them in the muddy waters, and then placing them on nearby bushes to dry. Each man seemed to have staked out his little area of river for the enterprise, as he stood waist deep in his territory. This colorful, even exotic scene, perfect for a "Kodak moment," didn't hide the fact the work was exhausting, unhealthy, and certainly unpleasant hour after hour in the relentless sun. By the time we reached the "slums" of Abidjan—some of the worst I'd seen up to that point—the bitter truths of the country's plight were clearly evident: (1) massive unemployment [no wonder grown men are reduced to selling a single toothbrush on the streets]; (2) an out-of-control population explosion [with a growth rate of 3.5% annually, half the population is younger than 16]; and (3) devastating illness affecting huge portions of the population [it is estimated 60 percent of the population is HIV-positive at this point and it's growing]. You wonder what even the best of governments could do with this dilemma.

When faced with such grim reality, it seems logical to worry about the hereafter and in the Ivory Coast elaborate caskets are designed, built, and paid for years before death is imminent. Each casket denotes a "theme" of that person's life—at least what he or she wants to be remembered as—and so we saw caskets "waiting" in the front yards that were designed like the car they always coveted or may have once owned; a motor boat they always wished they had; or designed to honor their occupation, complete with carved wood fishing nets or carpenter's tools or the metal wrenches of a mechanic, embedded part and parcel into the coffin itself. It's the only country I've been in where such a sizeable portion of your available income seems to be invested in your death.

But Senegal, the country we'd visited just a few days earlier, had done something that worked, when faced with problems almost identical to the Ivory Coast. First, massive public education, combined with dispensers offering free condoms evident on every street corner and village dispensary throughout the country, had cut the AIDS plague in half within one decade. Second, heavy emphasis on family planning and modern means of birth control had lowered the birth rate to a manageable level of near zero-population-growth. And, third, government organization of small goods and craft production for export had helped restore a healthy trade balance and significantly decrease chronic unemployment, perhaps the most depressing and debilitating of all human conditions in that it constantly reminds you you're not worth anything.

But none of this seemed to be evident in Cote d'Ivoire, where the small amount of foreign aid coming in had been directed toward the construction of a colossal concrete monument to its first president, an immense new cultural museum building with practically nothing in it, and two huge cathedrals and a mammoth soccer stadium that were imposing, but did little to alleviate the country's basic problems, beautiful stained glass windows or not. The cathedrals were especially strange since Muslims outnumber Catholics here, and "animists" outnumber both of them, but then the current President is Catholic.

The Ivory Coast is ill-equipped for tourists at this point. Every bus that could possibly still run and anyone breathing who could speak English had been gathered for the occasion of our ship's visit. Our particular guide was a high school teacher named "Tete" (a rather unoriginal name since it simply means "second son" which he was), who had taken the day off from his normal teaching for this rare windfall of tourists who were likely to tip well. Having sampled his English, I couldn't imagine how he could teach it, but when I got a chance to talk to him privately, it turned out he taught English at the national college in the evenings as well as French, which made we wonder about the quality of teaching at the national university since he had only had two years of college himself. Like most ambitious persons caught in a bad situation, he spent a good deal of his time exploring job opportunities in America via his busload of tourists, mainly retirees and those too wealthy to need to work, not knowing they were probably the least helpful group possible in this area.

After a long and tiring day of witnessing Cote d'Ivoire firsthand,

I turned to my wife and asked her with a straight face how she'd like to retire here since our money would go a long way at the current exchange rates. Her incredulous look of disbelief summed up my impression of the country too. It was Africa at its most colorful—and its worst!

Ghana was as different from the Ivory Coast as England is from France, reflecting the heavy residual influence of colonization to this day. More of the European built infrastructure still works and there's a sense of orderliness to the place that tends to mask huge unemployment and overpopulation problems that combine to stifle any government efforts for economic growth and development. Ghanian English is so accented I barely recognized it as my mother tongue, but anything Africa produces seems to have found its way to Ghanian shops and we were able to buy a bolt of the bright yellow and orange Ashanti tribal print that has recently gained popularity in this country. Our plan was to be the only home in Madison, Indiana, featuring Ashanti curtains at our bedroom windows.

But while in Ghana, I found out the Ashanti Empire's biggest industry for centuries was the slave trade and Ashanti chieftains got very rich from selling non-Ashanti Africans to foreign merchants at huge profits. Those foreign "slave factories," where hundreds of thousands of Africans were sorted, stored, and "broken" to slavery are still on the Ghanian coast and serve as a stark reminder of this country's grim past. Despite this, the Ashanti Empire was a very large, powerful, and extremely rich kingdom for many centuries occupying much more territory than the current boundaries of Ghana. Gold was so plentiful it was widely used for decoration by both men and women—the Ashanti King had an entire "throne stool" made out of solid gold which proved to be too soft to be practical, but certainly showed other, probably poorer, kings who had money to flaunt and who didn't. When the British took over, they did so by making sure the Ashanti monarchy stayed in command and enjoyed all the luxuries they were used to.

Like Cote d'Ivoire, the capital of Accra is at a higher elevation than the port itself, and is quite modern with high-rise luxury hotels, convention centers, and a large airport. Considerable effort has obviously been expended to attract tourists and numerous opulent beach side resorts, fancy restaurants, and modern highways stand in sharp contrast to where most Ghanaians live, where running water spigots in the streets, TV antennas stuck perilously on rooftops, and gangling electric lines distinguish the have's from the have-not's. Malaria continues to be a major health problem, and Ghana is not immune to the AIDS plague of the rest of Africa (although one does see many more hospitals and clinics than in some other countries).

Togo, the country right next to Ghana, is only ten miles wide at its narrowest point, crammed in between Ghana and Benin as it is. It's one of the few countries actually designed around tribal settlements (The Togos), but even here there are acrimonious tribes located in the northern areas of Togo. And there really is a King of Togo to this day, seemingly highly respected, complete with gold nose cover, a most corpulent body which he displays proudly as a sign of prosperity, and numerous wives and concubines and courtiers who accompany him in all public appearances.

Togo was the first country we had reached on this trip where neither Islam or Christianity seemed to have made a dent in public consciousness. Animism, the belief that prevailing and influential spirits reside in physical and/or animal presences, is by far the religion of choice and Togoan life reflects those beliefs. Fetish markets, featuring everything from sheep embryos to chicken feet to virgin's menstrual blood to hair of a dead person who died happy, is all available to aid in the various ceremonies and rituals, all conducted by spiritual advisors and priests we label "witch doctors." To anyone in health care of any type, medical or psychological, it's fascinating. Cases of severe depression, hysteria, obsessive-compulsions, and phobias are routinely treated by the "witch doctors" with a "cure rate" rivaling, and often bettering, American pharmaceutical therapies. If nothing else, it shows the power of belief in altering brain chemistry, at least with some psychiatric disorders.

And often without all those nasty side-effects we are expected to tolerate in the drug therapies so pervasive in American medicine today.

But the fetishes for sale were mainly sickening to American eyes, and the "witch doctors" instilled more fear than confidence in their strange costumes and jerky little dances. Nevertheless, I bought a small amulet from a witch doctor which was supposed to ward off all evil spirits causing sickness and he was good enough to "bless it" with a little dance and some muttered sayings for added zip when the time came to use it. (I gave it to my family doctor at home who stated it might come in handy sometime.)

I didn't want to visit Togo without visiting an actual animist ceremony (or voodoo as Westerners tend to label it) and the opportunity presented itself that very afternoon. I had anticipated something about the same length and sobriety as a church service. What we witnessed was over four hours long with no sign of really stopping then, a free-for-all with people coming and going, wandering in and out of various physical contacts with the "priests," a few people jerking in and out of short-lived trances or seemingly drifting off into coma-like states, chickens keeling over from the sight of a witch doctor alone, a great amount of shrieking, yelling, and moaning, and the incessant, almost hypnotic rhythmical cacophony of the loudest drums I have ever heard. Parts of the ceremony were explainable: a chicken doesn't die from the evil eye of the witch doctor—any chicken held upside down with its neck extended downward will suffocate to death just as a man on a cross dies of suffocation from having his lungs extended by his spread arms; and people jerking into trances has been known for centuries, especially in people who harbor intense belief systems and are in an environment where such behavior is thought possible, if not expected; and dancing for hours as physically as one can, especially under the metronome effect of constantly beating drums, leads to out and out physical exhaustion, a state which resembles a person lapsing into a temporary coma. All the shrieking, yelling, and moaning reminded me of a particularly spirited tent revival

I'd once attended as a kid in the Ozark Mountains. So overall, I was hardly converted over to animism, but it was interesting and I felt privileged to be able to witness the event. Certainly, that too was a part of Africa.

The next country, Benin (pronounced Ba-Neen), turned out to be my favorite of equatorial Africa. Surrounded by Togo, Burkina Faso, Niger, and Nigeria, (four of the five in almost continual civil war) keeping their neighbors happy and off their backs must be a major problem. But the people here, sort of a uniform rich brown in color, seem self-assured and happy despite the ever present poverty, too many people in too small a space, and the sickness of malaria and AIDS evident everywhere.

One of the most fascinating sights I've seen anywhere was in Benin: an entire village of 2000 people living in houses built on stilts in a large, marshy lake. The villager's ancestors had resorted to this way of life as the only way they could see to escape their enemies and survive, since the waters of this area are considered by the mainlanders to be unhealthy. Indeed, it is an area still rife with malaria. What is astonishing is that no one has moved back to wherever it was they came from. Generations later, their survivors are still huddled in the little reed houses perched atop long bamboo stakes driven into the swallow lake bottom. Garbage is simply thrown out the window for the fish, naked children, even babies, occasionally fall off the small porches outside each door, but here babies learn to swim long before walking, and school children could be seen paddling their way to the school (itself a larger reed shack perched upon stilts) in their bright yellow school uniforms which matched the exterior of the school longboat, a carved out log. Men fish from small one-person reed boats where they artfully cast homemade nets for the large takes, but they also fish from their front porches with a simple string wrapped around their fingers for the single take. Women weave reed baskets, bassinets, even bird cages, with amazing dexterity. Life looks like it hasn't changed in a 100 years and the thought of spending an entire life in a tiny little community on a given shallow lake in a constantly damp house (that only lasts 30 years before it rots) was unfathomable to me. But then I grew up with expectations a little different than these boys and girls who interrupted their play in the water only a few seconds to stare at the strangers staring at them.

We visited a small forest where, allegedly not too long ago, enemies had been turned into trees through "good magic," but where a tribal king and his court still reside with considerable pomp and circumstance. While there, as part of an ongoing religious ceremony, we witnessed the "royal" courtiers recreating some of the tribe's rich history through symbolic and colorful pageantry that was "pure" African: heavy drums, unwearying dancing, and a concentration on what they were doing that seemed almost hypnotic. At first, I thought all this was for the visitors, but when I realized the players in the game were exhausted long before we arrived, that it was far too serious and "heavy" to have anything to do with tourism, and that the people involved could care less whether we were there or not, I suspected we were seeing some genuine Africa.

Only an hour or so away was the "Temple of Pythons" where scores of the huge snakes were kept as objects of worship and where snake handling skills were so valued even children or four or five were being shown the basic rudiments by the "priests" in charge. I'd never seen a python outside a zoo and was astonished how big they really are when there's not at least two inches of plate glass between us. I thought they'd be cold to the touch, but they weren't—maybe because others had handled them right before the thing was thrust at me.

More has been done in Benin to commemorate the trans-Atlantic slave trade than in the other countries on the Gulf of Guinea where such commerce was concentrated. With the help of the United Nations, the "Road of No Return" has been reconstructed. Starting with the slave market 14 miles from the marshy shore where thousands of slaves were sorted and sold each week, the road follows their route to the waiting slave ships. Naked, with manacles tearing the skin around their ankles, they were psychologically "prepared" for their destiny at various stations along the way. One such station required each slave to circle a large tree seven times: this, he was told, would insure his spirit would come back to Africa after he died in the new land even though he would never again see his homeland. Close to the market was the area where slaves judged too old, too tired, too sick, and too feeble to make the horrendous trip were simply killed in front of the others and dumped in a huge mass grave. The final station gave the survivors their last taste of African food and fresh water before the crossing where death estimates range from one-tenth to one-half of the human cargo. At the very place the slaves boarded the boats, the United Nations has placed a huge arch looking out at the sea which gives the visitor today the same scene of the open sea the African slaves would have seen at that time. Imagine the feelings of hopeless despair that must have engulfed them as they looked out at this same sight.

NAMIBIA

"THE STRANGEST DESERT IN THE WORLD AND PART GERMAN TO BOOT"

Namibia, the old German Southwest Africa, is appropriately named after the Namib Desert, one of the oldest and driest deserts in the world and home to the oldest living plant in the world—the Welwitschia, no thing of beauty, but certainly unique at an estimated 1500-2000 years old.

Namibia is as different from the countries clustering around the Gulf of Guinea as day is from night. First, it's dry; second, it's German influence still shows; and third, it was controlled by the apartheid rulers of the Union of South Africa since Germany lost its colonies at the end of the First World War. Germany had colonized this huge arid land at the beginning of the century because they found gold, copper, diamonds and most other precious and semi-precious stones in abundance mainly along the few riverbeds and coastlines. As the first settlers quickly became millionaires, they built precisely neat and surgically clean little towns along the coast that were miraculously small replicas of the Hamburgs or Colognes they came from, and which remain the same to this day. When the Germans were defeated in World War I, the League of Nations "gave" this area to Great Britain who promptly handled it over to one of its Commonwealth countries, the Union of South Africa, to administer—which they did with a heavy hand and considerable exploitation (and industrial development) of the remaining mineral resources. After World War

II, the United Nations granted the Union of South Africa temporary "administrative control" of the area with the idea of self-governance as early as possible. But the post-war Union of South Africa had other plans and that meant Namibia didn't become an independent country until 1990, the rise of Nelson Mandela, and considerable pressure from the United Nations. In the interim, poor Namibia was subjected to all the apartheid policies prevalent in the Union of South Africa, including the forced "settlement towns" for blacks and "colored," different wage scales for whites, blacks, and the mixed coloreds, and highly restricted educational and job opportunities dependent on your racial classification.

Despite the collapse of apartheid, the separate living areas still largely remain and separate schools still seem to be the norm. And job status still seemed to be largely determined by skin color. But there was some evidence this wasn't going to last too much longer now that, at long last, the majority were in power.

Our first stop, the coastal city of Walvisbaal and the nearby Swakopmund, were as German as one could make a waterless desert look German. [When passing the Swakopmund Gymnasium (high school), I wondered to myself what it would be like to be a cheerleader for their soccer team and come up with a catchy little cheer for the Swakopmund team members.] German Victorian would best describe the architecture; Lutheranism seemed to be the predominate religion, and German is still the main means of communicating, even for the darkest Namibian around. Water comes from deep wells of "ancient water" estimated to be over 3000 years old and tastes like it; the electricity comes all the way from South Africa; and almost all goods in daily usage and certainly all foods except goat are imported. What's exported are diamonds, gold, and fish. The diamonds here are small but of the highest quality—we were told 98 percent of the diamonds in engagement rings are Namibian in origin whereas practically no industrial diamonds come from this region. Certainly, DeBeers, Inc., the famed diamond cartel, had the most modern office buildings wherever we went, but the buildings always looked strangely like white bank vaults with their heavily barred windows and doors and thick concrete walls!

The country now has good paved roads in all directions from its capitol of Windhoek, but usually just one in each direction and the only airport able to handle jets is in the capital. Originally, Namibia was made up of three tribes and the majority of the population still identify accordingly, while the sprinkling of foreigners are Germans, English, and South Afrikaners who seem to control the industries even today. The American presence is small, but we did use the Namib desert to train our astronauts in moon walking—a good choice since the Namib desert landscape does look exactly like the pictures I've seen of the moon's surface. When I was in the middle of the vast and forbidding Namib desert with its alien, otherworldly, look, I wondered what those astronauts thought of this strange country as they were training under the curious stares of the locals.

Namibians held a strange outlook on life, in my opinion. When asked what they would do when the rapidly depleting "ancient water" reserves were gone, the answer was simply "something else will turn up" without a furrow of concern; when asked if they had plans to produce their own electricity, since it's mighty expensive to import it all the way from South Africa, the answer was "no" without further elaboration; and when asked how they would pay for the import of food when and if the diamonds were gone, you simply don't get an answer. And I'm not talking about the indigenous undereducated population—I'm talking about the first generation Namibians who are now the leaders of industry. When someone in our group voiced their concern that the Hottentots (the southernmost tribe) was reportedly holding another minority tribe in virtual chattel slavery, the answer was "this may be true because the Hottentots have a long history of that sort of thing." I suppose Americans appeared to them as worried about everything.

But if different is your thing, Namibia is about as exotic as it gets. The people were invariably pleasant, scrupulously clean, and so carefree it was charming. The government is making a concerted effort to attract tourists and the new airport, new roads, rental car agencies, and a few lovely new hotels at incredibly low rates would make this a fascinating visit. Even the imported food was well prepared and sumptuous. After all, how many people do you know can casually say, "When I was in Namibia last month, I saw the oldest plant, picked up the biggest diamond, walked across what looked like the moon, etc."

SOUTH AFRICA

"YEARS OF APARTHEID HASN'T QUELLED BLACK'S HOPE FOR EQUALITY"

I'd always heard Cape Town was one of the world's most beautiful cities and it certainly was. When those early Dutch settlers picked this place to set up shop, they knew exactly what they were doing. But it's not Africa as we think of it—it's Europe transplanted to a site almost magical in its beauty. Mixed in with the soaring mountains sheltering Cape Town from the Cape of Good Hope, the rich fertile soil seemingly everywhere, the perfect protected harbor, are interstates ten lanes wide, cars and trucks everywhere, factories pumping out pollution, and a healthy tanned blond race of people now playing side by side with their fellow black citizens on the beautiful beaches of the new post-apartheid South Africa of Nelson Mandela.

Most Americans, myself included, wouldn't have dreamed of visiting this country just a decade ago with its Nazi-like feudal state of forced racial segregation that determined where one lived, the work one did, the education one received, the standard of living possible for any given person, and even who one could socialize with. And the idea of a black "servant class" brought up too many memories of our own historical injustices in this area. Since apartheid "died" less than a decade ago, I expected the situation to be much bleaker than it appeared. Yes, most blacks and the mixed coloreds still live in segregated areas, but it's obvious the color lines are breaking down due to economic pressures. And the universities are now open to all through government mandate. As many blacks were already enrolled in higher education as was true for whites in the country just 20 to 30 years ago. Supervisory jobs weren't all held by whites by any means. Restaurants had black maitre de's with white waiters as well as the other way around; some road crews were certainly mixed by color, and socializing wasn't entirely along racial lines by any means. So considerable progress seems to have been made in a remarkably short time, considering the length of our own civil rights struggle.

Still, there's obviously a long, long way to go before equal opportunity has any real meaning in this country. Blacks remain largely uneducated and hence lacking in job skills; the "coloreds" are mainly locked into clerical and mercantile jobs, and the professions are predominantly white. But it's obvious there's a will to change and some progress has obviously been made in short order.

Equally impressive is the sheer beauty of the country. Everywhere one goes, you're reminded of the best of Switzerland, of Austria, of California's Napa Valley, or our great Southwest. It's almost as varied as our own country and rivals it in beauty. Like the U.S., it's an industrial complex as well, and huge Mercedes and Volkswagen plants produce most of the many cars and trucks needed in this modern country; some of the world's best trains are in daily operation here, roads are excellent, but housing is one of two extremes: either remarkably modern and luxurious or the horrid squalor of overcrowded squatter's slums with modest newly-built government housing trying to make a difference in-between the two extremes.

We visited the famous vineyards producing some of the best wines in the world, the farming ventures of Cecil Rhodes, the controversial British entrepreneur, and the beautiful coastlines along both the Atlantic and Indian Oceans covering the southern tip of this continent. At times, you simply forget you're in Africa—it seems like you're in the U.S. or Australia or New Zealand and places like Namibia and Benin and Senegal seem like another planet. This feeling was heightened by the fact we were staying in one of the world's finest hotels—located right on the newly restored Capetown waterfront and built into a side of one of the world's largest shopping centers. As we walked across the beautiful rugs scattered across the polished marble floors with the quiet hum of the air-conditioning in the far distance, you tend to forget all about the open sewers of Togo, the desperate poverty of the Ivory Coast, the AIDS epidemic plaguing equatorial Africa, and the hunger barely hidden in so many African eyes. The contrasts were unbelievable and you suddenly realize this is part of contemporary Africa too—contrasts that are unfair, perhaps unneeded, but constantly there.

It was time to go home. Facing us was the world's longest commercial airline flight at that time—Capetown to Miami, Florida—15 hours long non-stop. My wife and I kept thinking the air-conditioning wasn't working as we waited in the Capetown airport. Little did we know it then, but we had already begun our whole new journey with the worst illness of our lifetime—a pneumonia with African origins and which took over six weeks to conquer!

GREENLAND

GREEN EYES, INUITS, and ICE

"Where are you going to go next?" a cheerful neighbor asked my wife.

"Greenland," she responded.

"Why?" the neighbor asked as she turned away, her brief interest in our travels now dashed.

When I first viewed the small port of Qaqortoq from the ship, I could see where my neighbor was coming from. Picturesque with its brightly hued houses, there seemed to be little else. Just a few days earlier, we had explored Iceland with its beautiful green pastures, its fascinating thermal geysers, its active volcanoes, and the thriving capitol of Reykjavik. This was so different. The thick glacier that covered 95 percent of all Greenland's land loomed like a dirty cliff just beyond the last little house. True, getting to Qaqortoq through the magnificent Prince Christian's Sound had offered some of the best natural scenery in the world, despite constantly dodging the omnipresent icebergs. But the little town, with its oil storage tanks, its small generating plant, its two churches, and a fish factory was a long way from exhilarating.

Undaunted, I eagerly sought out the local boat trip to the Norse Church and Hvalsey Farm, the last site of Viking settlement before they all starved to death in the late 1400's. After an hour on a crowded boat, we arrived at a small stone pier in a cold misting rain. No one had bothered to build steps up the steep slope to the remains of the old church and, as a result, most of our group were stuck on the peer since the soil was primarily mud and slick reindeer grass. But a few of us made it.

"In Denmark, there's a record of a wedding in this church," the guide said pointing to the roofless walls and the holes in those walls that must have once been windows. We wiped the rain out of our eyes and glanced around at the rubble of stone. "Twenty-six ships of Vikings started out to settle Greenland, but only 13 made it," she stated matter-of-factly. "No one knows what happened to the other ships. Since the climate was getting colder and colder in the 1400's, they could only grow a little barley and oats, so they eventually starved to death here," the guide continued flatly.

"The lucky ones were in the 13 ships that sunk," my wife added glumly as she tried to wipe the mud off her rain-soaked clothes.

"And their farm was next door there—we call it Hvalsey's Farm," the guide indicated waving her hand at a nearby pile of rocks.

"How do you know it was a farm?" one in our group queried.

"That's what the sign says," the guide responded with no further explanation forthcoming.

We staggered back to the boat for the ride back to Qaqortoq where no further information on the Viking settlement was forthcoming. Disappointed that we'd traveled 6000 miles for this, we signed up immediately for a "walking tour" of "fascinating Qaqortoq."

This guide turned out to be a most handsome man, 24 years old, with piercing green eyes. He explained he was from north Greenland, "where it gets cold," that he was a student at the Qaqortoq Business College for a two-year stretch, and that he was the product of a Danish father and an Inuit (Eskimo) mother.

"I get my height and green eyes from my father; my smooth skin and black hair from my mother," he said proudly in fairly good English. "They hired me today to tour you because I speak English," he explained.

He walked us to all the town highlights: the two churches, the "museum," the general store, the elementary school, and back to the pier. The "museum" consisted of two rooms: one full of black and white photos of various dignitaries visiting Qaqortoq (almost anyone from out of town it seemed like) along with a restoration of "how we used to live before electricity" (a sod house with a tiny door I wasn't sure I could get through, no windows, but warm and cosy inside). The generating plant ran on diesel fuel shipped all the way from Denmark.

"Isn't your electricity expensive?" I asked.

"No, it's made with diesel fuel, not gasoline. Gasoline very expensive here for cars," he responded.

"But still," I persisted, "imported diesel fuel is expensive."

"No, he said, "Denmark pays for it."

"What else do they pay for?" I asked.

"Schools, medical care, pensions, and unemployment pay," he replied.

"Aren't you a separate country, independent from Denmark now?" I countered. "Why do they pay for it?

"They owe it to us," the good looking half-breed replied.

"Owe it to you?" I asked incredulously.

"Yes," he explained as if I were retarded, "they're responsible for Westernizing us, so now they're responsible for what happens to us. If it hadn't of been for them, we wouldn't have gotten use to electricity and things like that."

"What happens if the Danes decide not to do that anymore?" I persisted.

"They won't," was his answer without a hint of concern evident.

The school children were almost all Inuits. They were in good health, curious about the rare visitors, and friendly considering they seemed to be basically shy. They faced a life of fishing or living off the unemployment dole since other options seemed to be void. Even the fish were dwindling, though, so a certain gloom pervaded the adult population.

"Too bad I have the flu," our guide explained, "or I'd give you a better tour."

I was happy to discover even the natives reacted sensibly to the horrid weather. But when I got back to my ship, I told them the tours of delightful Greenland weren't worth the money. They must have agreed—they refunded half the amount I'd paid. Still, if you like glaciers three miles thick . . . . . .

APPENDIX

All of this book has been about my travels within my adult married life. But the first extended trip I took was with my parents and younger brother in the summer following my first year at Antioch College. The trip, in the late fifties, was representative of millions and millions of other American families venturing forth for the first time since the poverty of the Depression and the restrictions of World War II. Since none of us had traveled much before, that trip to California was a great adventure and whetted our appetite for a similar trip to Canada and the Eastern Seaboard the following summer. For me, it established a desire to travel that has never diminished and so I view it as the nucleus of all later trips. That's why I decided to include this trip, taken much, much earlier, as an "Appendix." It's not related to the other travels and it's written from an entirely different perspective, but some of you may enjoy it and I've included it for that reason.

GOING WEST IN THE FIFTIES

"The First Trip: California"

It was 1955 and the prosperity following World War II had saturated even the most remote crannies of the U.S., meaning, of course, it had somehow reached the worn out mining town of Webb City, buried in the midst of the Ozarks, where my family had lived for many years. In an almost blatant advertisement of their newly attained affluence, my parents had purchased a flashy two-tone green Plymouth sedan complete with whitewall tires, fender skirts, and PowerFlyte, the automatic drive controlled by a little lever sticking out from the dash itself (a system which lasted exactly one year before it was replaced with an ever fancier dash-mounted pushbutton control).

As if the new car itself wasn't sufficient reward for surviving the Depression and World War II, a vacation involving a motor trip outside the town was planned, an idea planted in our heads by numerous magazine and newspaper articles which claimed without too much substantiation that unnamed "rich and sophisticated" persons had actually undertaken such trips for a number of years now.

Inspired by John Steinbeck's novel, "The Grapes of Wrath," we decided to go all the way to California just like our Dust Bowl predecessors. Instead of an old truck, however, we would be traveling in a sleek new Plymouth. Instead of sleeping in tent camps along the way, we were planning to stay in the explosion of "tourist cabins" which had sprung up along Highway 66 leading to the Coast. Compared to Steinbeck's tale of courage against all odds, it was sort of an upscale, even spoiled, way to travel but more in tune with the times.

We planned to visit my mother's sister, Aunt Gwen, who ran an orchid ranch with her husband and mildly retarded son in Oxnard, California. My father had a long lost sister who lived near the ocean in Long Beach that was going to be contacted, whether she wanted to be or not. One of my many cousins, another of the four sons of Aunt Gwen and Uncle Wayne, was a psychiatrist living in San Francisco and my mother assured us he would want to show us that city himself, being her nephew and all. Aunt Maple, a mysterious sister of my father who had allegedly married a man lodged in the Colorado State Prison and now ran a ranch "singlehandedly" in Western Colorado, was another marked destination.

Between these family obligations, we planned to take in all the things we'd read about in the magazines: the Grand Canyon; Hoover Dam; the new city of Las Vegas sprung out of a desert; the wicked city of Hollywood; the "freeways" of Los Angeles where people drove with reckless abandon at great speeds; the Golden Gate Bridge and Fisherman's Wharf; the Mormon Tabernacle; Pike's Peak; and the amber waves of grain of Western Kansas mentioned in "America, the Beautiful." A most ambitious undertaking scheduled to take a full month in the new Plymouth.

My older brother and sister were now married and gone. The family headed to California consisted of: my mother Florence, 55, a welfare caseworker for the State of Missouri, who longed for a life beyond Webb City; my father Paul, 60, in his 35th year with the local electric company, who couldn't see looking beyond Webb City for the good life; my younger brother, John, 14, struggling with early adolescence and getting even passing grades in junior high; and myself, then 20, a sophomore at Antioch College in Ohio, as full of myself and as self-righteous as college students are wont to be. It was about as disparate a grouping as could be assembled, but our spirits were high.

When the great day finally arrived for departure, nature hadn't cooperated too well. It was beastly hot, as the Ozarks tend to be in late July, but we had an early start before the sun began really bearing down.

As titular head of the family, Dad took the wheel despite his discomfort with driving. This was based on years of passengers screaming, other drivers shaking fists and swearing at him, the constant screeching of brakes, horns blasting, and tires squealing. He was self-taught and, as was common in the early twenties, had been grand-fathered into a driver's license with no test of any kind required.

The engine was fired up, the little command lever for PowerFlyte was slipped into "D", and his small foot jammed down on the accelerator as he pulled out into the traffic of Highway 66, which passed right by our front door. We were off!

"You damn son-of-a-bitch," we heard above the chorus of horns. Out of the corner of my eye, I saw a huge irate man, beet red in his anger, shaking his fist in rage as our car pulled right out in front of him without warning. To avoid hitting us, he had swerved over into the other lane, causing a huge trailer truck to hit the berm, blatting the huge diesel's horn in protest. We were quite use to this when my father drove, and more or less ignored it as the Plymouth speeded into its place in the flow of traffic. Mother, though, started to cry from her position in the back seat—perhaps from fear of impending death, but more likely from raw embarrassment at the language used by the uncouth drivers.

As we headed south on Highway 66, the person we'd almost sideswiped desperately passed us, giving us the horn and a final fist shake. He obviously wanted to get as much distance between us and his car as possible. My father saw the car sported New York license plates.

"Damn New Yorkers," he muttered, "shouldn't be allowed on the road. Should ban those know-it-all people from ever entering the state," and he leaned on the horn in protest against all New Yorkers as our car drifted over into the oncoming lane. As we saw a huge truck aimed right at us, my mother let out an awesome shriek just as my father swerved back into the right lane with a horrific squealing of tires.

"What's the matter with you now," my father yelled at Mother as the car swerved once again, this time onto the right berm. "Can't go anywhere without you carrying on," he continued. "Hell, I'm not going to California with you crazy people, screaming and crying," he announced as if somehow he had been locked into a car with a group of total strangers. "Damn, I'm not going anywhere with you at all," he angrily choked out as he jammed on the brakes.

We squealed to a complete stop in the middle of Highway 66 amidst horns sounding, people shouting, and brakes screaming. Leaving the car in the middle of the highway, he jumped out. "You damn fools can go to California if you like, but not with me—no sir—I'm going home right now," as he walked past the rest of us still in the car, totally disregarding the screaming motorists piled up behind us, and opened the trunk where he pulled out his small suitcase.

As he started the two mile walk back to Webb City, I slid into the driver's seat and pulled the car over so the traffic could pass. When all the piled up traffic in back of us had cleared, and everyone had exercised their frustration by hurling oaths and shaking their fists at us, I turned the car around, drove back two blocks, turned again, and pulled the car onto the berm at the point my father was now at, lugging his suitcase toward Webb City. I reached over and opened the door next to the driver. Without a word, he hopped in, threw the suitcase in the backseat, and grabbed some maps to study as if nothing had happened. All of us had the good sense to not pursue the matter further and settled down for the long day's drive.

Within 12 miles, we had crossed the Oklahoma state line and were nearing the small town of Commerce. Mother was beginning to compose herself and plan for the trip ahead.

"It's going to get unbearable," she announced as she fanned herself. "Pull over at a store in Commerce and we'll get some dry ice. I've heard if you put dry ice on the front floor under the ventilator, it keeps the whole car cool. And I'll put aluminum foil on the windows, just so we can still see out some, that'll reflect all this Oklahoma heat."

I spotted a general store that looked like it might have dry ice and started to pull the car over.

"What's going on?" said Dad. "If you're going to stop every mile along the way, I'm not going with you. Stupidest thing I've ever heard of—getting dry ice and putting junk all over the windows—I'm not riding with a bunch of crazy people. Already complaining and we're not even through Oklahoma yet. Pull over, Harve."

I was pulling over anyway. My mother, undaunted, alighted from the back and entered the store.

"A dollar's worth of dry ice," she said to the grizzly, unshaven clerk.

"What fur?" he shot back, the tobacco juice running down his chin.

"Why, to cool the car," she purred. "We're on our way to California," she added proudly.

"It won't cool no car," he replied, apparently unimpressed by the fact she was going to California.

"Nevertheless," she said in the icy tone she could quickly assume when she was crossed, "I want a dollar's worth of dry ice."

"It's your money," he grunted back, "but I tell you it won't cool no car."

"We'll see," she retorted, her tone beyond the frost level by this time. "Here's your dollar," she delivered in a withering tone.

"Yes, ma'am." He returned with a small package of the icy substance with vapors drifting from it.

Back in the car she instructed me, "Harve, they say to put it right below the ventilator—right there on the hump," pointing to the transmission hump on the front floor. I did as she said. My brother John scampered into the front passenger seat. "I'll make sure it stays put," he said, making his presence in the front seat appear necessary. My mother busily draped aluminum foil over the back windows carefully leaving spaces where I could see out.

We all assumed my Dad had gone to the restroom, but after waiting and waiting, I decided to go into the men's room to hurry him up. I checked and he wasn't there. John and I looked up and down the street, thinking he had gone to another store. Mother re-entered the store to see if he was still there. He wasn't. We couldn't imagine where he had disappeared. Finally, panicked, we began going up and down the street.

A block away, in the Greyhound bus station, Daddy was calmly sitting with his small suitcase. He pretended he didn't see us and sat staring out the window.

"What are you doing here, Paul?" Mother asked.

"Going home," he answered as if this were an everyday occurrence. "It's too far to walk."

"Don't you want to go to California with us," Mother pleaded.

"No."

"You're going to ruin the whole trip," Mother replied, starting to cry. She sat down and her sobbing became more and more noticeable to other waiting passengers.

"Oh, all right, if you're going to carry on like that," Daddy relented, "but I'm going to take the bus home the minute you get acting silly again." Without another word, he grabbed the small suitcase and we all walked back to the car. This time he got in the back seat, where he stayed for the next 6000 miles.

The store clerk was right. The dry ice didn't do a thing to cool the car with every window closed, and the fumes coming off the ice were strange smelling. The foil did give the illusion of cutting the sun's rays, but after a while we felt it wasn't worth cutting the air circulation by having the windows closed. But a scrap of aluminum foil was left on the rear window the remainder of the day so Mother could be proven right.

The trees in Oklahoma were stunted by Missouri standards, the land was so flat it was difficult to believe the earth was round, and, as the heat pounded down on the green Plymouth, the dust swirling around seemed just like the Dust Bowl.

By two in the afternoon, we were reduced to wiping ourselves with wet rags and wearing headbands to keep the sweat out of our eyes. By three, all conversation had stopped because our throats were parched and raw. We were in a stretch of Highway 66 with no gas stations, no restaurants, and by supper time the loneliest section of road I've ever seen. Our stomachs were growling by 8 P.M. when we saw the distant lights of Amarillo, Texas. We pulled up to the first restaurant we saw, a big Texas barbeque joint with "all you can eat for $1". They lost money on us that night.

We found an old tourist court only half full and glad to give us a cheap rate. There were bugs in the bathroom and the sheets were strangely warm, but I was too naive then to know what that meant. The room came with a small electric fan but the Amarillo night brought some cool, so we quickly fell asleep. We were one day down the road to California.

****

The next day was even hotter, but our excitement over the sheer vastness of Texas overcame the heat until mid afternoon when Highway 66 began to look sort of wavy. But we became fascinated with the tourist attractions on both sides of this major artery to the West Coast—restaurants made to look like hamburgers, motels disguised as concrete Indian tepees, "authentic Texas bear wrestling pits," "Wild Bill Cody's Do-Drop Inn," and the "Must See: Calf with three heads."

By late afternoon, we felt we couldn't go any further and a cheap motel advertising "ice-cooled" rooms lured us into an early stop. "Ice-cooled" turned out to be a pitcher of ice water and one small drinking glass with a rotating fan fastened on one wall. The small Texas town was fascinating not only for its dusty bleakness but in the resident's cowboy clothing and their Texas drawls.

The next day was supposed to be "a real scorcher" according to the diner's waitress. Considering we were to cross the great American desert that day, we stocked up on jugs of water, went to bed at twilight, and started out at 3 A.M. in the cool of the morning.

With the sun's morning arrival, we saw millions of one-seed junipers, a few isolated cactus trees, some of the fabled sagebrush, and a strip of asphalt across an ocean of dust and sand. By 10 AM, the heat was unbearable and most of us kept our eyes glued to the temperature gauge of the Plymouth. We'd read stories of cars boiling over and leaving occupants to rot in the desert. The few cars that were coming in the opposite direction all sported two accessories we didn't have: canvas bags of water draped over the front grill where the evaporation could presumably keep the contents cool and handy to add to the radiator if needed; and long cylinder devices called a "car evaporative cooler" hooked to the top of the passenger's window that scooped up the hot desert air to flow over a grill of straw kept moist by water in an attached tank.

Although running noticeably hotter than usual, our car never reached the red mark on the temperature gauge, and we got to Gallup, New Mexico, right on schedule. We became so wrapped up in the Navaho influence there we thought we were the original Western settlers, and couldn't help staring at the Native Americans who predominantly populated the town. Buying groceries and fixing our own supper of bologna and cheese sandwiches, we splurged on a motel with a pool that we used for hours.

The next morning, we left for Boulder City, Nevada. Aunt Gwen's husband, Uncle Wayne, had lived at Boulder City while working on the construction of Hoover Dam. This made the hastily constructed town more interesting to us as we imagined him living there in the army of thousands needed for the colossal engineering feat.

Hoover Dam itself was mind-boggling to the four of us who'd never seen anything bigger than Riverton Dam in Gravette, Arkansas. It was like comparing a doll house to the Empire State Building. Few tourists traveled this far west in the heat of the summer so we were able to stop and take pictures as we drove across the top of the dam. The tour of the Dam itself took three hours and took you into the very bowels of the colossus where I imagined I could feel the pressure of the water against the walls.

The Park Ranger taking us through really wanted us to appreciate this wonder of the world and asked us a lot of questions to make sure we understood and were listening carefully. The tour included every detail about the actual production of electricity with visits to both types of generators utilized as well as the control room. [Thirty years later, I took the same tour, except this time the traffic going across the bridge was so great there were minimum speeds to be maintained, the "informational tour," which you had to wait in line about an hour for, had degenerated down to 20-30 minutes so the sheer crush of tourists could at least say they'd been in the dam itself, and the tour guides were so overworked and harassed they could care less. Sadly, you could leave the tour not even knowing they produced electricity there.]

By evening, we were driving down the "Strip" of Las Vegas, although in the mid-fifties the Strip was still a lot smaller than Downtown Las Vegas. But the big bright signs were there for the Sahara, the Sands, and the Aladdin, while the Imperial House and Caesar's Palace were under construction. The lights on the Strip were worth the trip alone and we ate supper at the Sands where we had a fabulous complete prime rib meal for 99 cents each. Later, we walked from one casino to another to see the lavish architecture, the scantily clad women around the hotel's pools, the neon brightness of the casinos, and the tired gamblers pulling the handles down on the slots with cigarettes hanging out of their joyless mouths. We were quickly made aware that a 14-year-old wasn't welcome in any of the actual sites of gambling, so we sort of had to peak around the edges to see the insides of the casinos and their inhabitants. Despite this small handicap, we got caught up in the ambiance of the city and decided to treat ourselves to a real Las Vegas show with half-naked women and all.

But problems arose. First, some of the shows wouldn't allow minors so John's presence again interfered. Secondly, the tickets were quite costly by Webb City standards, but we decided to go ahead although we all understood without being told this meant more meals out of a grocery store bag. Thirdly, even after you had the expensive tickets in hand, it was obvious the best seats were going to those who tipped the gatekeepers generously. Such open graft offended the very being of my social worker Mother who loudly announced this was wrong and then added to our embarrassment by pointing out even louder that everyone engaged in this open bribery looked like New Yorkers to her. I was astonished. Was this the same woman who lambasted people for their bigotry at the mere hint of prejudice? But her strategy, right or wrong, worked and to shut her embarrassing comments up, the gatekeepers motioned us up front and led us to a decent table inside, not without comment from those still waiting in line about the unfairness of it all.

The show was great, although my brother and I felt for the first half hour that the people we'd passed over in line were still staring at us. The dancers were beyond anything we'd ever seen, the costuming was properly revealing, and the vocalizing by Tom Jones, a person we'd never heard of as a Las Vegas newcomer in one of the lesser priced shows, was spectacular. John and I were most uncomfortable to be with our parents while the sexy singer thrust his hips around suggestively in his skin-tight pants, but neither one of them seemed embarrassed in the slightest. When I commented they must have sewn the singer into his pants, my mother announced in her most sophisticated tone that "all the good singers nowadays dress like that," as if I was hopelessly provincial and out-of-date.

After Vegas, we headed for the California border. Barstow, our first stop, was, then as now, the hottest place on God's earth. As we pulled into the little row of tourist courts on both sides of the highway, the temperature topped out at 115. The tourist court we rented featured an evaporative cooler mounted in the flat roof that really worked with a steady blast of cool wet air flowing directly down toward the two double beds and the linoleum floor. The heat must have exhausted us because all four of us fell fast asleep in the cooling breeze and didn't wake up until long after sunrise the next morning.

Los Angeles, our next stop, was exciting before we even got into the city itself. We'd all heard horror stories about the multi-lane freeways of California. Actually driving on one was something else again. Determined to not appear like an Ozark hick, I tried to keep up with the traffic as the freeway grew from four to six and finally to eight lanes. My father, true to his nature, was perched on the edge of the back seat and I could feel his hot breath on my neck as he scanned the overwhelming traffic.

"Dad, get back," I yelled at him in my nervousness over driving under such conditions.

"Four eyes are better than two," he yelled back as cars seemed to be passing us on all sides. "Go faster, you're not going fast enough."

"If you can't drive, pull over and let someone who can," John added his two cents worth as if he had a valid license or vast experience to offer.

I loved to drive, but this traffic was something else again. I looked down at the speedometer and to my astonishment saw we were doing a cool 80. I didn't even realize the six-cylinder 85-horsepower Plymouth with full load could hit 80. And still cars were passing us and were right on our bumper in back.

"It won't go any faster," I announced with chagrin as I felt my foot mashing the accelerator into the floorboard.

Dad, eyes bright with excitement, blocked the rear view mirror as he adjusted himself on the very edge of the back seat to afford the best view of the situation.

"I can't see out back," I screamed as a horn in back of us sounded and another car passed us on the right.

Suddenly, Dad just disappeared. At least, I could see out the rear view mirror but I couldn't divert my attention long enough to inquire as to where he went. Finally, miles later, I was able to edge myself out of the center lanes and over to the outer lane where I could slow down to 60 and catch my breath. I felt my heart pounding from the driving challenge I assumed was very akin to the Indianapolis 500.

"Looks like you'd just rot at the wheel," John announced as he noticed the speed reduction, "always hogging all the driving even when you can't drive any better than you can play football," referring to my embarrassing lack of success as a high school football player and further implying there was someone else available to drive even better, namely a 14-year-old from Missouri.

"What happened to Dad?" I asked, amazed he had just instantly vanished into thin air.

"I dunno," John answered disinterestedly. "Whatdoyoumean, what happened to Dad?" and he turned around to look in the back seat where he saw only my Mother sitting serenely happy that she had arrived in the City of Angels at last. "Well, where's he at?" he shot back in an accusatory tone, as if I had arranged his quick exit.

"I don't know. That's what I asked you, dummy," with a little panic creeping into my voice. I glanced in the rear view mirror to check that the rear doors were shut.

John turned in his front seat position to better check out the spot where Dad had been perched on the edge of the seat he usually preferred. "What're you doing down there, Dad?" John asked in an amazed, but relieved tone.

"Where's he at?" I asked excitedly as I continued to cope with the worst traffic I had ever even imagined.

"He's on the floor—on all fours," John said in amazement. "Dad, what are you doing down there?" John asked, obviously chagrined but also bemused.

"Harve said to get out of the way so he could see," Dad answered as if everyone in a car always hit the floor on all fours to clear the view.

I didn't know whether to feel guilty, laugh, cry, get mad, or just drive. I choose the latter in view of the traffic.

John said, "You can get up now, Dad. Harve can see OK. He was just mouthing off as usual."

But Dad didn't get up until several miles later when I asked him, as the chief navigator, where to get off the damn freeway. He quickly grabbed his maps and provided the answer as if nothing had happened. That night, safely abed in a nondescript hotel on Santa Monica Boulevard, I got thinking about the incident and couldn't get it out of my mind. Finally, I started laughing at the memory and when everyone told me to shut up, I couldn't, and when they asked what I thought was so funny, I told them. At that point, everyone, including my Dad, got caught up in the contagious laughter and I bet it was 30 minutes before we could stop. By this time, tears were streaming down our cheeks and we slept like babies. But we never got on another Los Angeles Freeway again on that trip.

****

Los Angeles was a lot smaller in those days and there were no touristy attractions like Disneyland, the Queen Mary and the Spruce Goose, Universal Studios, and the Simon Museum. All that was there was Knott's Berry Farm with its chintzy little rides, the entrances to Fox and Paramount Studios off of Santa Monica Boulevard, Grumman's Chinese Theater (still in operation then), and the "Walk of Fame" where they still imbed star's names in the Hollywood sidewalk. Miraculously, with my Dad's maps, we found all of those things and dutifully sat through the movie at the Chinese Theater, walked down the "Walk of Fame" hoping to see a real live movie star, saw Schwab's Drug Store where Lana Turner was allegedly discovered as a young girl from the Midwest, complained disappointingly about the high prices, big crowds, and general tackiness of Knott's Berry Farm, and thought Santa Monica Boulevard was pretty with the palms lining both sides. But the biggest treat was seeing the Pacific Ocean through the oil derricks of Long Beach. We'd never seen the ocean before and its vastness overwhelmed us.

******

One of my father's sisters allegedly lived near the ocean and when we found her small house, it was indeed a block from the ocean itself. He hadn't seen Aunt Laura since he had been a boy in his teens and John and I were curious what the long awaited reunion would be like after a 40-year lapse. It was memorable but not the way you'd think.

"Laura, I'm your brother Paul," my Dad said, waiting a long time after knocking before the door was answered by a craggy small woman who looked exactly like my Dad but older.

"Yeah," she answered in a flat tone. "How're you doing?" she asked as if she'd seen him last week.

"I'm OK, and this is my wife, Florence and two of my sons, John and Harve," he said pointing to us politely lined up on her front porch.

"Yeah," was her answer followed by a long period of silence.

"Well, what do you do with yourself, Laura?" Dad asked.

"Not much," she snickered. "Not much."

"You married?" Dad asked.

"Yeah," she answered.

"Got any children?" he persisted.

"Used to," she said without emotion.

"What does your husband do?" Dad didn't give up easily.

"Sits around and fishes some," she said still standing in the door staring at us through the screen.

"Sort of hot out here," Mother said suggestively but with all her gracious charms on full display. "Your house is so cute," she lied.

"I got your letter but I didn't really think you'd come," Laura said without grace.

"I bet you've got it fixed up cute on the inside too," my Mother asked as she delved into her social worker ploys.

"Nope," Laura answered my mother.

"Well, I was planning on getting some fishing in this afternoon,"

Laura said pointedly as she glanced at her wristwatch.

"We're planning to visit Mabel out in Colorado," my Dad said, knowing she was closest in age to this sister than any of the others.

"That ought to be interesting," Laura said, revealing nothing by her comment.

"We'll say hello to her for you," Dad continued.

"Well, if you want to," Laura granted as she looked at her watch again and grabbed a fishing pole next to the door. "Good to talk to you, Paul," she said as she strode across the porch and down the street to the ocean hugging her pole next to her. Dad never again mentioned the incident nor did the rest of us. Some things are best left unsaid.

Although we were in strong agreement that Los Angeles wasn't much for us, after that episode we all reached a quick consensus that we would never want to live in Los Angeles under any circumstances, and, once this was decided, we moved on to Oxnard where my Mother's sister and her husband lived with Bruce, their mildly retarded son.

****

It was Uncle Wayne, a man I'd only met once before in my life, who first gave me the idea that Californians just think differently than the rest of us. At the time we visited their modest little home in Oxnard with the greenhouses for the orchids in back, he was working on some construction project miles away and only accessible via the famed California freeways. He returned from work long after we'd arrived in a 1940 Packard business coupe, now 16 years old, and the perfect description of a "heap." Every fender was crushed as was the front grill and the back trunk; two of the windows were cracked and a third was gone; the chassis was a study of how rust can hold things together. Black smoke poured out the back as he roared into the driveway sans muffler. He slammed the door as the Packard burbled a last protesting backfire and greeted us warmly. Everyone sort of stared at the still smoking coupe in wonderment.

"Great car for the freeway," he announced proudly. "Packard's back then were made out of 18 gauge steel instead of those tin cars they're making now," glancing disdainfully over at our new Plymouth. "With the Packard, I can just forget about people hitting me—doesn't hurt her a bit," he said affectionately, "and if a person needs a nudge now and then, the ol' Packard's always game for it," he said with a jolly little wink. "No sense wasting a car worth anything out on the freeways," he pontificated as if the limousines and expensive cars of the stars out on that same freeway were pure foolishness. The Packard wasn't his only car as it turned out. He did just use it for freeway battles and had another fairly decent car to use around Oxnard and for family trips. But the idea that you went to battle just getting to work, that you had the "right" to bang another person's car up, and that you couldn't afford to have anything out in the public domain that you minded getting damaged were all new concepts to me and I thought at the time, uniquely Californian.

Aunt Gwen reminded me of my mother and growing orchids seemed like an interesting business. During our brief overnight stay, it was decided that Aunt Gwen would ride with us to San Francisco as we went up coastal Highway 101, visit with Dr. Wayne (as the son living in San Francisco was always referred to), and return by bus later. Bruce and his dad would "batch" it while she was gone.

Aunt Gwen, Mother and John started out in the back with Dad and his maps in the front passenger seat as we started up the coast on the beautiful but curvy scenic road. We weren't five miles of navigating the bluffs until we had to pull over for John to vomit from "car sickness."

"It's all these curves," Mother diagnosed.

"It's going to be this way for 400 more miles," Father grandly announced, glancing up from the maps temporarily.

"He'll have to sit up front," Mother announced. "It won't sway around so much up there."

John vomited up another stomach full, wiped his mouth off with his arm, and climbed into the middle of the front seat, crowding the three men together while Aunt Gwen and Mother spaciously arranged themselves anew in the back seat like Queen Elizabeth and the Queen Mother on an afternoon drive in the royal Rolls-Royce.

John's foul breath, laced with vomit, quickly ended all conversation in the front seat. He did look sort of sickly, but we all forgot about it in that the scenery was spectacular: the ocean on one side, tall cliffs with waterfalls on the other. But before long, it was obvious there was something wrong with the steering as we navigated the endless curves and horseshoe bends. It got harder and harder to steer. Finally I pulled the car over onto the narrow berm, suspecting one of the front tires was semi-flat. But, after checking, the tires seemed OK and we started up again. Within five miles, the steering was even worse and it took great effort to turn the wheel. I pulled over again and Dad, dirtying himself on the pavement, slid under the car to check out the tie-rods and steering linkage. He popped out announcing, "It's fine. No damage there at all." The mystery continued, but we started up again and within three miles the same problem reoccurred except this time turning the wheel was practically impossible. Again, we pulled over and found nothing wrong with the car. There wasn't a repair shop within fifty miles at this point so I didn't know what we would do even if we could identify the problem. So again we started out and soon the same problem was even worst. But this time, I happened to glance down and saw John's thigh pressed as hard as he could get it to the bottom side of the steering wheel. How he could hold the tension so long without his leg paralyzing is still a mystery to me, but the strategy had worked. The feel of the car was exactly like it had two flat tires in front and a broken tie-rod in the steering mechanism.

"Brat," I screamed as I hit his thigh as hard as I could with my right hand. The car swerved as the tension was relieved from the wheel and we almost hit a car coming toward us on the narrow strip of road.

"Watch what's you're doing," Daddy yelled and Aunt Gwen, who'd been snoring loudly in one of her endless "cat naps," suddenly awakened with "Are we in San Francisco already, Paul?"

After getting the car back into the right lane, I proceeded to give John a number of other blows for good measure as I ranted once again what a mistake it had been to take a "spoiled brat like him" on any trip anywhere. "You", referring to my parents, "should have known he'd ruin the trip." I pulled the car over once again on the minuscule berm and demanded he be seated elsewhere. Dad moved to the center and John sat by the front window where he promptly fell asleep.

"Sick my eye," I mumbled. "The brat will use any trick to ruin the trip. He's no more sick than I am—he should be sitting in the trunk," I struggled to get the last word in.

But no one was listening. Everyone was asleep but Dad and I and he was pouring over the city maps of San Francisco.

****

Someone should have warned us that 400 miles of Highway 101 equals about 1500 miles of any other highway with all its curves and twists. But late that night, we finally got to a modest tourist home on the outskirts of San Francisco. I thought it strange we weren't staying with "Dr. Wayne," but he was a bachelor so I just assumed he didn't have room, even though I'd been given the impression by one and all that his success had surely led to a mansion by now. And I thought it was strange we weren't visiting another cousin of mine, Jean Lozier, my Uncle Harve's only daughter, who lived near Stanford University as the wife of a "famous neurosurgeon," especially since I knew a visit with her highly successful brother was scheduled when we got to Des Moines, Iowa. When I inquired, Mother haughtily replied that her niece "hadn't even bothered to answer my letter, so obviously she has better things to do now." Aunt Gwen's stern look seemed to confirm that their niece Jean Lozier was now a lost cause, so I didn't pursue the matter.

The next morning, we delivered Aunt Gwen to "Dr. Wayne's" apartment and proceeded to take in all the sights of San Francisco. As we drove across the Golden Gate Bridge, we all agreed we could feel it swaying in the strong winds, the cable cars were even more fun than we thought they would be, the extensive harbor tour in the small boat was fun for Midwesterners and Fisherman's Wharf was actually used by fishermen and wasn't very crowded. We were too busy to eat lunch so when suppertime rolled around, we were starved. Adventuresomely, we treated ourselves to an abalone dinner right on Fisherman's Wharf, a fish we'd never heard of but loved instantly. As we ate, we stared out at the foreboding lights of Alcatraz, still in use at that time.

The next day we were scheduled to meet with the mysterious "Dr. Wayne" for lunch at a "famous Chinatown restaurant Dr. Wayne himself has picked out." I noticed my mother had picked up the presumptuous habit of referring to a relative as "Doctor" by this time. Chinatown was exciting and the restaurant, on the third floor of a building right in the middle of the district, was really something in terms of decoration and menu. "Dr. Wayne" arrived right on schedule with Aunt Gwen and ordered a fabulous "Dinner for Six" which included every conceivable dish. He seemed little interested in the aunt and uncle he hadn't seen in over two decades, and it was obvious from the start he had even less interest in the likes of John and me. It was my introduction to a person who had never once thought beyond himself and his conversation reflected this single-minded purpose of "I". Even Aunt Gwen seemed embarrassed and would try to introject with asides like, "Aunt Florence and Uncle Paul drove the whole way out here—all the way from Missouri" or "Aunt Florence is a social worker now" or, getting more desperate, "Your Uncle Paul helped your Dad find a lot of lead and zinc samples when we visited them in the Ozarks" (Uncle Wayne was a rock hound). Undaunted, "Dr. Wayne" never once deviated from his steady discourse on himself. Finally, Aunt Gwen raised her voice and interrupted with "Your cousin Harve here goes to that college in Ohio the American Legion says is Communist," which embarrassed me. But even this alleged treason swept over him. He never even stopped to catch his breath in his unrelenting mission of self-aggrandizement—all in a tone of such incredible self-importance I can hear it to this day. He seemed to always refer to himself in the third person, such as "Well, Dr. Wayne thinks that . . ." or "Would you believe it, Dr. Wayne told him . . . ". At first, I thought he was talking about someone else with the same name, but then it dawned on me he was, as usual, talking about himself. If he was a psychiatrist, I can't imagine him ever stopping his endless vocalization long enough to hear anyone else say anything, let alone get a chance to describe their problem. On the other hand, he was single, then as forever after—a fact I for one could clearly understand—and maybe he never had a chance to talk to anyone so he couldn't stop once he found somebody to listen. It was the last anyone of us ever heard of or about him. As my brother John summed it up in his 14-year-old mind, "What a loser."

As I recall, he didn't even pay for the meal, but handed my father the bill for all six of us with the instructions, "I wouldn't tip him too much, Uncle Paul. Dr. Wayne's certainly had better service than this."

****

Luck was with us in Salt Lake City because we'd no sooner arrived at the Mormon Tabernacle than the choir marched in and the magnificent organ boomed forth the overture to the first cantata. We heard all about the Tabernacle being built with no nails and how the organ pipes were just hollowed out logs dragged from some 200 miles away and listened to a simplistic explanation of Mormon beliefs. The whole tale of Brigham Young leading the true believers clear across a barren desert and setting up a whole city was enough to capture anyone's imagination, especially when I found out the majority of those pioneers were women. I was especially impressed that back in those days of horse and buggies they had laid out main streets eight lanes wide because the visionary Mr. Young said that someday Salt Lake City would be a huge metropolis and would need streets that wide. On a more secular level, John and I rode the best and fastest roller coaster I've ever been on, a high rickety affair of rotten looking wood that was built out over the Great Salt Lake itself. I remember Dad yelling at us from a tiny spot on the ground to hang on tight. Later, we all got into swimsuits and got right into the Salt Lake where the alkaline waters burnt everyone's crotch so we didn't linger—something no one had warned us about. But we did test out the theory that you can't sink in such waters and we bobbed around to prove it as a white scum of salt adhered itself to our skin.

At Yellowstone, we saw the bears and "Old Faithful" and "Morning Glory Pool" and weren't disappointed. But getting to Yellowstone was a trial. Dad had studied the route endless times. He had poured over the maps like Prince Henry the Navigator planning a trip to the East Indies. Finally, the route to Yellowstone was announced: State Highway 79 would take us right there. It was just a tiny little line on the maps, but my Dad announced it was probably an "overlooked shortcut." It existed, but that's about the best that could be said about it. Two lane at best, it sometimes deteriorated into one lane and once in while became unpaved; no effort had ever been attempted to straighten the road. After 10 miles, I concluded it was simply a cleared Indian path to a salt lick and unsuitable for motor travel, but Dad was listening to none of that kind of talk. After miles and miles without ever seeing a house, a teepee, even a tent, it started to get dark and the thought of being hopelessly lost in the mountains crossed everyone's mind but my Dad's. By 10 PM and a gas tank only one-tenth full, we suddenly burst upon a filling station with a real live attendant. After the attendant filled the tank, my Dad rolled down his back seat window to talk to the fellow, maps firmly in hand with a flashlight aimed at the critical routes.

"Mister, I know we're on Wyoming 79 but right up ahead there's Highway 44 and then to the left of that is Route 36. Seems to me if we turn on 44 and go over to 36, we can then get onto 22 and that should lead us over to where 44 joins up with 22 and then if you take that going north, looks to me you end up on US 30 heading on up to Idaho," my Dad said in the vocal style of a rapid-fire machine gun. The attendant stared dumbly in amazement as this apparition from the back seat trying to figure out who he was talking to, if anybody, since no question had actually been asked.

"Well, if 79 here leads to 44 and . . ." my Dad repeated the entire dialog as if the man hadn't heard him and spoke twice as loud. Again, the man just stared at this voice from the dark. Dad was a patience man, so he repeated the entire dialog a third time in an even louder voice, but this time added a lot of "turning right onto" and "turning left onto" into the proposed route. Again, the man said nothing and just stared in amazement. Apparently, my Dad figured he needed visual aids to amplify his dialog, so all the maps, the flashlight, and the Mobil Travel Book were thrust out the window along with his head so he could point and talk at the same time in a multimedia blitz. When finished, Dad looked him straight in the eye awaiting his verdict on the proposed itinerary. The man, now holding the money for the gas, stared, took a deep breath, hefted his overall straps, and was apparently preparing to utter a sound.

"Drive on," my father snapped sharply, "the man knows nothing," quickly withdrawing his treasured maps and flashlight back into the car and rolling up the back window in a gesture of finality. "Nothing at all."

I drove off as ordered to God knows where and we headed north in the gloom of night. After 15 minutes, I heard a small female chuckle from the back seat, followed by a similar muted laugh from my brother. It was contagious and all three of us started laughing so hard we cried as the Plymouth headed into oblivion in the blackness of Wyoming. Finally, my Dad started laughing as we mimicked the one-sided conversation over and over, going into peals of laughter with each retelling and eventually we had to pull the car over until our laughing fit was over. The truth was, we really didn't have the vaguest idea of where we were. But, as it turned out, the route my Dad had in mind panned out and we actually got to where we were headed. It was so typical of the best of my Dad.

****

Mother had to get her hair done, a sacrosanct ritual to be performed every week regardless of where she was or what she was doing, somewhat above in priority but similar to going to church. Upon the seventh day since her last hairdressing we were in one of the most desolate spots of Wyoming and the idea of finding water, let alone a beauty shop, seemed infinitely remote. But, true to her instincts, a front bedroom of a ramshackle farm house converted to a "beauty parlor for particular women" as the sign, hanging by one loose nail announced, was spotted and we stopped for the absolution. The weekly rites didn't take much more than an half-hour or so and gave the rest of us a chance to inspect an old graveyard right across the street next to an abandoned church. What grabbed our attention was the old iron bedsteads sticking up out of the ground. Apparently, the practice was to literally bury you in your deathbed. The bed and all was stuck down in the dug out hole, your body was covered, but the head and foot of the old rusty metal beds stuck out among the weeds at the top. None of us had ever seen the practice before and, upon closer inspection, we found most of those buried were Christianized Indians with names attached to the emerging bedframes like "Crazy Horse Jesus" or "Running Deer Smith." It was fascinating. As we poked around in the weeds, I was shocked to find "Sacajawea, Indian scout for the Lewis & Clark Expedition." I'd just seen a movie about the Lewis &

Clark expedition starring Gregory Peck in which Hollywood claimed the mission would have been a bust without the help of this brilliant, beautiful, multilingual, wondrously diplomatic Indian princess played by the American-as-apple-pie movie star Donna Reed with a lot of brown makeup. There really was such a person! And to think she lay before my feet at this very spot! The thrill of discovery swept over me. As I pulled the weeds out to better read the fine print of this Native American heroine who, according to the movie, had been personally thanked for her magnanimous help by no less than the President of the United States when she was a guest in the White House, I couldn't imagine her ending up in this nondescript deserted graveyard. I had imagined I would have found her remains in a national monument, not here! But when the weeds were removed, the simple little description below said, "Buried with her two sons. Claimed, but never confirmed, to be a princess of a Canadian tribe, she served as guide, cook, and interpreter for many of the members of the early exploration of the Northwest Regions. Dying at the age of 77 in great poverty, she and her sons are buried here in recognition of her conversion to the Baptist faith."

I was excited at the discovery and the rest of the day was filled with my tales of Sacajawea and her role in the Lewis & Clark Expedition. But it did give me a greater appreciation for the trials and tribulations the American Indians had experienced in coping with the invasion of the White Europeans over and above our diseases.

My Mother had not been idle in her own time in the "beauty parlor for particular women." She came back with tales of the "jackalope," seen only this morning by the local beautician who swore it was a common enough sight around these parts for the alert. A "jackalope" was a jack rabbit so big it was often confused with a small antelope and, if you hit one on the road, it would wreck your car so you had to be careful out here in Wyoming. And the lady had told her there was an Indian Princess buried right across the road but that's about all she knew about her. "Buried right in her own death bed," the woman had claimed.

*****

Heading east, we got within 30 miles of the Kansas border before we turned off US 40 and started heading north in Colorado to visit Aunt Mabel's ranch. Dad had all the maps and letters of instruction from Aunt Mabel laid out across the back seat like the command desk of General Rommel in the Africa Campaign. The first hour was uneventful in that the road was paved. The fact we never saw one living soul the entire time wasn't too alarming at that point. It was when we got to the "main town" where Aunt Mabel bought her groceries I began to wonder. The "town" consisted of a gas station/grocery store with a post office tucked in one corner and a couple of wires stretching across the desert—one for electricity and the other presumably for a phone but I wasn't sure of the latter. There wasn't a tree, a bush, a flower, a blade of grass in sight anywhere. We wisely gassed up, got a bottle of pop out of an electric cooler (so I knew they had electricity), and checked our directions to Aunt Mabel's, who was well known to the Postmaster since she picked her mail up here, along with "supplies once a month regular as clockwork."

"She's quite a character," the Postmaster said with little warmth. "Quite a character," he repeated. "Quite a little drive out to her spread," he warned, "You think your car can make it?" as he glanced dubiously over at the Plymouth sedan.

"Mabel's expecting us," my Dad replied as if that alone answered the postmaster's question.

From there on, the "road" was one-lane and pure dirt. I'd call it a trail more than a road, but Coloradans tend to be optimistic due to need. We drove 10 miles on the trail, dodging the potholes and sagebrush accumulations until we got to the first fence where we had to stop, unhook the barb wire gate, drive through and refastened the gate since we were now, apparently, on private property. After another 15 miles, where at times the trail seemed to disappear until you could spot tire ruts again in the distance, we came upon another barbed wire gate and went through in the same way. The entire way, we never saw one living thing—not a prairie dog, not a rabbit, not a cow, nothing. Mother, following her usual behavior patterns, had begun to sob quietly in the back seat but no one paid any attention since crying seemed the sensible thing to do under the circumstances. We drove another five miles, forded a dry creek bed, went over a small hill, and there it was: a medium sized one-story unpainted house made out of adobe brick with a flat roof and surrounded by barb-wire to keep the animals *out*. The trail ended in the front yard and as we climbed out of the car in relief, Aunt Mabel burst out of the back door.

"Jesus Christ, it's Jake," she exclaimed in a voice they surely heard in Denver as her right hand reached down and grabbed the neck of a passing chicken. She snapped the chicken's neck with her thumb and forefinger before the chicken even knew what happened and grabbing a bucket, apparently out of thin air, with her other hand, dumped the chicken into the bucket as it flopped around in its death throes. "I knew you'd make it, Jake," she added, "and, God Damn, whose the little blushing bride here," she said looking at my Mother who had been married for close to 30 years now, had four children the youngest of which was 14, and was always big boned enough to never be called "little."

"Mabel, this is my wife Flo and two of my boys, Harve, he's in college, and John here, 14 last February," Dad said proudly.

"Well, Jesus Christ, I'm glad to see you all," Mabel boomed out. "Jake, how the shit are you?" as she grabbed him in a bear-like hug.

"Fine, Mabel, Fine," Dad gasped, not used to being hugged.

I was totally bewildered. Who was Jake? I looked around to see who she was talking to or about, but could see no one but my Dad. Had he had a secret nickname all these years? Did he play a role in his strange family I knew nothing about?

John and I snickered when we realized the Jake she was talking about was actually our Dad. Jake seemed as remote to his character as any name we could imagine and the strangeness of the name struck us as funny, especially since my Dad looked so embarrassed by her use of the name. Mabel hefted herself down in a old metal lawn chair and putting the dead chicken in her lap, plunked the feathers out of that bird so fast it reminded me of a movie I'd seen where a school of piranhas attacked a small piece of meat in the Amazon. There was a blur of flying feathers and suddenly a naked chicken's carcass was lying limp in her lap.

"We'll have the little fucker for supper," she said sweetly as my Mother gasped. About then, another innocent little chicken strolled by and the great hand again swooped down, cracked the neck, and plucked the second bird while it was still thrashing around.

"Hell, it's going to take two of these scrawny things to feed the bunch of us," and she laughed uproariously as she grabbed a butcher knife out of her apron and cleanly whacked their heads off right there in the front yard. My mother turned pale white and stared wide-eyed at the bloody chicken heads lying at her feet.

"Don't you worry none, Flo, the dogs will clean it right up. No need for a pretty little thing like you to be getting all dirty." With that, she led us into the house which she claimed she'd made herself.

"Took me a year or so, but here it is, such as it is. Serves me well enough, I reckon. I ain't got too many years left in me anyway," she reflected as she motioned for us to sit in some homemade wooden chairs she'd obviously also made.

John and I had never met anyone like this. The truth is, we've never even been anywhere remotely like this. And we were fascinated. Mabel seldom stopped talking. About fifty percent of her talk was made up from words forbidden to John and me; the other fifty percent we were used to. "Jesus, Jake, it's good to see you in flesh and blood, you ol' shit," she went on warmly. "How'd you ever meet a pretty little thing like Flo here, a shy old bastard like you . . . I'm surprised anybody would marry the likes of you, Jake, mean as you are," and she'd break into another gale of laughter. "And, Flo, why, I just feel I've known you all my life . . . I just knew the moment I saw you standing there with Jake in the yard I was going to like you . . . Now, Flo, don't you let my talk hurt your ears none, you hear me? That's just the way I am . . . Learned to talk that way long time ago . . . Lived around men—rough men—most of my life and ended up talking just like the ornery bastards myself . . . Don't let it offend you none, Flo, a nice decent lady like yourself.. Shit, I had to talk like this to get any respect where I've been at . . . I'd probably be dead now if I talked any different . . . God damn it . . ." and she'd go into another round of laughter.

"It's all right, Mabel," Mother lied. "I understand perfectly."

"Oh, Jake there done run away and got himself educated. I should of done the same thing, probably if I had any God damn sense at all. But I don't," and she roared in laughter at her own joke.

As she hurriedly fixed supper, refusing to let my mother help her, we discovered she had escaped the back-breaking work demanded by her parents at their Kansas homestead by running away with a man who'd later committed a murder and was given a life sentence to the Colorado State Prison. Mabel had opened a small diner right across from the prison entrance catering to the prison guards to be near her husband for visitation and to keep in touch with him through the prison staff eating at her diner. After a number of years, her husband was killed by another inmate, she sold the diner for what she could get, and eventually found a aging French immigrant who was looking for someone to tend to him in his old age. They were married and this second husband had taken her to his ranch where we now sat. There, she was the only woman within a fifty mile radius; she had to work and care for the dying Frenchman; and wash, cook, and cope with 10 to 15 ranch hands "as tough as Hell itself" as she delicately put it. Somehow, she'd managed. The Frenchman, Claude DuValle, eventually died after years and years of a bedridden illness and left her, for good or bad, with the huge but desolate ranch still run by the 10 to 15 ranch hands "as tough as Hell itself." They lived in a bunkhouse a mile or so away and Mabel said she'd told them she'd get the gun out and shoot 'em dead if they didn't keep their distance when she had family visiting. "Shit, I've already cooked up enough stuff to keep them off my back for a week, you'll think." Her threat to shoot them dead must have been taken seriously because the only sign of life we saw was a jeep going by in the distance now and then stirring up a cloud of dust.

The next morning, Aunt Mabel had fired her wood stove up good and hot to make biscuits for us among other goodies. But she was overzealous and the stove got red hot—too hot to suit her for baking the biscuits. Without as much as a how-to-do, she calmly picked up a pail of water by the sink, threw the entire bucket onto the stove producing a huge cloud of steam accomplished by a lot of hissing sounds, and announced proudly, "There, that'll cool the God damn thing down," and proceeded to bake her biscuits which, I might add, turned out delicious. Mother, a very fastidious person, looked like she was going to faint as she saw all the steamy water on the kitchen floor, but managed to retain her usual graciousness through the farewell breakfast. We said our farewells and Mabel knew she'd never see us again, but it was obvious the visit meant a lot to her and apparently no one else had ever bothered. I knew as I headed the Plymouth out on that little dirt trail back to US 40 it was a visit none of us would ever forget.

When we were safely back on the main highway heading into Kansas, my mother told and retold the story of Aunt Mabel cooling down the oven leaving out the "God" before the "damn" to clean it up a bit. But to the day she died, she loved to tell about the visit to Aunt Mabel's ranch. And, you know, despite all the roughness around the edges, I think she liked her far better than anyone else in my Dad's whole family. I know John and I did.

****

The next stop was Des Moines, Iowa to visit my mother's relatives there. They were quite a contrast from my father's family. Uncle Harve's son, Dick Lozier, has spun his father's florist business into a statewide chain and Aunt May's son, Joe Strausser, was now President of Des Moines' largest bank. One of Aunt Winnie's sons, Melvyn Temple, was Vice-President of the Pioneer Seed Company, the "inventor" of hybrid corn headed by Henry Wallace, the Vice-President of the United States under Franklin Roosevelt. So we were suddenly traveling in quite different circles.

We first visited my cousin Dick Lozier's new home, the former mansion of Gardner Cowles, founder of Look Magazine and once publisher of the *Des Moines Registrar* newspaper. The estate took up seven acres complete with swimming pool and bath house and featured seven bedrooms with seven baths along with one of Des Moines' only elevators in a private home. President Herbert Hoover had been a house guest of Gardner Cowles and the bedroom he'd stayed in was marked with a special plague. Dick Lozier was handsome with a charming although quiet wife with four good-looking children who seemed to fit right into the fairy-tale existence complete with brick driveways and white-coated servants. John and I sampled the private pool, unheard of in those days among the middle class, and marveled at the windows to the pool's depths from the basement of the bathhouse. Down in the basement of the main house, the water heater for the mansion looked like a hotel's and I couldn't even imagine how much gas it would take to heat all that water on a cold Iowa winter day. After a formal lunch there, we were whisked off to my cousin's bank and then shown a new housing development in Des Moines Joe Stausser and Dick Lozier were underwriting together as business partner cousins. Everyone was gracious and charming, but you felt the distance between their world and yours. Even John felt the strain and mumbled something cynical like "we'll never see any of that again." He was right. It was the last time we ever saw those cousins as they moved on up the corporate ladders and, after my mother died, we never even heard from them again.

By the time we got to Kansas City, we were on the last leg of our trip and were getting eager to get home, the goal of any great trip I suppose. Kansas City, true to its reputation, was an inferno in August. All that concrete, left over from the Pendergast Machine scandals a decade earlier, was everywhere you could see in Kansas City and simply stored up the heat to make it even hotter. But we managed to visit a famous dairy on Troost Avenue that had a world-renowned hot fudge sundae that was well worth seeking out, visit the Nelson Art Gallery on the energy from the ice cream, and took in the free tour of the Russell Stover Candy Company where we got to eat all the free chocolates you wanted at the end. That night, gutted with the chocolates for supper, we headed for the Starlight Theater, one of the first outdoor theaters in a city park in the U.S. Our seats were way to the back since we hadn't been able to reserve them earlier, but at least we were there and Carol Channing, a young star from Brooklyn, was starring in the road version of a fairly new musical "Hello, Dolly!" After the show, the star appeared on stage and croaked out in her strong Brooklyn accent how "Hap-p-p-y I am to be in Kansas City" as the crowd went wild in admiration. [Thirty years later, I again attended the Kansas City Starlight Theater to see Carol Channing in "Hello, Dolly!". She hadn't changed any more than the musical had and, at the end, exactly like thirty years before, she appeared on stage and croaked out in her strong Brooklyn accent how "Hap-p-p-y I am to be in Kansas City" as the crowd went wild in admiration.]

After "Hello, Dolly," we were ready to go home. Home was only five hours away so we decided to not stay overnight but save our money and get home in the early hours of the next day. By three the next morning, we were rolling into our home driveway—we'd made it to California and back. We were already thinking about where we'd go next summer when we headed East.

Printed in the United States
3416